S M A R T   S T A R T

C O L O R A D O

How to Start a Business in Colorado

D1511651

EP
Entrepreneur® Press

Editorial Director: Jere Calmes
Cover Design: Beth Hansen-Winter
Editorial Development and Production: CWL Publishing Enterprises, Inc., Madison, WI,
www.cwlpub.com

This publication is designed to provide accurate and authoritative information in regard to
the subject matter covered. It is sold with the understanding that the publisher is not
engaged in rendering legal, accounting, or other professional services. If legal advice or
other expert assistance is required, the services of a competent professional person should
be sought.

> —From a Declaration of Principles jointly adopted by
> a Committee of the American Bar Association and
> a Committee of Publishers and Associations

ISBN 13: 978-1-59918-119-6
       10: 1-59918-119-3

Library of Congress Cataloging-in-Publication Data

How to start a business in Colorado / by Entrepreneur Press. — 2e with CD-ROM.
   p. cm.
ISBN-13: 978-1-59918-119-6 (alk. paper)
ISBN-10: 1-59918-119-3 (alk. paper)
1. New business enterprises—Colorado. 2. New business enterprises—Colorado—
Management. I. Entrepreneur Press.
HD62.5.H68516 2007
658.1'109788—dc22

                                        2007019633

11 10 09 08 07   10 9 8 7 6 5 4 3 2 1

Contents

Preface

The zipper, the helicopter, and the artificial heart valve. What do these inventions have in common? They came to us through small business ventures—not major corporations. In fact, small businesses are responsible for more than half of all the innovations developed during the 20th century. Today, small businesses play an integral role in our daily lives as Americans, whether we are directly involved with one or not. Small businesses (fewer than 500 employees) represent about 99.7 percent of all employers. They also employ half of private-sector workers and 41 percent of workers in high-tech jobs. Over the past decade, small businesses created between 60 and 80 percent of the news jobs. About 53 percent of small businesses are home-based.

Another factor contributing to the move towards small business in this country is the erosion of public confidence in large, established corporations. From the fear of falling victim to downsizing, to a perceived lack of concern for employees' well-being, former corporate workers are turning away from big business and embracing the opportunities and rewards offered through entrepreneurship. In turn, these entrepreneurs are bringing new sources of innovation and creativity to the marketplace. Given the current social and economic climate in the United States, there has never been a better time to start your own business.

Support for entrepreneurship at the federal, state, and local levels is at an all-time high—further evidence that the time is right for starting your own business. Many government agencies understand the important role small business plays in America's stability and economic future, and are acting accordingly when it comes to funding various ventures. In fact, the House Committee report concluded that small businesses receive one third of all federal prime and subcontract dollars.

Yet with all this potential success and personal fulfillment comes the risk of failure and disappointment, so it is crucial for you to understand the ins and outs of small business ownership, from what it takes to fund, open, and manage your company through how to make the right decisions when times turn difficult.

How to Start a Business in Colorado is a state-specific start-up book designed specifically for entrepreneurs. The following is a sampling of what you'll find:

- State and federal information on specifics for starting your business from choosing the right legal forms to filing taxes and incorporating.
- Tips for operating your business once you have officially conquered the start-up phase. There are helpful hints regarding proper accounting methods, how to market your product or service, and how to choose and keep quality employees.
- Guidelines for developing a business plan—possibly the most important step in forming and operating a profitable business.
- Statistical information about your state to help you anticipate trends and give you the ability to compare economic and social factors affecting your business.
- Several appendices filled with addresses, phone numbers, and Web site addresses for the agencies and resources you will probably need to contact for licenses, permits, business registration, financing alternatives, workers' compensation, unemployment taxes, and more.

It's all here, in one helpful, easy-to-use volume. If you find errors, or if changes to existing laws are not reflected, please let us know so we can better help others who will be using this information in the future. Thank you for choosing SmartStart and we wish you much success in your new enterprise.

Part One

Setting Up Your Business

1 | *Initial Business Considerations*

smart *(smärt) adj. 1) characterized by sharp, quick thought: intelligent; 2) shrewd in dealings: canny*

start *(stärt) v. 1) to begin an activity or movement: set out; 2) to have a beginning: commence; 3) to move suddenly or involuntarily; 4) to come quickly into view, life, or activity: spring forth*

A smart start—this phrase certainly has a ring to it. In fact, it sounds like what all burgeoning small business owners and entrepreneurs strive to achieve. And, yet, the statistics show that only one out of 20 new ventures will survive to celebrate its fifth anniversary. So what is it that will give you the edge on starting your new venture? The answer involves knowledge and preplanning.

Look back at the definitions of "smart" and "start." Both words imply action—action on your part. You have a dream: starting a business. You are the one responsible for making that dream come true. You won't be working for a boss; you will be the boss. You won't have a set nine-to-five schedule; you will work whatever hours are necessary to stay on course.

Of course, with any dream comes inherent challenges. A study published by Dun & Bradstreet lends some insight into the common challenges faced by today's small business owners. These are the top ten challenges:

1. *Knowing your business.* This aspect entails in-depth industry knowledge, market savvy, and a certain practical knowledge.
2. *Knowing the basics of business management.* The basics include accounting and bookkeeping principles, production scheduling, personnel management, financial management, marketing, and planning for the future.
3. *Having the proper attitude.* Realistic expectations coupled with a strong personal commitment will carry you through.
4. *Having adequate capital.* From establishing a good relationship with a bank to maintaining a business credit report, sufficient capital is vital to surviving the first year.
5. *Managing finances effectively.* In a phrase—cash flow. Cash flow entails ongoing capital, inventory management, extending credit to customers, and managing accounts receivable.
6. *Managing time efficiently.* A combination of discipline, delegation, and planning (your business plan has already set the priorities) is essential for effective time management.
7. *Managing people.* Finding and keeping qualified personnel is critical to building a successful business.
8. *Satisfying customers by providing high quality.* You will establish and maintain credibility with your customers when you constantly deliver the best possible product or service.
9. *Knowing how to compete.* New ways of selling, knowing the marketplace, a clear understanding of your niche, and sticking to your original plan all qualify as things you must do for the stiff competition that may lie ahead.
10. *Coping with regulations and paperwork.* Welcome to red tape central—where you may be required to file anything from quarterly tax payments to withholding taxes, from employee manuals to profit-sharing and pension plans, from sales tax records to industry-related reports.

> Finding and keeping qualified personnel is critical to building a successful business.

You have heard the phrase "work smarter, not harder." Working smarter means overcoming these ten challenges by knowing what lies ahead of you. A smart start for your business means understanding the course, possessing the skills to overcome the obstacles, and knowing the right way to clear the hurdles. Whether you've competed in athletics, academics, or a simple game of cards, if you are starting a small business then you're in for the race of a lifetime. Before you run out and buy a pair of the best and fanciest running shoes, take a moment to consider what it takes to be an effective and profitable small business owner.

The Entrepreneurial Archetype

entrepreneur (än´tra pra nur´) n.: A person who organizes, operates, and assumes the risk in a business in expectation of gaining the profit.

Today more than ever entrepreneurs are playing a vital role in America's diverse economic structure. According to the John F. Baugh Center for Entrepreneurship at Baylor University, the number-one source of new jobs in the United States will continue to be entrepreneurial ventures and emerging firms. Even large corporations are beginning to recognize the value and importance of the "entrepreneurial spirit." Numerous books have been written on this so-called entrepreneurial spirit and the subject is the focus of many research groups at business colleges throughout the world. A cursory look at what many believe to be the entrepreneurial archetype may help you discover if owning your own small business is right for you.

> Even large corporations are beginning to recognize the value and importance of the "entrepreneurial spirit."

Some Serious Self-Evaluation

What lies within you? Today's researchers believe some of the necessary traits for successful entrepreneuring are drive, commitment, passion, energy, leadership, and pride of ownership. As a fledgling entrepreneur, it is important to understand your strongest talents and skills and realize your areas of weakness. Successful business owners choose a business that allows them to do the things they love to do. Ask yourself questions, such as:

- What kinds of things do I most enjoy doing?
- What do I like to do on my day off?
- What have I always wanted to do but have never had time to do it?
- What do other people compliment me on?
- Do I enjoy interacting with others?
- What types of things do I not enjoy?

These types of questions and many others are listed in self-assessment worksheets in the small business development centers (SBDCs) throughout the nation. SBDC counselors are located in various communities of all 50 states and the District of Columbia to help you plan your business startup. (See Chapter 12 for more details on how SBDCs can assist you.) As you identify your strengths and weaknesses you become more aware of what business type will compliment your personality. Once you have done some self-assessment, you will need to ask yourself some more practical questions related to four major areas of concern:

- Your experience and motivation
- Your product or service
- Your customer
- Your competition

Your Experience and Motivation

You may have all the drive and ambition in the world. But without some experience or way to gain experience in the type of business you plan to start, you may be facing some major hurdles. If you don't have direct experience in the business you want to start, don't be discouraged. Start now by plugging in to the right resources for your industry or trade. For instance, you can join one or more of the trade associations that represent your industry. By joining an association you will get information about legal and other issues of interest to your industry. Membership or affiliation with these associations will also help you support lobbying efforts to represent your interest in the state legislatures and Congress.

Other types of assistance and support you will receive from membership in an association include:

- Periodic newsletters or magazines that keep you abreast of important changes occurring in your industry;
- Seminars and meetings that you can attend to get information from other business owners and experts; and
- A network of small business owners like yourself to help you stay in touch with what others are doing in their communities.

Your local library should have association directories. If you prefer, you can access information and oftentimes direct links to the associations via the Internet.

Your Product or Service

Nearly all businesses fall into one of two categories: selling products or selling services. If you have an innovative product and the know-how to produce it cost-effectively and know a distinct market for it exists, then you have the

> As you identify your strengths and weaknesses you become more aware of what business type will compliment your personality.

basis for a successful venture. In addition, if you want to start a service business you may be looking at quicker start-up and lower start-up costs due to reduced or no inventory.

Have you clearly identified what you will be selling? In attempting to answer this question, make sure you know how your product or service is different from those of your competitors. Determine what is unique about your product—is it less expensive or of better quality than your competitors'? Maybe it is the same price as your competitors' but you offer guarantees and place warranties. Does it have more options at the same price? You will need to know (not to mention be able to convince) your customers that your product or service is better than the competition's. Further, you will need to know how to measure the demand for your product or service.

Your challenge, among many, will be to establish your product or service upfront—that is, before you open your doors for business. The true test of whether you have clearly identified what you will sell will be sitting down to write your business plan. Your business plan will guide your business to achieve its purpose, its product's or service's purpose, and its long- and short-term goals. You will learn more on this critical aspect of business planning in Chapter 3. A sample business plan for a service-type business is at the end of Chapter 3 to help you create your own plan.

> Your business plan will guide your business to achieve its purpose, its product's or service's purpose, and its long- and short-term goals.

Your Customers

Part of knowing your product or service is knowing who will buy it. To smart-start your business you must have a clear idea of who your customers are and where they are located. You should understand the demographic and psychographic makeup of your customer base. Make sure you know the answers to questions, such as:

- Which age group, income range, and gender will my product or service target?
- Will my product or service appeal to a specific ethnic group?
- Do I know the marital status, education level, and family size of the people I will be selling to?
- Do I know the lifestyles and buying preferences of the target market I've identified?

In addition, you must determine such things as the number of potential customers that exist in your geographic market area and how you will attract and retain buyers. You will want to understand the purchasing patterns and buying sensitivity of your potential customers. It is important to understand the current size of your market and its growth rate. Things like social values and other concerns will influence your customers' buying habits.

As a prospective business owner, your top-priority goals should be establishing a strong sales and marketing plan and a smart business plan. As you gain a thorough understanding of your target market you will begin to reap the benefits of repeat business from loyal and satisfied customers. Customer loyalty is a challenge for all businesses; but with the right sales and marketing plan and quality control measures, you can establish a solid customer base.

Your Competition

> Your top-priority goals should be establishing a strong sales and marketing plan and a smart business plan.

As important as knowing your customers, you will be one step ahead of the game if you have clearly identified your competitors. Make sure your start-up efforts involve researching your competitors. Who are your major competitors? What advantages and disadvantages do you have compared with the competition? Does your business face any barriers for entry? How do customers perceive your competitors? For instance, do their customers remain loyal because of perceived quality, image, or value? Further, determine how you will gain a sufficient share of the market. For the most part, unless you are part of a new industry, your market is probably already served by one of your competitors. Your goal is to carefully plan how you will snatch some of this market share and show that you will continue to reach new markets.

You can be confident about one thing as you start your business—the competition will be fierce. To gain the business street smarts to beat the competition you must know your industry and the number of businesses in your field that have succeeded and failed. Knowing why these businesses survived or died quick deaths will help you in your planning efforts. In addition to understanding where you fit in the entrepreneurial world, you will need to carefully consider how you want to get into business.

Methods of Getting into Business

As a potential business owner, you have three primary choices for starting your business.

- Start a business from the ground up—from home or elsewhere;
- Buy a business; or
- Buy a franchise.

Each method has its pros and cons and it is up to you to decide which is the best alternative for your situation.

Starting a Small Business

Starting a new venture allows you to let your imagination and efforts take you to wherever they may lead. You may be able to start your business on a shoestring in your home or small office with little capital. If so, you can design all the business identification signage, logos, letterhead, and business name. If you are very successful, you may even be able to franchise your idea.

The main factor in starting the business is you. As previously discussed, you will need to have the drive, energy, passion, and determination to make the business work—no matter how many hours, days, or weeks it takes. If the business succeeds, you will reap the financial rewards, pride of ownership, and sense of accomplishment that a new venture can bring. And, if the business fails to live up to your expectations, you can make changes on your own.

> The main factor in starting the business is you.

The reality of starting a new venture—not buying a business or buying into a franchise—is shouldering the responsibility for each and every detail of business operation. You will have to build the business from the ground up and attract customers based on your own efforts and reputation. You and, if applicable, your partner(s) are the individuals solely responsible for anticipating problems, defining marketing, finding the proper location, and achieving your business plan goals.

Buying a Business

When you purchase a business, you buy many unknowns. For instance, what is the true reputation of the previous owner and did the business truly make a profit or do the books give a false impression of the business's true profitability? How current and usable is the inventory and equipment? Will you inherit employees that you don't want to retain? These and numerous other concerns face the would-be buyer. Research and investigation are critical to buying a business.

As the buyer of an existing business, you need to have your attorney or other qualified professional look at all accounting records for the last three to five years minimum. In addition, you need to arrange for a thorough inspection of the inventory and all contracts. Your goal in doing this research is to protect yourself from future liabilities. For instance, make sure your attorney checks for any judgment liens or other recorded security interests. Usually, the secretary of state will have this information. Further, if you will be purchasing real property, get a title search done to make sure the seller has good title and that there are no recorded claims or deeds against the property.

Today's business owners are faced with many environmental responsibilities for their businesses, including proper handling of hazardous materials, maintaining proper water or air quality standards, proper waste disposal methods, or removal or monitoring of underground storage tanks.

Also, although not necessary, you may want to have a licensed professional conduct an environmental audit of the property. The last thing you want to deal with are federal or state liabilities for environmental hazards. (For more information on business environmental issues, see Chapters 10 and 11.)

> When purchasing a business, be aware of the current status of the bulk sale law in your state.

The method of amortizing the amount paid for a business changed as a result of federal legislation. As a buyer of an existing business, you may now amortize intangible items such as goodwill, customer lists, patents, copyrights, and permits and licenses. The old law allowed amortization only of tangible items. The new law requires amortization to occur over a 15-year period. Ask your tax accountant about the best tax treatment for your situation before buying a business.

Many states have repealed their bulk sale laws that required sellers and buyers of certain types of businesses to notify creditors of the impending sale of the business. When purchasing a business, be aware of the current status of the bulk sale law in your state. You can obtain information from your secretary of state's office or consult your attorney.

The IRS now requires the buyer and seller to file Form 8594, Asset Acquisition Statement. Whether you are the buyer or seller, the business's taxable situation will be affected. A copy of Form 8594 is available via the Internet at www.irs.gov. If you prefer, contact an IRS field office near you. See Appendix B for addresses and phone numbers.

PURCHASE AGREEMENT

Another important factor of buying an existing business is that both parties agree to a purchase price, terms of payment, and the items involved in the sale. These matters are all addressed in a purchase agreement. Consult your attorney for more information on drafting a purchase agreement.

Buying a Franchise

Approximately 850,000 franchised outlets exist nationwide and it is estimated that a new franchisee opens for business approximately every ten minutes. With figures like these, it's no wonder that people across the nation are buying into the more than 3,000 U.S. franchise operations. Even the U.S. Small Business Administration (SBA) has found that your chances of business success are higher with a franchise than with a typical start-up. And, Department of Commerce figures show that 92 percent of all franchise companies formed during the last decade are still in business. But before you jump the gun and decide a franchise is your best bet, consider the advantages and disadvantages of franchising.

Overall, you may have a lower risk when you buy a franchise than when you start a business from scratch.

The biggest advantage is that the franchisor has done most of the work for you. For instance, the franchisor will have already developed the product(s) or service(s), a positive name recognition, eye-catching signage and interior and exterior store layout, training methods, and effective ways of operating the business. The franchisor should assist you in finding a location for the business as well. Since the franchisor wants you to succeed, the franchisor often provides help for developing your business. Much of the trial-and-error that all business must experience has been learned by the franchisor or by other franchisees and this knowledge is passed on to new franchisees. Overall, you may have a lower risk when you buy a franchise than when you start a business from scratch.

In looking at the downsides of franchising, the first concern is cost. Some franchises cost $500,000 in total capital investment and may even require ongoing payments of up to 20 percent of gross sales for rent, marketing, royalties, and advertising. Also, when you buy a franchise you give up a lot of freedom. Because the franchise has its own protocol, you will have very specific limits on what you can and cannot do.

The Federal Trade Commission (FTC) regulates the franchise industry. The FTC has a hotline that will give information on:

- Federal disclosure for franchises,
- Getting a copy of a disclosure statement for a specific franchise, and
- How to file a complaint against a particular franchisor.

An attorney is available to answer your questions regarding franchises. For more information, contact the Bureau of Consumer Protection of the Federal Trade Commission. The address and phone numbers for the FTC headquarters are in Appendix B.

State governments also have shown their interest in franchising by publishing guidelines like those issued by the FTC. Several states have franchise investment laws that allow potential investors a chance to review pre-sale disclosure information—also known as an offering circular. But remember: all states are subject to the FTC regulations whether or not they have statutes that govern franchises. For more information, refer to Appendix B for the addresses and phone numbers for the FTC headquarters or a regional office that serves your state.

Although legal guidelines exist, this is not to say that the legislation has prevented bad business practices. If you are considering purchasing a franchise, you are encouraged to look at all FTC disclosure documents before signing any agreements. Also, review the franchisor's financial statements and Securities and Exchange Commission (SEC) quarterly and yearly filings to determine its financial strength. You can also contact other franchisees to determine if they are satisfied with the franchisor. In addition, know how to read and understand the prospectus offered by the franchisor.

Research, Research, Research

Research is to small business what location is to real estate. With so many businesses, so many personalities, so many approaches, it is easy to get overwhelmed. Although numerous variables exist, the reality of starting a business is actually more tangible now than ever before. But where do you start?

> Research is to small business what location is to real estate.

One of the most important things you can do for your start-up is to research all matters related to your business. You can conduct preliminary research via numerous routes, including:

- Local, public, and college libraries;
- Federal, state, and community business organizations and assistance programs; and
- The Internet.

After reading through this book, you will have a jump start on your research and be able to significantly reduce the time it will take.

CHAPTER WRAP-UP

This chapter has helped you consider many of the initial factors of starting your small business. Despite what the experts may tell you, there is no "right" way to start your business. You cannot follow ten easy steps to ensure success of your venture. What you can do, however, is know the various tasks that lie ahead and approach each task with a can-do attitude. Use the following worksheet as a primer for the many business decisions you will need to make. For your convenience, use the chapter reference column of the worksheet to learn more about the various tasks you must complete.

Planning Primer for New Entrepreneurs

YOUR PRODUCT OR SERVICE	YES	NO	N/A	IN CHAPTER
Have you clearly defined your business?				1 and 3
What distinguishes your product or service from your competitors?				2 and 3
Do you plan to manufacture or purchase parts?				3
Do you know the turnaround time for ordering parts and are they guaranteed?				2
Is there a discount for purchasing a larger quantity?				2
Do you know how your product or service will reach its market?				6

YOUR PERSONAL NEEDS	YES	NO	N/A	IN CHAPTER
How long can you survive financially without drawing your assigned salary or wage?				1
Are your family members prepared to withstand the time constraints placed on you as a new business owner?				1
If yours will be a home-based business, how will your home office space accommodate your customers, vendors, and family members?				8
Are you ready to work long hours and weekends?				1
If you will have partners or co-owners, have you clearly identified what each member will bring to the overall operation? (Think in terms of time, money, equipment, and commitment.)				9

YOUR PERSONAL NEEDS, CONTINUED	YES	NO	N/A	IN CHAPTER
If yours is a partnership, do all partners have similar goals and can you work with them?				9
Are you a self-starter and can you maintain a disciplined approach to making your business succeed?				1

YOUR INDUSTRY	YES	NO	N/A	IN CHAPTER
Have you explored the risks associated with selling or manufacturing your product or service?				3
Do you know the seasonal or cyclical nature of your industry and how these changes can affect your ability to sell?				3
Have you researched the credit terms that your suppliers offer and can these terms accommodate your business's needs?				2
How much control do you want or are you willing to give up based on your choice of legal structure?				9

MARKETING ISSUES	YES	NO	N/A	IN CHAPTER
Are there sufficient willing buyers who will be attracted to your current price, quality, and convenience levels?				2
What is the demographic makeup of your customer base?				1 and 2
Do you know your target consumers' buying habits?				2
What advertising media will you use to promote your business' image and/or message?				2 and 3
How will you reach your customers?				2 and 3
Do you know your target consumers' buying habits?				6
What advertising mediums will you use to promote your business' image and/or message?				6 and 7
How will you reach your customers?				6 and 7

THE COMPETITION	YES	NO	N/A	IN CHAPTER
Do you know who your competitors are?				1, 2, and 3
How does your business measure against the competition (e.g., higher quality or lower price)?				1, 2, and 3
What sets your business apart from the competitors?				2 and 3
Will your product or service meet a need for an under-served market?				2 and 3
How do you plan to communicate your business's uniqueness?				2 and 3

YOUR FINANCES	YES	NO	N/A	IN CHAPTER
Where will your start-up funds come from?				3 and 4
Do you know of the numerous federal and state government loans available to your type of small business?				4
Are you aware of how many months (or years) it will take before you start to see a profit?				3, 4, and 5
Do you know the cost of sales (merchandise, freight, labor, etc.)?				2
Have you calculated the monthly fixed costs of your business, including rent, utilities, and insurance?				5
Do you know what your monthly net profits will be?				5
Will you use money from profits or other sources to fund expansion of your business?				3 and 5
Do you know where to get a loan for your start-up or expansion efforts?				5
Have you developed a pricing strategy for your product or service?				2

YOUR FINANCES, CONTINUED	YES	NO	N/A	IN CHAPTER
Do you know the costs associated with obtaining insurance and bonds to cover your business's liability issues?				6
Are you familiar with the basic pro forma financial statements—balance sheet, income statement, and cash flow analysis?				3 and 5
Can you interpret your pro forma statements?				5
Have you found a bank that will meet your business's needs?				5
Are you aware of how your business structure is taxed?				9 and 10

START-UP EXPENSES	YES	NO	N/A	IN CHAPTER
Do you know the down payment for leasing or purchasing office space? (Keep in mind, negotiating the lease or purchase price of property is usually an option.)				9 and 12
Have you calculated the expenses of equipment leases, inventory needs, fixtures, and office furniture and supplies?				9 and 12
Are you aware of all the necessary deposits you must make for things like sales tax, utilities, credit card acceptance, and leases?				7 and 5
Do you have enough funds to cover your start-up employee salaries?				3
Do you know the costs associated with paying estimated taxes and obtaining permits and licenses to operate?				7 and 8
Are you familiar with the financial requirements for withholding taxes, unemployment tax, and workers' compensation?				11
Have you projected your initial advertising budget?				2
Have you thought of allotting money toward paying a professional, like a lawyer or accountant?				5

START-UP EXPENSES, CONTINUED	YES	NO	N/A	IN CHAPTER
Do you know the cost of setting up a fax machine, getting Internet access and an e-mail address, and setting up a Web site?				8
How many phone lines will you require?				8
Will you need a separate post office box for incoming mail?				8
Do you know the fees for setting up your business's legal form (sole proprietorship, partnership, corporation, or LLC)? (Keep in mind, if these expenses become overwhelming, then calculate only the major priorities now and budget the other expenses later.)				6

EMPLOYMENT ISSUES	YES	NO	N/A	IN CHAPTER
Will you need to hire employees?				11 and 6
Have you considered using independent contractors or leasing employees instead of hiring permanent employees?				11 and 6
Are you familiar with the wages for your industry?				13
Do you know your state's minimum wage laws?				11
Does the area in which you wish to locate have a skilled labor pool from which you can hire and retain the best-qualified employees?				13
Do you know the federal and state regulations that govern employee and employer rights (e.g., fair employment practices and antidiscrimination issues)?				11 and 3
Will you offer a benefits package to your employees?				6
Have you written a clear set of company policy and procedures for your employees?				6
Do you have all employer posters required for display (minimum wage, equal opportunity, etc.)?				11 and 6

INSURANCE ISSUES	YES	NO	N/A	IN CHAPTER
Do you know what kind of property coverage your business will need (e.g., fire, burglary, robbery, business interruptions)?				7
Do you know what kind of casualty insurance your business requires (e.g., liability, automobile, employee theft)?				7
LOCATION	YES	NO	N/A	IN CHAPTER
Are you aware of any environmental issues relating to your business?				10 and 11
How will you address safety and health issues and do you know how to stay in compliance with both federal and state OSHA laws?				8
Does your product or service have specific location requirements?				8
Have you checked the makeup of the population and the number and type of competitors in the area?				8
Can the area support a business like the one you propose?				8
Do traffic count, parking facilities, and other business establishments play an important part in location?				8
Do you know the four critical factors for locating your business?				8
Do you know the zoning restrictions and permit requirements for the area in which you will locate?				10

2 | *Successfully Marketing Your Product or Service*

Most new business owners understand that they will have to partake in some degree of marketing and promotion to make their products or services visible to the world. But all too often, these same business owners forgo developing a solid marketing and public relations strategy so they can deal with the more immediate aspects of starting a business, such as obtaining financing or filing the right paperwork with state and federal offices.

Regardless of the type of business you plan to open—whether a retail shop or a home-based consulting business—you will need to know how to attract and retain customers to ensure your business remains profitable. By choosing to look at your market before you open your business, you will be able to do the following:

- Understand the specific habits and characteristics of your customers;

- Safely evaluate your pricing based on your production demands and your market demands;
- Be better prepared for the cycles of your field of business or your industry; and
- Know what your business's best methods of communication are.

All of this information will give you the keen insight to be more responsive to your business's needs and financial stability.

This chapter will help you gather information about your business and formulate it into a meaningful marketing and public relations plan. One of the first steps to building a sturdy framework to your plan is to understand some basic principles behind marketing and public relations. If you are familiar with this field of business already, you know that there are innumerable books, articles, and seminars on marketing and public relations. Unfortunately, not all of them follow the same definitions or standards. So, to maintain some sense of clarity, this chapter treats marketing and public relations as two separate vehicles of communication.

Public Relations or Marketing First?

A favorable review of your business in a local newspaper and sponsoring a student in a 4-H program both qualify as good public relations.

Public relations is the practice of developing and maintaining a positive connection between your business, the community, and those who either are or will soon become loyal, satisfied customers. A favorable review of your business in a local newspaper and sponsoring a student in a 4-H program both qualify as good public relations. The options that are available for you to position your business in a favorable light are limitless. Marketing, on the other hand, defines and perpetuates demand and is directly related to the goal of "making a sale" or creating revenue for your business. Advertising your products or services on television and deciding to have a sidewalk sale are functions of marketing.

Many business owners decide to jump into marketing and advertising before dealing with how the public perceives them. Obviously, if you can first establish an awareness that you will soon be open for business and ready to meet your customers' demands, then your marketing efforts to make sales will be more effective and show better returns. In other words, by first establishing healthy public relations, you will clear the way to make sound decisions about marketing and generate money back to your business.

Don't be misled by the lure of marketing and advertising professionals. You would be amazed at how quickly salespeople will catch wind of your new business. Not far from the snake oil peddlers of decades past, they will want to sell you on a variety of schemes to bring in immediate revenue. Whether it is selling advertising space in phone books, designing a Web site for your company, or selling you a blimp emblazoned with your company name to hover about your city's skyline, you are in no position to determine what will actually work unless you understand how the general public will perceive these promotional attempts—assuming the public will even notice.

Until you can identify who your best customers are and who can help you further your business exposure, you are at the mercy of salespeople and general advice givers. Since it is unlikely that your start-up will be able to afford a marketing and public relations staff, much of this responsibility will be on your shoulders.

Define Your Key Audiences

Your public relations and marketing efforts will be much easier if you start off by identifying the groups of people who will (or could) affect the livelihood of your business. Your key audiences might include:

- The general public,
- Your customers,
- Your employees,
- Your investors,
- Government and civic leaders, and
- The media.

Regardless of the type of business you own, it is important that the general public supports your company.

This is a general list of potential audiences; you should take time to think about any additional groups of people who may influence the success of your specific type of business. For example, keeping unionized truckers on your side may be a top priority if you plan to start a big-rig transportation brokerage, but certainly not if you intend to run a typing service for college students. You will definitely want to add those specific groups to the more obvious key audiences in your public relations strategy.

The General Public

Regardless of the type of business you own, it is important that the general public supports (or at least tolerates) your company. If the general public does not support your business, it is very likely that even your best customers or clients will be swayed to support another business. You may want to focus primarily on your money-spending customers; however, the general public should always be on your mind too. Developing a favorable standing with the general public is sometimes referred to as community relations. The idea is to establish your company as a "good neighbor," not a money-hungry entity with little regard for the environment or community.

To illustrate the importance of community relations, consider the following scenario. Suppose you want to open a skateboard shop that targets teenagers. You take a lot of time to cater to the likes of your young customers and, as a result, they view your store as a hangout. On the other hand, the general public is far from being fascinated by the sport and may view your shop as an eyesore—"full of kids out front with nothing better to do." This does not bother you because you have established a loyal following among your customers and are reaping the financial rewards. That is, until one day a skateboarder accidentally knocks down an elderly woman in front of your shop. Suddenly you are faced with a crisis as the media takes hold of the negative publicity this brings to your store as an indirect cause of the accident, not to mention the impending lawsuit filed by the woman. Because you have not maintained a positive image among the general public, you must spend a great deal of effort to reclaim your business from rumors, angry parents who no longer want their children to support your store, and negative media reports.

> Developing a favorable standing with the general public is sometimes referred to as community relations.

If, on the other hand, your business had promoted a "responsible use campaign" before the accident—without alienating the kids who support it—you would have been in a better position to recover from the crisis. You could have accomplished this by offering free "responsible use" workshops or by bringing a well-known personality in the skateboarding world to demonstrate safer places to skate. By writing press releases, you might lure the local newspaper or television stations to cover the event.

Although the time and money spent on such a campaign may not show any financial return—as the same amount applied to advertising a sale might—being aware of your business's overall perception and its place in the community can help you prevent or at least recover from situations that could dramatically affect future sales.

Your Customers

Naturally, you will want your business to be the first choice of your potential clientele. This means you will have to conduct some research as to who specifically will be your best type of customer. Determine the common characteristics—age, ethnic group, gender, income level, education level, interests, and buying habits of the public who want your goods or services. This will be a crucial element to any of your future marketing needs. Specific methods for defining your best customers are discussed in greater detail in the marketing section of this chapter.

As soon as you have a good idea of who your customers are, you should always put your best foot forward when you choose to communicate to them. Your customers keep your business going. You want to create a comfortable experience for your customers to buy and use your products or services. Begin thinking about what will appeal to your customers on a subconscious level and what steps you can take to meet their interests. Will they identify and be drawn toward the design of your company logo or letterhead? Will the fixtures, furniture, and colors in your office or store appeal to your customers? All of these small details affect the big picture of your business and you should not overlook their importance.

> Your customers keep your business going.

Your Employees

If you will have employees, train them on the importance of portraying your company image in a favorable fashion. That includes how they greet your customers or clients when they call on the phone or walk in the door or how they receive customers who have a problem with a product or service. Inform employees about your company's goals and objectives and motivate them to make the business work. If you include your employees in your efforts and get them excited and proud of their roles, you are more likely to see the positive effects trickle over to your customers. Being concerned about staying in a favorable standing with your employees can improve morale, lessen employee turnover, cut down on rumors and gossip, and offer crucial information about company policies. For more information on establishing a healthy relationship with your employees, refer to Chapter 6.

Your Investors

Although your business is not publicly held and you will not have to worry about how shareholders and security analysts view your business, you may want to make an effort to establish a healthy relationship and company image with your banker or other financial consultants. Of course you will focus the message that is relevant to your investors from a different standpoint than you would use in projecting to another key audience, like your customers. In other words, you will want to take steps to ensure that your business appears financially sound to your investors.

Taking time to educate yourself and project your willingness to work and communicate with your investors are preliminary steps to reaching lasting healthy relations with your investors. This time spent may be just as, if not more important than the efforts you make with other key audiences, especially when you need funding. See Chapter 5 for more details on working with your bank.

Government and Civic Leaders

Developing a good relationship with local, state, federal, and even international officials can be crucial. Simply put, since these officials have a direct hand in creating legislation that could affect your business, make certain they know about your business and industry.

> Developing a good relationship with local, state, federal, and even international officials can be crucial.

By maintaining a productive and active voice with the various levels of government, you are more likely to improve or maintain the working standards, taxes, and other government interventions that your business faces. If your business has a voice and a strong image, you are more likely to be respected and heard.

The Media

Last, but certainly not the least important to your public relations efforts, is the role of the media. Work with the media to build your image. The media can include everything from your local newspaper to an international cable news network like CNN and even the Internet. By sending a press release about your company to editors and journalists, the chances are you can influence positive coverage of your business in news stories. If journalists can rely on you or your business for advice or pertinent information for their news stories, then the chances are they are more likely to listen to you when you have something to say about your business.

THE MEDIA CAN BE MORE THAN AN AUDIENCE

The media can serve not only as an audience, but as a definable conduit to communicate to several of your key audiences. Because the media—television, radio, newpapers, magazines, and Internet—can reach so many different quantities and types of people, you can use this to your advantage and pinpoint press releases to better serve your different key audiences. For example, you may discover through interviews that your customers primarily watch the evening news on television for information about the community. With this insight, you know that you should direct news releases to the television news programs with a focus on your customers' interests and needs. But you can also position that same news story for a different medium with elements that would interest your financial backers if you know, for example, that they prefer to read the local business journal. By continually learning about your key audiences' habits and characteristics, you will also be better able to assume which is the best medium for the key audience you want to reach.

Keep in mind: a third-party endorsement from the media can often be more effective than a high-priced advertisement. In fact, the Wirthlin Group for Allen Communications, a New York-based public relations firm, found in a landmark 1994 study that 28 percent of its 1,023 respondents over age 18 said a news article would impact their buying decisions, as compared with 8 percent who said they would be influenced by an advertisement. The respondents also said that they felt magazines and newspapers were more reliable for information than television or the Internet.

> Carefully establish a relationship with any useful media contacts.

Take Time to Build Relationships with the Media

Carefully establish a relationship with any useful media contacts. Make it as easy as possible for them to know you're available to provide insight into a particular issue and available for their needs. They want resources to rely upon—experts in a variety of fields—and if they can determine that you are an acceptable resource, the chances of promoting your company are greater too. Don't expect to submit a press release and then watch the story unfold on the six o'clock news. Avoid a press release that is just a strong sales pitch. Instead, try to gauge what the media is likely to want to report—what would make a newsworthy story. If you can provide the lead to a good story within the realm of your business, then you may very well have an "in." If not, it's probably better to wait until you do, rather than alienate essential media contacts.

Use the Internet as a Media Tool

Although subject to a lot of current media attention, the Internet is proving to be an invaluable medium for all types of business communication. Beyond developing a Web site for your business, you can monitor discussion groups about your business and industry that might generate ideas for press releases and potential news stories. Use e-mail to communicate with journalists and send press releases, if it is an acceptable form of submission for them. You can even use the Internet as your medium of choice to reach specific segments of your key audiences to communicate your message and to further your business image, rather than blatant marketing or sales pitches.

Build a Public Relations Strategy

Now that you have information about your key audiences, you are ready for a more formal plan of attack—a public relations strategy.

Your first step is to look at the overall picture—or the place of your business in the world. Paint a portrait of your business in the marketplace by finding articles about similar businesses, statistics or information about your customers and the community in which your business will serve, or any other indicators that will help you overcome potential image problems and stay in good standing with all your key audiences. You can find this information in the library, in magazines and trade journals, on the Internet, and even by surveying the public about its attitudes and opinions.

> Consider what messages you need to communicate to what key audiences to position your business favorably.

Analyze Your Information

When you feel you have gathered enough information to start, write down what you believe to be an accurate representation of your business in relation to its competitors and the issues that face you and your competition. Consider what messages you need to communicate to what key audiences to position your business favorably. Consider the limitations that your business has to face in order to communicate those messages to the key audiences. In addition, determine if there are government regulations that could affect your company or contribute to your problem.

Identify Potential Problems

You may discover that there are potential image problems that could affect your business operations immediately or down the road. Although you cannot predict the future, if you suspect an issue lingers ahead, it may be wise to publicly address the issue before it balloons into general consciousness or, even worse, a crisis. Be as specific as possible in determining these problems and their source, as well as what might happen if you chose to ignore them.

For example, if you have decided to start a timber-harvesting operation in the Pacific Northwest, you could face some fairly tough battles trying to keep your business image favorable in the minds of both people who consider your business destructive to the forest ecosystem and the industry that relies on timber for income. By siding with one or the other, you could face repercussions such as environmentalist demonstrations or a loss of support from your vendors and other business allies. Ideally, you may want to take steps to remain acceptable with both parties to a certain degree, assuming that you don't want to risk boycotts or other actions. You may also discover that you can bend only so far to meet the demands of either extreme side to the issue in order to keep your business profitable. Of course, there may be simply nothing you can do in some cases, other than monitor the noisemakers and hope they do not become the majority of your key audiences. The process of identifying and monitoring problems should be ongoing from the point you decide to open your business to the day when you sell or close it.

Set Goals to Prevent and Resolve Problems

Now you are ready to set goals and identify the methods to position your business in an agreeable manner. Once you have identified any problems, try to come up with ways to resolve them. Find solutions to your questions, based on research, surveys, and instinct. You might ask yourself some questions to find an answer. Will holding a grand opening meet your goals of more exposure for your business? Would coming up with a relevant news story for the media meet your goal? Could your goal be achieved if you find more time to identify and meet the needs to some of your identified audiences' needs? Would creating a newsletter or a Web site help?

> Once you have identified any problems, try to come up with ways to resolve them.

Always keep in mind which members of your key audiences will be most affected by the problem and your solution. Your message should cater to their specific interests and needs. Using different types of media—such as a business journal that your vendors and distributors read or a national news program viewed by your general customers—will help you target your message.

Imagine that your business develops a better way to reduce production costs and, in return, increase profit. Information such as this might be very newsworthy for a business journal that is read by your financial supporters. However, the information is not useful to your customers, since you are not passing a lower price for the goods on to them. From your research, you may have discovered that your customers are concerned about the environment, so instead of restating the news about your cut in costs, you can slant the focus of the story to show the added benefit for your customers of having less packaging to throw away.

Once you have identified your business's potential image problems, define your target audience and determine how to best shape the information to suit your audiences' needs. Then, you must develop your strategy. You have four options:

1. *Ignore the problem.* You may not have time to deal with the issue now or may think it is simply too early to address it effectively.
2. *React only if you absolutely have to.* You may decide that it is best for the business if you don't address the problem unless any of your key audiences become concerned about it.
3. *Prevent the problem.* It may be best to be proactive before the problem becomes uncontrollable or too time-consuming.
4. *Involve others.* You can sometimes involve groups (the media, government officials, or even media consultants) to solve or head off an image problem for your business.

Don't be concerned if you choose to ignore the problem; it may be in your best interest, considering your other business demands. Weigh your decisions according to your workload, other demands, and the importance of keeping up with your business image. There will always be a tradeoff, and it is OK to decide that dealing with an image problem may be the least of your worries at any given point.

In a larger context, however, do not write off the power of solid public relations throughout the lifespan of your business. If you choose to actively pursue a goal, you will want to outline exactly what you are going to do to reach your goal.

You might determine that it is best to have an activity, such as holding a special event, an exhibit, or some other sort of community involvement project. The involvement of the news media will be crucial to publicize these sorts of events and to get your message across.

Of course, you may decide that it would be better to pursue communications tactics instead. This might include distributing a newsletter, a brochure, a press release, or a direct mail advertisement. It might include coming up with a business logo, developing a Web site, or renting that blimp mentioned earlier with your company name across it.

> If you choose to actively pursue a goal, you will want to outline exactly what you are going to do to reach your goal.

Make a Timeline

Taking time to create a schedule will help you reach your planned goal. Suppose you are going to hold a grand opening for your business. You must determine when your business will be ready to hold the event, how long it will take to get a "Grand Opening" banner made, when a string quartet can come to perform for your guests, and whether the day and time will be convenient for your key audiences. By planning ahead and doing some research, you can ensure a much more successful launch than if you went without any insight or planning.

Allot Money and Resources

Along with creating a timeline, you will also want to examine the cost and time it will take to meet your goals. It is wise to create a detailed line-item budget, especially for the larger events you may be planning. Be sure to look for hidden costs as well.

Evaluate Your Efforts

At some point, you will want to determine if your efforts were successful. You determine success based on your goals, initial strategy, and the methods you used to achieve those objectives. You can survey your customers or potential customers to find out if their perceptions of your business have changed. You may simply notice that a news story featuring information about your business activities has brought in more curious customers. Whatever the case, you will want to weigh the effort it took to meet your objectives and what you have learned from the event. You may discover that your goals were not realistic or find a very effective way to build a healthy image with your business. This process can provide some real, qualitative insight into your business and its market.

How to Market Your Positive Image

Suppose you want to increase public awareness that your business is going to be open soon. After careful consideration, you decide that having a grand opening is the best method of meeting your objectives. You have fliers printed, alert the media, and even book the string quartet mentioned earlier to add some atmosphere. Your intent is to introduce yourself to the community and provide it with an enjoyable evening. And, after carefully orchestrating something close to the social event of the season, you can't help but feel your business is off to a great start.

Yet, in the weeks that follow, you may notice that interest in your business is waning. More importantly, you aren't earning enough money to keep your cash flow at a healthy level. What may have appeared to be the grandest of grand openings may leave you frantically searching for any means to attract customers.

> Along with creating a timeline, you will also want to examine the cost and time it will take to meet your goals.

It is important to establish a positive image for your business, but you will still need a certain amount of sales to keep your business alive and profitable. It is now time to transition your company's positive image into healthy sales. In short, you are ready to work on marketing your product or service.

Marketing is the pursuit of keeping your business financially stable through promotion. This can include running an advertisement in a magazine or taking the time to identify your best potential customers and then using available resources to communicate to their interests and needs through the type of business you operate.

By taking steps prior to opening your business, you will be better equipped to meet the needs of your best customers and help ensure that they continue to support your business throughout the months and years that follow.

> Marketing is the pursuit of keeping your business financially stable through promotion.

Define Your Ideal Customers

Go back to the key audiences you identified earlier in this chapter. Out of these groups, which do you see as your cash-spending customers? Base your assumption on indicators such as:

- What you already know about the industry and its consumers;
- What your competitors have done and continue to do to market to specific groups of people; and
- What business journals, association newsletters, industry magazines, and other resources are saying about your ideal customers.

Your marketing efforts—which take time and money—should be calculated and precise. You want to hit the right segment of people who are likely to support your business and, you hope, support it loyally.

Of course to achieve this, you may want to pinpoint your general customers even further. To find your best customers, learn as much as you can about them.

One excellent way to do this is through interviews or surveys. You can choose to do them on the street, near a competitor's store, or even over the telephone. By developing useful questions about your potential customers' likes and dislikes, you develop a better understanding of what exactly makes your customers tick. By getting to know their habits, knowing what types of entertainment they like, and understanding their motives for seeking out your business, you will be much more capable of making decisions about how to communicate to your best customers.

Defining your ideal customers through market research may even turn up a few surprises. For example, if you are planning to open an automotive parts store, you might assume that your primary customers are middle-aged men who either are mechanics or like to do things themselves. However, through your surveys of the general public, you discover that many women would be interested in supporting a retail store that offers automotive parts. By examining your competition, you realize that this segment of the general market is virtually ignored. You decide that it is worth allocating some money toward trying to develop women as a primary customer segment in your store. By taking steps to appeal to this group's interests and needs, you are building additional sales and gaining a competitive edge.

> Defining your ideal customers through market research may even turn up a few surprises.

Use Your Competitors' Strategy to Your Benefit

Although it may seem strange at first, you can learn a lot from your competitors. Observing how they run and promote their businesses and who visits their stores can provide insight as to who might migrate to your business.

Examine your competitors' prices. Document the pros and cons of their products or services. Find out as much as you can about their operating costs. Visit their Web sites and determine what types of customer they are trying to reach. Find out who their distributors and suppliers are, if any. Determine whether their locations are convenient and to their benefit. You have the luxury of evaluating their work and deciding whether or not they are doing something as well as it can be done. If not, you can try to find a better way of performing these functions in your business.

Distinguish Yourself from Your Competitors

After you have finished obtaining as much publicly available information as you can on your competition, compile it and analyze it. Compare your results with what you intend to do as a new business. Compare everything from your customers to what costs will affect daily operations. From this information, you can build ways to gain an advantage over your competitors. Maybe you can operate at a lower cost and reduced prices. Maybe your business is in a better location. Whatever the differences, your business will need to develop some unique selling points to lure customers. These can be as subtle or blatant as you want, from providing a more comfortable atmosphere in your business to heavy promotions for your rock-bottom prices.

Blaze Your Own Creative Marketing Trail

Unfortunately, as a new business you are not likely to have much money for any major marketing efforts. Certainly don't try to keep up with your competitors if they are large and can sink millions into highly targeted advertising campaigns—you will only drain your resources and put your business in financial jeopardy. Yet, don't be discouraged by having Goliath corporate competitors. Creativity, research, and public image can give you an advantage to sway your customers "to support the community" rather than some corporate giant.

Determine the Factors That Will Affect Sales

Of course, before you can really partake in a creative marketing idea to bring in customers, you need to examine some essential factors that could influence your overall marketing and sales. You will need to find inexpensive, yet quality ways to produce your message. You may have to find a reputable printer or television production crew to produce your marketing message. However, before you commit to creating and producing a marketing message, you need to be firm on what your internal cost demands are, the revenue you can commit to marketing, and how much you can invest to generate a quick return on your money.

> You will need to find inexpensive, yet quality ways to produce your message.

Beware of the Impacts of Pricing

Your operating costs may play a larger role in your marketing decisions than you may think. You may discover that your potential customers seek lower prices. So it may seem best to reduce your prices. Without prior examination, you may be doing more business, but not able to keep your production or operating costs in check.

Pricing your product or service will have an extraordinary impact on the success of your business. If you price your product or service too low, you will experience low profits and may even experience significant losses. Price your product or service too high and your customers will migrate to your competitors or never support your business.

Analyze Costs

Fortunately, most of the mystery associated with pricing can be easily dispelled with a simple analysis of your costs. Once you know the cost of goods and cost of sales, you have most of the information you need to determine the correct pricing for your product.

For example, suppose you plan to start a tie-dye T-shirt business. Each shirt you make requires $2.50 for raw material and costs $1.50 to dye and treat properly, including all of the overhead manufacturing expenses. After discovering it is more lucrative to run a mail-order business, you determine that the average shipping cost of a shirt is another $0.50. Your distributor near Haight-Ashbury in San Francisco warehouses your shirts by the thousands and ships them to clothing stores throughout the nation on demand. The distributor's average handling cost is $1.25 per shirt. The clothing stores determine the final price for the shirts based on a standard markup that takes into account many of the sales costs. So the total for your tie-dye shirts works out like this:

> *Once you know the cost of goods and cost of sales, you have most of the information you need to determine the correct pricing for your product.*

Raw material	$2.50	
Manufacturing	$1.50	
Shipping	$0.50	
Cost of goods		$4.50
Distribution		$1.25
Your profit		$0.50
Cost to store		$6.25
Markup—100%		$6.25 (50% of selling price)
Selling Price		$12.50

The final price the customer pays is $12.50. If the price is slightly lower than or equal to your competitors' prices, you're in business. If, however, the final price is higher than your competitors' pricing, there is something wrong with your process and you will need to rethink your production.

Production Considerations

When you set prices for your goods or services, consider what costs will be after you get into full production or to a production level that you consider adequate to support your business. Do not price your product or service with low overhead costs if you may have to rent other space or obtain equipment and hire employees to deliver your product or service. As production increases, you will obtain some efficiencies of sale. If you could purchase ten items at a unit price to make up a product, purchasing 500 will probably decrease your unit cost substantially.

However, the need for cash will also increase as production increases and you risk not being able to deliver to meet demand. You may not get paid for a finished product until several months after you have produced it and shipped it to your customer. You may also find that your vendors cannot meet the increased demand in the timeframe you expect. You should have alternative sources of all materials when possible.

Get your suppliers to guarantee prices and supplies of material. Discuss potential orders with suppliers in plenty of time for them to obtain the material they need to deliver to you. In today's global market, you can expect that foreign-made items will constitute some of your manufactured goods. Unless the materials can be easily air shipped, you may have a significant delay in getting items from manufacturers that depend on raw materials or finished goods from other countries. You may also find that price and quality vary considerably from one shipment to another, so you will probably want guarantees on the deliveries and the ability to return defective or substandard-quality materials.

> Get your suppliers to guarantee prices and supplies of material.

USE SALES TO DRIVE PRODUCTION GOALS

Production goals are directly driven by sales. It does no good to make 10,000 tie-dye T-shirts if nobody buys them. Conversely, if you are unable to provide T-shirts on demand, your customers may choose to take their business elsewhere. Your goal, then, is to manufacture T-shirts at full capacity and sell 100 percent of your inventory as it is made. Of course, the reality of actually doing this is very difficult, but certainly not impossible.

Determine Other Factors That Will Affect Sales

Other factors may also influence your best methods to market your business. You may want to consider the economy of the community you serve, looking at its population and where your business is located in comparison with competitors or other businesses that your customers may support. If you are catering to only a small population or to a small percentage who desire or can afford your product, you may want to be very careful about what money you spend to communicate to that select group.

Your location can play a big role in your sales too. If you are located near a competitor, you may find that you can draw upon its customers who may be comparison shopping. If you are not located near any other business that your customers may support, you may also discover that they have to find more reason than impulse to come to your business. See Chapter 12 about other considerations for choosing your business site.

Devise a Workable Sales and Marketing Plan

By taking into account the information you have gathered about your customers, your competitors, and your operating costs, you should be able to
determine how much money you can devote to reaching your customers.
Document your objectives and goals as you documented any public relations
strategy earlier.

The process of coming up with an idea to increase sales is never a sure-
fire thing, despite what salespeople's gimmicks may tell you. Realize that you
will be taking a risk—although necessary to build your sales and profits—
anytime you partake in a marketing effort. Fortunately, with some early planning and some research to determine who your best customers are and what
they are seeking in a business, you can feel a little more assured that your
decisions will show positive results. Marketing and gathering information
about your market is an ongoing process. You may start out small and grad-
ually build enough additional revenue to market your business with more
expensive methods, such as television advertising or large promotional
events.

> The process of coming up with an idea to increase sales is never a surefire thing.

Chapter Wrap-Up

How you choose to promote your business will largely depend on your costs
and your time; but, keep in mind that there are several interconnected factors. Your marketing will be based largely on your production costs, the economy, your location, and the size of your market. Your company's image is just
as important to your banker or financial lender as it is to your customers and
other key audiences. Although the desire may be strong to delay your marketing and public relations until after you have opened your doors for business, the ability to be more responsive to the demands and costs of your
business will come much sooner if you begin considering your market now.

3 | *Your Smart Business Plan*

Before undertaking any endeavor, you must have a plan. This is true whether you are going on a ski trip or launching a new business. Even if you haven't yet written a business plan, you probably have at least a general idea about your business goals, your customers, and your product. But have you considered such things as business expansion, second- or third-year profits, or financing?

Writing a business plan will force you to consider the management of your business for the next three to five years. A top-notch business plan will take a lot of work. You must think through your entire business at least once.

Drafting a business plan causes you to think about yourself, your product or service, your market, your customers, and your finances at least once before you get into business. A smart business plan will convey prospects and growth potential. A smart business plan will give you greater control of your business.

Frequently, new business owners do not write a business plan until forced to do so by a bank or other financial institution as a part of a loan application package. By taking this approach, they miss out on some of the most important benefits associated with having a business plan. If you write a business plan, you gain the following benefits:

- A clear picture of the financial condition of your business projected over the next five years;
- Critical marketing information related to your business;
- Specific business goals and milestones for the foreseeable future;
- Key information for making goal-related decisions; and
- Ready documentation available, if needed, for business financing.

You have a story to tell—that is not enough. The way you present the story is crucial to your success. This chapter will help you present your story in the best possible light to attract the investors and give you the control you need.

Most plans follow a specific format that has been largely standardized throughout the business community.

Get Help Before You Begin

A business plan is not difficult to create. Most plans follow a specific format that has been largely standardized throughout the business community. This specific format is not to be used as a boilerplate for your plan; rather, use it as a guideline to incorporate your business's unique characteristics. The basic elements are the same for all plans. Feel free to modify or expand on the basic elements of the business plan to better describe your business.

In preparing your business plan, you may refer to any number of resource materials on the market, including *Entrepreneur* magazine's *Business Plans Made Easy* (David H. Bangs, Jr., 3rd edition, 2005). Written for both start-ups and established businesses, this guide demonstrates how a business plan can vary depending on your type of business.

In addition, there are software packages on the market that will lead you through the process of preparing your business plan. One such product is OfficeReady Business Plans. This application is an add-on to Microsoft Office and integrates documents from Office applications into a single business plan document that is very effective.

Essential Components of a Smart Plan

Several examples included in OfficeReady Business Plans are used throughout this chapter and in the sample business plan at the end to illustrate the essential components of a successful business plan, which include:

- Section I: Executive Summary
- Section II: Company Background
- Section III: Owner/Management Background
- Section IV: Market Analysis

- Section V: Product/Service Offering
- Section VI: Marketing Plan
- Section VII: Financial Plan and Analysis

Read through these essential components and the sample business plan before you start your own plan. You may include other aspects of your business that you feel are important to understanding it, but are not in the outline above. Modify your plan to present your business or business idea and clarify in the reader's mind why you think the business idea is viable. Feel free to add or delete parts of the business plan described in this chapter. However, be careful not to delete parts of the plan that are essential to understanding your business. Also, do not provide information that the reader may not read or digest.

Section I: Executive Summary

The executive summary is considered by many experts to be the most important part of a business plan. It functions as the front door to your plan and presents your entire business in condensed form. Many lending officials read the executive summary first. If it doesn't make a good impression, they often ignore the rest of the business plan. The end result: your loan proposal doesn't receive the level of attention it might deserve.

Because writing the executive summary requires you to have an extremely clear picture of your business, many business planners advise writing this section of the business plan last. In this way, you benefit from the information and knowledge gained by writing the rest of the plan, and all aspects of your business are fresh in your mind. Even when a business plan is prepared for internal use only, the executive summary plays an important role. It provides a snapshot of your entire business concept—all your goals, marketing plans, and financial predictions. The overview should include the following:

- Type of business;
- Company business summary;
- Financial objectives, including the highlights of your operating performance;
- Management overview; and
- Product/service and competition.

If you will be using your business plan to obtain financing, include two additional sections—funds requested and use of proceeds.

> The executive summary is considered by many experts to be the most important part of a business plan.

If you feel intimidated about writing a plan, you can obtain help from a consultant or a small business development center. You should actively participate in developing the plan and clearly understand all the financial calculations and what is said in the text. If a lender asks a question about the plan and you indicate that you don't have an answer because a consultant wrote the plan or at least that section of the plan, the lender will not be positively impressed with what you know about your business.

CONTENT

Because the executive summary is such an important part of your business plan, its content and tone must clearly convey to the reader the unique structure, capabilities, and expertise of your business and its management. Show your business as:

- Well planned,
- Competently managed,
- Positioned where a clear market exists based on market research,
- Competitive against similar businesses, and
- Financially sound and likely to remain so.

By convention, these points are generally made in the order listed, following the content of the business plan. The executive summary summarizes the remaining sections of the business plan. If it is written well, it will motivate the reader to examine the plan in detail.

STYLE

Writing the executive summary requires a little skill. As a narrative discussion of your business, it must have all of the compelling elements of the opening pages of a novel, yet be firmly based in reality. A well-written executive summary will tell the story of your business, and it will entice, excite, and motivate the reader. At the same time, it will avoid exaggeration and outright fantasy. Creative, concrete, and compelling, an executive summary is business writing at its best.

When writing an executive summary, use language that presents a positive, confident business attitude. Write in an active voice, presenting your points in a clear and logical manner. If you don't feel confident writing the summary yourself, hire a professional writer or prevail upon a friend or family member with strong writing skills to write it for you.

> If you feel intimidated about writing a plan, you can obtain outside help from a consultant or a small business development center.

Ideally, the executive summary is short, one to three pages. "White space is my friend" is a common mantra for professional business writers. What this means is that you should avoid having huge blocks of text dominating your page. Break up text by putting space between paragraphs and by using bold headings and bulleted points in much the same way as this book is designed.

Refer to the executive summary portion of the sample business plan at the end of this chapter. This summary is very well written and uses a compelling, easy-to-read page layout.

Section II: Company Background

This section of your business plan discusses the basic structure of your business as well as your business goals. It provides your readers with a detailed description of your business, preparing them for later discussion of your product line and marketing strategy. The company background section includes the following basic information:

> The mission statement briefly describes the character, purpose, and goals of your business.

- Your mission statement or purpose of your business;
- A brief history of your business or business concept;
- A discussion of your personal business goals, including anticipated growth and financial objectives;
- The legal form of your business and its ownership structure;
- A discussion of your business location and facilities;
- A discussion of the financial status of your company, including how you will finance the operation; and
- Other information that has a bearing on your company.

YOUR MISSION STATEMENT

The mission statement briefly describes the character, purpose, and goals of your business. In short, the statement tells about your business and your business philosophy. Part declaration, part philosophy, part rallying cry, a well-thought-out mission statement provides the focus for all major business decisions.

Here's an example of a well-written mission statement:

Fortune Branch Market is a mom-and-pop convenience store specializing in friendly, neighborly service to an isolated, rural customer base. We concentrate on serving our customers' needs and work to maintain a diverse inventory, which includes special-order items requested by individual customers. Our goal is to maintain moderate annual growth through good, old-fashioned service, a friendly smile, and word-of-mouth advertising.

If you prefer, you can use this section to point out to your readers that you have clearly identified your market and the opportunity for steady sales and future growth.

BUSINESS HISTORY

Next describe the history of your business, including when it was founded, milestones achieved, such as a breakeven date, and the attainment of specific goals. State which phase of development your company is in—whether it be in the start-up or expansion phases.

If you are developing a new product, this is the place to discuss the extent of its development, which might include:

- The completion of product testing;
- The acquisition of patents, copyrights, or trademarks; or
- The acceptance of initial orders.

For a start-up business, an important thing to include in this section is a discussion of the basis for the business concept. The business could be an original idea aimed at an all-new market niche or it could be based on a successful business concept with which you will employ a unique approach or advantage. It could also be a proven business concept being introduced into an untapped or underserviced market.

BUSINESS GOALS

In this section of the plan, describe your business's future, including sales, growth, and expansion plans. To bolster this information, include charts, tables, and figures that show your sales, profit, and income projections. If there are industry-standard sales figures for your business, use them to back up your assertions regarding projected sales and growth. Use this section to describe how you will take advantage of your unique niche or concept.

In the goals section of the business plan, describe your business's future, including sales, growth, and expansion plans.

LEGAL FORM OF BUSINESS

Describe the legal form of your business. Is it a sole proprietorship, a partnership, a corporation, or a limited liability company? Explain why you chose the form for your business. Identify the state where your business is registered and any other state in which you are operating. Identify the owners, managers, or corporate officers. If your business is a corporation, identify major shareholders and discuss the number of shares that are outstanding.

LOCATION AND FACILITIES

You can describe the location of your business and explain why the location is particularly suitable for your business. Include demographic and psychographic factors that contribute to the location's suitability. For example, list the number of potential customers within a ten-minute drive based on income, education, interests, or other factors that you identified in your assessment of reasons why your business will be successful. List any branch offices or multiple locations. Identify the geographical area serviced by your business.

If your company requires specialized facilities for its operation, include a description of the facilities. You might, for example, include machinery, equipment, computer software, display counters, cash registers, alarm systems, a loading dock, storage facilities, or even a railhead for loading and shipping by train.

> If your company requires specialized facilities for its operation, include a description of the facilities.

FINANCIAL STATUS

Briefly discuss the financial state of your business, including funding sources to date, profitability, outstanding loans, owner equity (the amount of ownership you have in the business), number of employees, and characteristics of those employees (experience, education, or other important characteristics). If you are currently seeking additional funding, briefly describe how much money you need and why, as well as how much of the required funding will be provided through owner equity and personal investment. Save detailed discussion of your financial condition and loan requirements for the financial section of your business plan.

OTHER INFORMATION

You may have agreements to distribute or manufacture products that will give your company a competitive edge. Or you may have applied for patents or have copyrights that are important in the development of the business. Also include leases, options, or letters of intent that materially affect your business. Include copies of prospective catalogs or other printed material that will advertise your business. Include a brief description of any of these documents in your executive summary and include complete copies at the end of your plan.

Section III: Owner/Management Background

The purpose of this section of the business plan is to describe the abilities, experience, and qualifications of the people who will run the business. The greater the wealth of experience being brought to bear on the success of the business, the higher the level of confidence potential investors will feel when considering your business's investment potential.

THE MANAGEMENT TEAM

While your business concept, service, or product is the core of your venture, it is the people who personify that business concept. For this reason, it is appropriate to provide an overview of the key people who will be representing your business to your customers. Describe the attributes of each key person, emphasizing their experience, background, and education as they pertain to your business.

Identify any professionals and consultants whose specialized expertise you will use or require. Examples of these professionals include technical consultants, accountants, equipment specialists, and attorneys. In those cases where you have planned to add specialists or additional management to your team, identify those skills you will be seeking and when you plan to bring those people on board.

MANAGEMENT RETENTION

When your business relies on the expertise of key employees, it is a good business practice to provide those key players with appropriate incentives to remain with your company. Potential investors will be interested in the steps you have taken to retain your most valuable employees.

The following incentives provide tangible evidence of your efforts:

- *Salary.* Salary is the amount of money paid to your employees on an annual basis, regardless of performance. If you pay a higher salary than your competitors, indicate how much higher and express the difference as a percentage.
- *Bonuses, commissions, and profit sharing.* A bonus is extra cash, generally paid at the end of the quarter or year, in recognition of superior performance at the company level or the individual level. A commission is cash payment in addition to salary, based on a percentage of total sales made. Profit sharing is a cash distribution to all employees based on the annual profitability of the company.
- *Stock.* Corporations can issue shares of stock to employees as a performance incentive, in effect making the employees part owners and giving them a stake in the financial success of the business. Alternately, they can give employees stock options that will allow them the opportunity to purchase stock in the future at today's prices.

While your business concept, service, or product is the core of your venture, it is the people who personify that business concept.

Section IV: Market Analysis

The market analysis section of your business plan is your opportunity to demonstrate a thorough understanding of your customer base. Developing a thorough knowledge of your market will require some research, but the effort expended here pays big dividends and it will show that you have done your homework. This homework will entail a comprehensive analysis of your industry, target market, customer profile, and major competitors and also a description of your product.

> The market analysis section of your business plan is your opportunity to demonstrate a thorough understanding of your customer base.

Summary

Begin with an overview of the market. Keep in mind that the person reading your plan is probably in a hurry and is likely to be scanning your document rapidly, so give the good news first, and then back it up with the facts. Give the reader an interest in the subject and a desire to learn the details presented in the next sections of your business plan.

Your goal in this section is to identify the most beneficial aspects of the market and present them in a positive, concise, and convincing manner. These sample paragraphs illustrate how.

> Industry statistics indicate that this form of retail business requires a minimum population base of 10,000 people to achieve breakeven sales. ABC Mousetraps serves a much larger population base of 25,000 people.
>
> There has been a growing concern for controlling mice infestations more humanely than by using poisons or the old spring traps. ABC Mousetraps' new trap design is a direct response to this issue.

Industry Analysis

Industrial growth or decline is an important consideration in determining the health of your business. Use this section to discuss trends in your industry as they apply to your market sector. For example, your particular industry may be enjoying an annual growth rate of 10 percent nationwide, while experiencing a growth rate of only 6 percent in your market sector.

There may be underlying factors that affect the growth of your industry. Identify these factors and explain them here. For instance, a decline in the economy either nationally or locally may have a significant impact on your business. Other factors may include seasonal influences, technological advances, government regulation, and environmental or ecological concerns. Include these factors and state them in a format similar to the following:

> A Department of Agriculture study predicts that mice populations in urban areas will increase approximately 12 percent per year during the next ten years.

> The mousetrap industry is seasonal, with peak sales occurring in early to late fall. ABC Mousetraps has efficiently responded to this industry-wide condition through the implementation of innovative production methods and the extensive use of temporary labor resources.

TARGET MARKET

Identify your target market in this section. Describe the type of people you expect your customers to be and why. Include those specific aspects of your product or service that will appeal to those customers and the marketing approach you will use to direct your sales messages to them. You will use demographic statistics to help you determine the characteristics of your market sector. This information is available in your local library, from small business development centers (SBDCs), and through some Internet resources.

> Describe the type of people you expect your customers to be and why.

Some of the characteristics of your target market that might be significant include income bracket, educational level, gender, lifestyle, and family makeup. You must describe the characteristics of your target market in a way that demonstrates that you can reach potential customers in sufficient numbers to sustain your business.

Here's an example of a target market statement:

> The market that ABC Mousetraps will serve is the middle-class, suburban, and rural consumer who desires to control mouse infestation humanely, at a competitively low cost. Additionally, rural customers who store feed or grain for livestock will benefit from a control method that excludes poison and the expense of conventional extermination methods.

CUSTOMER PROFILE

Based on the target market analysis in the previous section, you will then develop a customer profile based on age, income, family status, geographic location, occupation, attitude, and motive for buying. Include any other factors that may be relevant to your product or service. Review the sample business plan at the end of this chapter for more information.

Major Competitors and Participants

If you are just starting out in business, more than likely your market is already being served by your competitors. Use this section of your business plan to identify those competitors. This will demonstrate that you have a full understanding of your market sector and the role your business will assume in it. Also, your research will help identify those parts of the market that are not being adequately serviced, and allow you to target your money, time, and advertising efforts accordingly.

Projected Market Growth

How will your business grow during the next year or during the next five years? Use this section to make some reasonable estimates regarding your projected market share for your product or service. Compare these figures against industry standards and adjust them according to the peculiarities of your market sector.

Section V: Product/Service Offering

Describe your product or service in this section of your business plan. Use detailed, descriptive phrases that clearly identify what you sell as well as any unique characteristics about your product that set you apart from the competition.

Product Summary

Describe your product or service in general terms, summarizing the detailed description that follows in much the same way as you first summarized your market analysis. Identify those other aspects of your business that enhance your product, such as personalized customer service, environmental considerations, or assistance after the sale. For example:

> ABC Mousetraps manufactures and markets a unique mousetrap that does not kill the entrapped rodent. The trap is constructed of recycled paper. Once the trapped mouse is released to the wild or otherwise disposed of, the trap is fully disposable as normal paper waste. ABC Mousetraps also offers free trap placement advice and an industry-unique mouse disposal service that allows the customer to return the trap and rodent to the store for humane disposal at no additional cost—all without having to directly handle the rodent.

If you are just starting out in business, more than likely your market is already being served by your competitors.

DETAILED DESCRIPTION

When your business has more than one product line, describe each one in detail in this section of the business plan. Your purpose here is to give the person reading your business plan a thorough understanding of what you sell as well as any services you provide before or after the sale. Identify how your product or service compares and contrasts with those of your competitors.

> When your business has more than one product line, describe each one in detail in this section of the business plan.

COMPETITIVE COMPARISONS

Most businesses have some sort of competition. Even if you have a new product or service, there are usually alternatives to the product or service you provide. Prospective customers will consider the alternatives and determine if yours has advantages in price, convenience, or design and any other characteristics that distinguish your product or service.

To help communicate your uniqueness among the competitors, list the strengths and weaknesses of your product or service against all those you can identify. List the characteristics that you believe will distinguish your company; then do the same for other companies that are likely to be your direct or indirect competitors. For example, if you plan to open a paintball field, your direct competitors may be the other paintball fields in your area—probably within a 30- or 40-mile drive from your location. You will also need to consider the alternative recreation opportunities that will attract people in your target age or income group who you think are interested in playing.

PRODUCT OR SERVICE UNIQUENESS

As you develop your list of competitive comparisons, you will probably identify characteristics that are unique about your business. If you own a restaurant, for example, you may emphasize speed of service, food quality, ambiance, price, taste, or friendliness of the staff.

Again, itemize these characteristics that make your product or service desirable to a specific group of people. You may want to interview customers or prospective customers to see if they agree with your assessment of the unique characteristics of your business. If you believe that you have a unique approach to a product or problem, but others don't recognize the value of it, there is little value to the perceived difference. In the long run, your customers' perceptions of what they believe is unique will hold the most weight.

RESEARCH AND DEVELOPMENT

Many businesses start with nothing but an investment in research and development (R&D). This investment usually leads to changes in the way something is manufactured or delivered. The value of R&D is difficult to measure until it is tested in the marketplace. However, R&D can give an important competitive lead over companies that have not invested in R&D.

PATENTS AND TRADEMARKS

Patents are processes for manufacturing an item that are protected by the U.S. government. In many cases the protection extends to other countries. The protection is for a limited time but there is normally enough time under patent protection to make a product commercially viable and for the patent holder to get a return on the investment required to take out a patent. Usually patents are obtained through the help of a patent attorney and can be very expensive to obtain. They can be an extremely valuable part of a business, giving the business the exclusive right to create a product under the patent or to license the patent for a royalty and allow other businesses to create the product.

Therefore, ownership of patents may be an extremely important part of a business plan. However, it is not enough to just mention that your business has a patent. You must describe how the patent can generate income for the business and contribute to its success.

Trademarks are identifiers of a product or service that is unique to a company and is protected by the U.S. government from anyone else using the same identification. Trademarks are not as expensive to obtain as patents but often require the help of an attorney to obtain.

Make sure you identify in your business plan any trademarks owned by your business. Trademarks can have a significant value to a business if they carry a positive image for the public. A trademark that has not been advertised or is not well known is of little value; trademarks must prove their value in the marketplace.

Section VI: Marketing Plan

A marketing plan is different from a market analysis. With a marketing plan, you will map out a strategy for reaching your customers and bringing them to you. The purpose of marketing is to get your message out to your potential customers.

THE MESSAGE

The first step in marketing is identifying your message. In addition to the product or service itself, determine what else you are selling. It may be convenience, value, quality, safety, fun, youth, or even sex appeal.

> Patents can be an extremely valuable part of a business, giving the business the exclusive right to create a product under the patent or to license the patent for a royalty and allow other businesses to create the product.

Then, whatever your message is, the advertising media you use must push your message and identify your business with the message. This part of your business plan describes your message and how you will use advertising to associate your business with your message. Overall, your message must be geared toward attracting and retaining customers.

PRODUCT PRICING STRATEGY

Describe your pricing strategy and how it will allow you to compete with other businesses in your industry. Determine whether you will set your prices to be higher than, lower than, or the same as your competitors' prices. Each pricing strategy has inherent advantages, and the one that you use will depend directly on your message. It would make little sense, for instance, to emphasize value in your advertising while pricing your product higher than the competition.

PRODUCT POSITIONING

Positioning refers to the process of ideally presenting your product to the segment of the market you are specifically targeting as your customer base. For instance, camping gear is positioned to attract younger, recreational consumers while garden tractors are positioned to attract older, primarily male consumers. Positioning will influence which advertising media you use to market your product or service. Briefly describe your product positioning strategy in this section of the business plan.

> Positioning refers to the process of ideally presenting your product to the segment of the market you are specifically targeting as your customer base.

PROMOTIONAL STRATEGY

Promotion is the art of associating your company with your product in ways and under circumstances that wouldn't occur ordinarily. To promote your business, you can do one or more of the following:

- Sponsor local amateur sporting teams.
- Contribute funds for public facilities.
- Provide scholarship funds to graduating seniors.
- Participate in charity events.
- Pay for publishing church bulletins or newsletters.

All of these activities provide you with the opportunity to promote and advertise your business as well as contribute to goodwill.

Section VII: Financial Plan and Analysis

The financial plan is the meat of your business plan. If you are preparing your business plan for the purpose of obtaining funding, this section will tell a lender whether the amount is reasonable and whether you are capable of handling the additional debt. Most investors expect to see the information in this section presented in a specific format. Essential elements include:

- Start-up capital requirements
- Financial highlights
- A three- to five-year projected income statement
- A three- to five-year projected balance sheet
- Future cash budgets or cash flow statements
- A breakeven analysis

INITIAL CAPITAL REQUIREMENTS

This section is sometimes called sources and uses of funds. You first mentioned the amount of required capital in the Executive Summary (Section I) of your business plan. This is the section where you develop an explanation of that amount.

Break down and identify the costs associated with the start-up or improvements to your business, detailing where you expect the money to come from and how you expect to spend it once you receive it. Potential lenders will expect to see this information in a table format. If you have the capability to produce a graph of your information, it is acceptable to do so. Refer to Chapter 4 for details on how to obtain financing.

As a new business you won't be able to provide any financial history. However, you can project your expenses and income based on some reasonable expectations. You should be able to defend your assumptions about sales as well as certain expenses. Too often, profits look very promising but fail to materialize because expenses such as taxes, repairs, insurance, and miscellaneous are not included in the projections. It is not uncommon for a new business to show a loss for the first year of operation. What lenders want to know is how much loss you project and how you will recover from the loss with profits in future years.

FINANCIAL HIGHLIGHTS

This section highlights key financial information calculated for the next five years. This provides information at a glance on the projected liquidity, leverage, efficiency, and profitability of your business for the planning period. Ideally, your debt-to-equity ratio should decrease over time while your gross margin should remain at or above the averages for your industry. For more information on how to prepare this section, consult your accountant.

THREE- TO FIVE-YEAR INCOME STATEMENT

The income statement is frequently referred to as the profit and loss (P&L) statement. It shows how profitable your business is after all expenses are paid. Income statements are read from top to bottom, and entries are listed in the following order: income from sales, cost of sales, and gross profit. These are followed by a listing of general and administrative expenses. Subtracting total expenses from the gross profit reveals net profit before taxes. Finally, taxes are subtracted to leave net profit as the bottom line.

> The financial section highlights key financial information calculated for the next five years.

Your accountant may help you prepare this financial form. If your business is too small to warrant an accountant, a computer program such as QuickBooks will generate this report for you from the information you enter into the program. Alternatively, many popular spreadsheet programs such as 1-2-3 (IBM Lotus SmartSuite) or Microsoft Excel provide the basic tools necessary to produce these forms.

THREE- TO FIVE-YEAR BALANCE SHEET

The balance sheet provides a snapshot of your business's financial position for each planning period. More than an income statement, the balance sheet includes such things as the values of equipment, facilities, and property. For this reason, it provides the potential investor with better information about the financial condition of your company than can be derived merely from your income statements.

The balance sheet compares all assets and liabilities. Excess value is the company's net worth. Net worth is distributed as equity or retained as earnings for the company to use. In either case, the net worth is listed as a liability. Once you've listed them all, liabilities and assets should balance out, hence the name "balance sheet."

Balance sheets may be difficult to prepare without professional assistance. Buildings, facilities, and equipment depreciate in value over a set period, property improvements result in appreciation of property, and inventory values vary with time and acquisition costs.

CASH FLOW OR CASH BUDGET STATEMENTS

Cash flow statements, sometimes called cash budgets, tell the story about your ability to conduct business on a daily basis. Most businesses are subject to seasonal or market fluctuations. It is important to be sufficiently liquid to survive lean times. Liquidity is important as well for businesses that maintain large inventories or that operate with a large credit base.

The cash flow statement is similar to your checking account ledger. You work to maintain a positive balance in your account at all times. If you run out of cash, you no longer have the resources necessary to conduct business, even if your income statement shows a continuous net profit. Many businesses have closed because of success. By trying to produce more products than the cash flow permits, a business may run out of cash and be unable to deliver products on time, thus losing contracts or not collecting receivables when expected.

Most lenders will be very interested in your cash flow statements and will check them against your policies for accounts receivable, aging, inventory turn, and other indicators of your business health.

BREAKEVEN ANALYSIS

> The breakeven analysis tells you how much income you must have from gross sales to meet all expenses.

The breakeven analysis tells you how much income you must have from gross sales to meet all expenses. Expenses include total fixed expenses plus the cost of goods. To arrive at a breakeven figure, you divide total fixed expenses such as rent, utilities, and insurance by your gross profit margin. Profit margin may fluctuate from product line to product line, so you will have to adjust your figures accordingly. The main reason for including a breakeven analysis in your business plan is to show that you have sufficient income to continue operations.

Chapter Wrap-Up

Your smart business plan will give you the edge your business needs to prosper in today's competitive environment. The key to your business plan is preparation and research. Make sure you allot sufficient time to researching the various aspects of your business plan. Use the basic outline in this chapter to stay organized. While you focus on the critical aspects of your business, consider the following:

- *Clearly identify your business concept.* What product or service will you sell and what type of business is it?
- *Know your industry.* Become familiar with the ups and downs of your industry. Is it seasonal or are there cyclical economic influences that will affect your operation? How big is your industry and at what maturity level is it currently?

- *Understand your target market.* Know the demographics and psychographics of your customer base. Find out what appeals to your customers and work those things into your sales and marketing strategy.
- *Familiarize yourself with your competitors.* Take a close look at what you're up against. What are your competitors doing that you aren't? What things will you do better than your competitors?
- *Know what distinguishes your product or service.* Investors will want to know what makes your business concept unique. Is it a new product or service? Did you improve on an existing idea? Are you serving a new market or filling a need in a market that has yet to be reached?

As you document the answers to these questions, you will begin to see the blueprint of your business. You can use this blueprint to approach investors and lenders and to build a successful business.

101 Wet Stone Hill Road
Wakefield, RI 02756
Telephone (401) 422-8888
evergreen@inter.net
Contact: Nolan Wentworth

S A M P L E   B U S I N E S S   P L A N

Evergreen Lawn Care

Professional Lawn Care

TABLE OF CONTENTS

Evergreen Lawn Care
Business Plan

EXECUTIVE SUMMARY

Evergreen Lawn Care is a start-up company that will provide fertilizing and weed and insect control. The sole proprietor of the company is Mr. Nolan Wentworth, who is contributing his own capital, significant lawn care experience, knowledge, and business skill. Mr. Wentworth is an area expert on lawn care with a very good reputation. His expertise and reputation give Evergreen a competitive service advantage. In addition to Mr. Wentworth's contributed capital, Evergreen will need another $75,000 for start-up capital. The business will operate in South County, Rhode Island.

Evergreen's marketing plan was designed to initially attempt to convert a large portion of the more than 2,000 customers that Mr. Wentworth helped to service when he was employed by GreenThumb, an area lawn care company. Additional marketing and advertising strategies are designed to target the business executives and professionals who don't have the time or expertise to maintain a beautiful lawn but understand the extent to which a nicely landscaped lawn increases property values. Evergreen's particular niche and positioning will be to appeal to the environmentally conscious homeowners who are concerned about their kids, the long-lasting health of their lawn, and the impact on Mother Earth.

Currently, the lawn care business in South County is dominated by one company—Mr. Wentworth's former employer, GreenThumb. Some landscapers and grass-cutting companies also offer fertilizing services, but these providers hold an insignificant portion of the market. From all indicators, the South County lawn care market has experienced little competition; therefore, Evergreen has an excellent opportunity to create a large customer base if it can persuade people that it can offer greater expertise and value-added services than the current supplier, GreenThumb.

While Evergreen will directly compete with GreenThumb, it is offering a service that differentiates it from GreenThumb. Here are some of the ways in which Evergreen's service will be different:

- *The 14-point lawn care evaluation.* Evergreen will offer every prospective customer a free lawn evaluation that can be used to develop a custom-designed six-step lawn care program. GreenThumb does not offer a comparable analysis.

- *Evergreen's organic alternative.* Evergreen will offer customers an organic alternative that is safer for the environment than the fertilizer used by GreenThumb. The facts will easily show how Evergreen's services will cost far less in the long run, while customers will appreciate the added safety the services afford their children and pets.

- *Evergreen's experience and expertise.* Evergreen is the only area company to have Nolan Wentworth, a lawn care professional who is highly respected in the South County region.

Type of Business

Evergreen Lawn Care is a service business specializing in fertilizing and weed and insect control.

Company/Business Summary

This is a start-up business that will be organized as a sole proprietorship, a business to be owned and operated by Nolan Wentworth. The firm will provide services for the care and maintenance of lawns, trees, and shrubs. The company will concentrate services on preventing plant life disease and promoting plant growth by using natural alternatives.

Financial Objectives

The financial plan and analysis section of this business plan details the projected operating results, financial position, cash budgets, and break-even point. Below is a chart that summarizes the financial objectives for the five-year planning period beginning in 2006.

OPERATING PERFORMANCE HIGHLIGHTS (all numbers in $000)

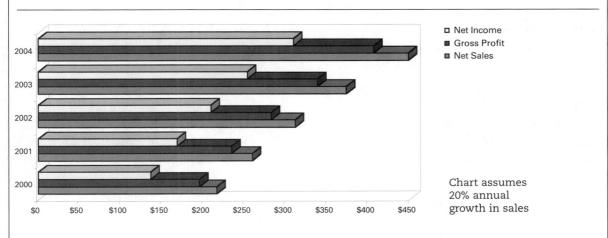

OPERATING PERFORMANCE HIGHLIGHTS

	2000	2001	2002	2003	2004
Net Sales	$216	$259	$311	$373	$448
Gross Profit	$195	$234	$282	$338	$406
Net Income	$136	$168	$209	$253	$309

Management Overview

Nolan Wentworth is a graduate of the University of Rhode Island's Turf Sciences program. Mr. Wentworth also worked for five years as a greenskeeper for a large public golf course in Massachusetts and worked for another five years as a landscape architect for a nursery in Rhode Island. For the last two years, Mr. Wentworth worked for GreenThumb as a lawn specialist, a position that required him to become company-certified. Mr. Wentworth worked under the direction of an agronomist for over six months while he was with GreenThumb.

Product/Service and Competition

Evergreen Lawn Care will offer a six-application lawn care program. These applications will be custom designed for the particular grass type and location. Evergreen will be offering the homeowner safe, all-natural fertilizers and weed controllers.

Funds Requested

Evergreen is requesting a five-year $75,000 loan to finance the start-up. Collateral of about $65,000 is available to secure the loan.

Use of Proceeds

The $75,000 loan proceeds will be used to purchase a truck and equipment that will cost approximately $65,000. The remaining loan proceeds will be used to purchase supplies (fertilizer and other related chemicals).

COMPANY BACKGROUND

Identification of Market Opportunity

Evergreen Lawn Care plans on providing fertilizing and weed and insect control services to

South County, Rhode Island. According to statistics provided by the Small Business Development Center of Rhode Island, the lawn care business is a $750,000 market in South County. There are no Rhode Island statistics on the rate of growth in revenues for the lawn care industry, but according to *Lawn and Turf Magazine*, a trade association publication, the national growth rate for lawn care services has been 20 percent for the last five years and the sector is forecasted to grow at that rate into the near future.

South County, Rhode Island is an excellent market opportunity for this service, with only one competitor, GreenThumb, a national company that has granted a franchise in South County.

The Professional Landscapers of America estimate that the homeowner's return at resale can be between $800 and $1,200 over the cost of lawn care improvements. However, there is no debate that the value of a home is enhanced through the use of lawn care services. The use of lawn care services tends to be common in areas where home values are relatively high and where home sales are vigorous.

While Mr. Wentworth was with GreenThumb, he observed several things that convinced him that his Evergreen start-up has excellent chances for success:

- There is an overwhelming desire by most customers for a safer alternative to the toxic chemicals that required flag notification at the end of a treatment.
- Traditional lawn treatment companies are wed to the past and have little opportunity to change methods because of equipment investment and reliance on old ways.
- Mr. Wentworth studied the organic trend closely and experimented with it extensively. He became convinced that his expertise, drive, and customer knowledge would provide a competitive edge.

Business History

Evergreen is a start-up company. Mr. Wentworth has recently resigned from his position with GreenThumb to start his venture. To date, he has invested approximately $5,000 of his own capital.

Growth and Financial Objectives

The first-year goal of Evergreen is to have 275 customers by the end of the first 12 months, with subsequent annual growth in revenues equal to the national projected rate of 20 percent per year.

FIVE-YEAR SALES FORECAST (all numbers in 000)

	2000	2001	2002	2003	2004
Lawn Feed and Weed	$156	$187	$224	$269	$323
Tree and Shrub Care	48	58	70	84	101
Other	12	14	17	20	24
Total Sales	$216	$259	$311	$373	$448

FIVE-YEAR SALES FORECAST (all numbers in $000)

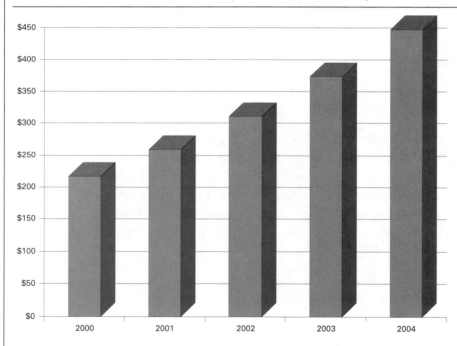

Sales forecast based on 275 customers the first year, followed by 20% growth

Legal Structure and Ownership

The company is organized as a sole proprietorship. Mr. Wentworth has filed all the necessary paperwork to gain a d.b.a. certificate and all appropriate permits.

Company Location and Facilities

Mr. Wentworth will conduct the business from his home office at 101 Wet Stone Hill Road, Wakefield, Rhode Island. The home office is equipped with a personal computer, a laser printer, and a fax machine. Mr. Wentworth has erected a 2,500-square-foot barn on this residential property that will be used to store supplies and equipment, including the company truck.

Plans for Financing the Business

Mr. Wentworth has contributed $5,000 of his personal funds to the business venture. He plans to contribute an additional $20,000 from a maturing CD and another $10,000 from a loan from his father-in-law. He will need an additional $75,000, in the form of a five-year business loan, to purchase supplies, equipment, and a truck. The loan can be collateralized, at least to some extent, with the title to the truck and the equipment. The truck and equipment will have a combined cost of $65,000.

OWNER'S BACKGROUND

Since the business is organized as a sole proprietorship, there is no management team. Mr. Wentworth will be the sole manager.

Background on Mr. Wentworth

Nolan Wentworth, who will run the business, is a graduate of the University of Rhode Island's Turf Sciences program. He has also had excellent practical experience, with much of this related to lawn care. Mr. Wentworth worked for five years as a greenskeeper for a large public golf course in Massachusetts and worked for another five years as a landscape architect for a nursery in Rhode Island. For the last two years, Mr. Wentworth worked for GreenThumb as a lawn specialist, a position for which he had to become company-certified. While he was with GreenThumb, Mr. Wentworth worked under the direction of an agronomist for over six months.

Mr. Wentworth also keeps up with developments in the industry. He is very much aware of the April 1990 public hearings held by the U.S. Senate to acquire information on the environmental impact of the use of chemical insecticides and fertilizers. He is keenly aware that the government may increase its regulation of this business and he is constantly reevaluating any impact this might have on the industry. He has researched new fertilizers and insecticides that are not harmful to the environment and is very much interested in organically based fertilizers. Mr. Wentworth plans to stay on top of the effects of new products on the environment through books, magazines, conferences, and workshops. His business knowledge will become a public relations tool.

Other Employees

The company will have two part-time employees. Evergreen will use the skills of two family members:

- Mr. Wentworth's wife, Jane, will manage the books for the company and manage the customer renewal process.
- In the summer, Mr. Wentworth will employ his son Jimmy (age 20), who is attending the University of Massachusetts Amherst. Jimmy is studying Architectural Landscape Design.

MARKET ANALYSIS

Summary

From all indications, the South County lawn care market is large enough to support several companies. At this time only one major player is in the market. The lack of competition in the market plus Evergreen's unique expertise and approach make success highly probable. The overall market seems large enough and is growing fast enough to provide plenty of business for a company that can successfully service its target market. Evergreen's target market has three factors that will also contribute to success.

- They are sold on the idea that a beautiful lawn and fine-looking shrubs and trees add significant value to a property.
- They lack the time needed to conduct their own lawn care program.
- They have the economic resources to afford a six-step application program.

While this factor is not essential to marketing, Mr. Wentworth believes that the large majority of customers will select the Evergreen alternative because of its organic approach.

Industry Analysis

It is estimated that more than 15 million homes nationwide use lawn care services. The size of the South County, Rhode Island market for lawn care is estimated to be potentially $750,000 per year. This estimate is based on the industry statistics that disclose the number of suburban households per thousand that contracts for lawn care. Evergreen's projected share of the market is modest, at approximately 14 percent of the market by the end of year one.

Target Market

The market that Evergreen will be targeting is the suburban upper-middle-class to upper-class market with household annual incomes from $60,000 to $100,000 and higher. In South County, Rhode Island, there are approximately 22,000 households with annual incomes in the range defined above. The six-application-per-year lawn care maintenance program, which costs an average of $360 (for 7,000 square feet), is affordable for this market. People in the defined market already see or can be easily convinced to see the merit of the six-application process as a way of ensuring a beautiful lawn. Statistics show that in neighborhoods where the average household income is $60,000 or above, one out of every three homes has a lawn care provider. However, market penetration in the South County area has not been great up till now, with only one local vendor providing service. Estimates show that only one out of ten homes in this demographic segment currently contracts lawn care services.

Customer Profile

The demographics of the homeowner market that Evergreen will serve are as follows:

- Income level: $60,000 + annual household income
- Occupation: executive and professional
- Median property values: $130,000 +
- Neighborhoods: suburban, upper-middle class
- More likely to have at least one child

Major Competitors and Participants

The only major competitor at this time is GreenThumb. Other competitors are lawn maintenance (grass cutting) companies and landscapers who offer lawn care as secondary to their primary business. GreenThumb is a national company that has had a South County franchise for the past four years. GreenThumb has had the market virtually to itself. Evergreen will be in direct competition with GreenThumb. Mr. Wentworth was employed by GreenThumb for the last two years and will attempt to persuade GreenThumb customers to convert to Evergreen at 5 percent below their GreenThumb cost. GreenThumb has over 2,000 customers.

Projected Market Growth and Market Share Objectives

Mr. Wentworth's sales goals are very modest, with a target of 275 customers by the end of year one. It is estimated that Evergreen's market share will be approximately 14 percent of the existing market but under 5 percent of the potential market. Mr. Wentworth is predicting that half of these customers will come from the current GreenThumb base and half will be new customers. Annual growth is assumed to be at least at the national projection of 20 percent for each of the next five years. These goals seem to be modest and achievable when compared with the customer list of over 2,000 customers from GreenThumb.

PRODUCT/SERVICE OFFERING

Product/Service Summary

The service that Evergreen will offer is a six-step lawn care program that involves fertilizing for growth and color and applications that will control weeds and insects. Each program will be custom-designed based on a 14-point, no-charge evaluation.

Product/Service Uniqueness

Evergreen's service is also unique because of the skill and knowledge that Mr. Wentworth brings to the business. In addition, Mr. Wentworth's customer relation skills help to make this venture unique and give a definite competitive advantage to the firm. Mr. Wentworth knows that being courteous to the clients and his expert qualifications are the most critical issues for this business. If a lawn care firm is unable to maintain a friendly, courteous relationship with its customers, it will not be successful.

Product/Service Descriptions

Evergreen will be in the business of selling a six-part application process that will give the homeowner a beautiful lawn. The service consists of a six specifically designed and seasonally scheduled service visits (applications).

- *Early season.* The first visit of the year involves an application that will promote spring green-up and lawn recovery from winter stress. The application will also help control weeds and crabgrass.
- *Spring.* This application is designed to give the lawn extra nutrients, which will make the grass greener and thicker. Weed and crabgrass control will be applied only if necessary.
- *Early summer.* This fertilizer application gets the lawn ready for the possible stressful summer (heat and drought) ahead. The lawn will be checked for isolated weed and insect problems and treated accordingly.
- *Late summer.* Like application 3, this is a fertilizer that will help promote color without pushing growth. Again, the lawn will be checked for isolated weed and insect problems and treated accordingly.

- *Early fall.* This application is designed to help thicken the lawn and to promote new root growth. Since weeds and insects can be present in fall lawns, the technician will check for those problems and treat the lawn accordingly.
- *Late fall.* This application consists of a special fertilizer that will promote root growth and food storage for the winter ahead. This application is critical for winter survival and will help bring about a healthier lawn the following spring.

Competitive Comparisons

Many of the services offered by Evergreen are comparable in price and value to those of GreenThumb. However, there are four differences.

Evergreen will offer a free 14-point evaluation that will help the technician design an appropriate program and will give the homeowner a better understanding of his or her lawn's needs. The 14-point evaluation is in writing (in a checklist format) and examines the following: grass type, turf density, color, thatch, diseases, soil type, weeds, mowing, insects, shade, watering, problem grasses, potential, and present conditions.

Another distinct difference between GreenThumb and Evergreen is that Evergreen will give the homeowner the option of using organic and environmentally safe fertilizers. The homeowner will be told, in writing, the pros and cons of organic and non-organic fertilizers and the difference in cost between the two will be clearly disclosed.

The third competitive difference is that Evergreen will not charge an additional amount for grub control, as is the case with GreenThumb.

Finally, another competitive advantage is Mr. Wentworth, who is well known in the community and has already developed a rapport with many of GreenThumb's customers. In addition to working with many homeowners in South County, Mr. Wentworth is a frequent guest on a local talk radio home and garden show. The benefits Evergreen can sell because of Mr. Wentworth's background, reputation, and experience include many intangibles: confidence, reliability, and answers to questions about lawn care.

Competition Comparison

The following chart summarizes the key differences between GreenThumb and Evergreen Lawn Care:

Feature	Evergreen	GreenThumb
Seasonal Cost	$10.00 per 1,000 sq. ft.	$9.75 per 1,000 sq. ft.
Customer Satisfaction	Money-Back Guarantee	Money-Back Guarantee
Treatment	Organic	Toxic Chemicals
Child- and Pet-Safe	Yes	No
Grub Control	Included	Extra Charge
Effective Long-Term Treatment	Yes	No (requires more and more chemicals)

Research and Development

Evergreen has access to a regional agronomist who is employed by Grass Roots, Inc., Evergreen's fertilizer supplier. Grass Roots, Inc. spends in excess of $500,000 annually on R&D and freely shares its findings with its customers. Grass Roots, Inc. also conducts quarterly seminars on lawn care at its Montvale, New Jersey, headquarters. In his study of the organic treatments, Mr. Wentworth spent a lot of time with Grass Roots, Inc. and has a strong working relationship with its research team.

Patents and Trademarks

Evergreen does not own any patents or trademarks.

MARKETING PLAN

Creating and Maintaining Customers

Evergreen will attract and maintain customers by pricing its service competitively and demonstrating, through hard work and a customer-driven approach, that the company can take the time and hassle out of lawn care. Evergreen will position itself as the busy person's safe and natural way to a beautiful lawn. Customers will quickly recognize that the company's main "asset" is its founder, Mr. Nolan Wentworth. And, as is often the case with service-oriented businesses, Evergreen will attract new customers as current customers begin to appreciate the skill, expertise, and knowledge of Mr. Wentworth. Those customers will recommend Evergreen to their family and friends and will help to broaden the customer base.

Product-Pricing Strategy

Evergreen's service will be priced to be competitive with the marketplace. Mr. Wentworth understands the pricing strategy of the competitor and he will monitor its pricing to stay competitive. GreenThumb's basic price is $9.75 per 1,000 square feet (with discounts given, because of economies of scale, when total square footage is greater than 12,000 feet).

Evergreen's sales literature tells customers that Evergreen will meet the price or promotional appeals of any competitor, as long as the customer has documented proof — such as a competitor's bid sheet, program estimate, or coupon. Existing GreenThumb customers will be given a one-year 10-percent discount enticement to convert their lawn care service to Evergreen. Mr. Wentworth is happy to give these discounts for the first year in order to establish the business base. He is confident that he will be able to retain the customers over a several-year period.

Product Positioning

While Mr. Wentworth brings some clear skills to the business, the most important positioning of the business is its safe, natural, and longer-lasting approach. There have been many negative reports on the use of lawn chemicals. Evergreen has contracted with a local artist to design a truck that will communicate this message loud and clear to the customer. The company has also secured a local telephone number that spells NATURAL. "Call NATURAL to find out more" will be one of the messages on the truck.

The Evergreen service will be positioned as the professional and executive solution to expert lawn care. Advertising will discuss how most homeowners could perform their own lawn care program, but the time and hassle of the task are a barrier. Emphasis will also be placed on the value of expert service. Mr. Wentworth's background and reputation and the 14-point evaluation will help substantiate the expert claim.

Sales and Service Delivery

The sales cycle in this service business is very seasonal: 75 percent of all purchase decisions are made between February 15th and April 15th. The service delivery begins on May 1st. There are five main ways to get a new client and the chances of success are in this order:

- Recommendation by a friend
- Article or other public relations opportunity
- Direct mail
- Newspaper advertisement
- Presence of the truck in neighborhood

The promotional plan below is designed to complement this sales cycle and customer buying mentality.

Mr. Wentworth will perform much of the direct calls on sales prospects and lead the follow-up efforts. He will also use freelancers in the area to perform telemarketing. Mr. Wentworth's wife, Jane, will handle the books, manage the billing, and sign up customers from one year to the next.

The service will be delivered to the customer using a variety of equipment and tools. Evergreen will initially purchase a GMC small flatbed truck that will be retrofitted with a tank-and-pump system for applying the fertilizer and weed control. The truck, tank, and pump system are the key equipment of the business. The estimated cost of the system is $65,000.

Promotional Strategy

The promotional strategy will consist of telemarketing calls to current GreenThumb customers to tell them about Mr. Wentworth's service and offer them the one-year 10-percent discount. In addition, any customer who refers two customers to Evergreen will receive one of the applications free. On average, the free application represents a $60 value. The company will also use a telemarketing service to set up appointments for the 14-point lawn evaluation. Homeowners will be contacted and informed that an Evergreen technician will be in the area conducting free, no-obligation lawn analysis. The calls will clearly differentiate the service from Evergreen's chemical competitor.

Evergreen will also use a local bulk mail coupon service that will mail monthly coupon savers and offers for the free 14-point lawn evaluation to households with median incomes of $60,000 or more. The mailing will include a special offer for 1,000 frequent flier miles on American Airlines or United Airlines, the two most popular affinity programs. Mr. Wentworth recently attended a convention that discussed the value of these programs when services of over $500 are offered to high-income purchasers.

Newspaper advertising campaigns, both in traditional hometown papers and in the free "shopper papers," will be executed in late winter/early spring and in early fall.

The service truck for the company will bear the company logo and a brief listing of services offered, along with the NATURAL business telephone number.

When a technician completes a written estimate, he will give a brochure to that potential customer. The brochure will describe Mr. Wentworth's skills and experience and the type of service the customer will receive. In addition, after a technician renders a service, he will give the customer a brochure describing what he or she needs to do to maintain the grass.

Evergreen will offer special prices in the spring and discounts to regular customers who contract for year-long services.

Mr. Wentworth plans to spend a reasonable part of his time working with local newspapers and radio shows to place articles about the advantages of natural lawn care. He has enlisted the services of some local college journalism students to write some sample articles that will be distributed to the media.

FINANCIAL PLAN AND ANALYSIS

Initial Capital Requirements

The initial start-up capital requirements of the business are expected to be about $110,000. A large portion of the initial capital (76 percent) is for the upfront costs for equipment and supplies. The remaining amount (24 percent) is for the monthly expenses needed to launch the business.

Financial Highlights

Key financial ratios have been calculated for the five-year planning period and are shown below. Although the debt/equity ratio is a bit high at the end of year one, it improves significantly during years two through five. Please note that since this is a service business, the gross margin is 100 percent because there is no cost of sales, just operating expenses.

Five-Year Income Statement

The projected operating results for the five-year planning period are shown below in the pro-forma income statements. Net profits range from $8,000 for the first full year of operation to $36,000 by the fifth year.

Five-Year Balance Sheet

The projected financial position as of the end of each fiscal year in the planning period is shown below.

Cash Budgets

Cash budgets have been prepared using two formats: a 12-month cash budget for year one and annual budgets for each of the five planning periods. Both reports are shown below.

Breakeven Analysis

The monthly breakeven point of about $5,200 in sales translates to about $62,400 annually. According to income statement projections, the store will operate above the breakeven point for all five years in the planning period.

ESTIMATED START-UP CAPITAL

	Monthly Expenses	Cash Needed to Start	% of Total
MONTHLY COSTS			
Salary of owner-manager	$1,000	$3,000	2.7%
All other salaries and wages	833	2,499	2.3%
Rent		0	0.0%
Advertising	250	3,000	2.7%
Delivery expense		0	0.0%
Supplies	1,250	15,000	13.6%
Telephone		0	0.0%
Other utilities		0	0.0%
Insurance	250	3,000	2.7%
Taxes, including social security		0	0.0%
Interest		0	0.0%
Maintenance		0	0.0%
Legal and other professional fees		0	0.0%
Miscellaneous		0	0.0%
Subtotal		$26,499	24%
ONE-TIME COSTS			
Fixtures and equipment		$65,000	59.1%
Decorating and remodeling			0.0%
Installation charges			0.0%
Starting inventory		10,000	9.1%
Deposits with public utilities			0.0%
Legal and other professional fees		1,000	0.9%
Licenses and permits		500	0.5%
Advertising and promotion for opening		2,000	1.8%
Cash		5,000	4.5%
Other			0.0%
Subtotal		$83,500	76%
TOTAL ESTIMATED START-UP CAPITAL		$109,999	

FINANCIAL HIGHLIGHTS

	2000	2001	2002	2003	2004
Liquidity					
Current Ratio	8.62	11.00	18.69	23.15	29.00
Acid-Test Ratio	6.31	8.31	14.85	19.31	24.38
Leverage					
Debt Ratio	27.86%	14.10%	8.07%	4.55%	2.39%
Debt/Equity Ratio	38.62%	16.41%	8.78%	4.77%	2.45%
Times Interest Earned	20.43	25.00	30.86	37.14	45.14
Efficiency					
Inventory Turnover	0.70	0.71	0.58	0.70	0.70
Average Collection Period	16.90	28.19	23.47	29.36	32.59
Total Asset Turnover	0.82	0.69	0.58	0.51	0.47
Profitability					
Gross Margin	90.28%	90.35%	90.68%	90.62%	90.63%
Return on Assets	51.91%	44.68%	39.21%	34.90%	32.12%
Return on Equity	71.96%	52.01%	42.65%	36.56%	32.91%

INCOME STATEMENT

For the Years 2000 through 2004
(all numbers in $000)

	2000	2001	2002	2003	2004
REVENUE					
Gross sales	$216	$259	$311	$373	$448
Less returns and allowances	0	0	0	0	0
Net Sales	$216	$259	$311	$373	$448
COST OF SALES					
Total Cost of Goods Sold	$21	$25	$29	$35	$42
Gross Profit (Loss)	$195	$234	$282	$338	$406
OPERATING EXPENSES					
Selling					
Salaries and wages	$3	$3	$3	$3	$3
Commissions					
Advertising	$5	$5	$5	$5	$5
Depreciation	$3	$3	$3	$3	$3
Other	$1	$1	$1	$1	$1
Total Selling Expenses	$12	$12	$12	$12	$12
General & Administrative					
Salaries and wages	$20	$25	$30	$40	$50
Employee benefits	$3	$4	$5	$6	$7
Payroll taxes	$3	$4	$5	$6	$7
Insurance	$4	$4	$4	$4	$4
Rent					
Utilities	$2	$2	$2	$2	$2
Depreciation & amortization	$5	$5	$5	$5	$5
Office supplies	$1	$1	$1	$1	$1
Travel & entertainment	$1	$1	$1	$1	$1
Postage	$1	$1	$1	$1	$1
Interest	$7	$7	$7	$7	$7
Furniture & equipment					
Total G&A Expenses	$47	$54	$61	$73	$85
Total Operating Expenses	$59	$66	$73	$85	$97
Net Income Before Taxes	$136	$168	$209	$253	$309
Taxes on income	0	0	0	0	0
Net Income After Taxes	$136	$168	$209	$253	$309
Extraordinary gain or loss					
Income tax on extraordinary gain					
NET INCOME (LOSS)	**$136**	**$168**	**$209**	**$253**	**$309**

BALANCE SHEET—YEARS ONE THROUGH FIVE

ASSETS	2000	2001	2002	2003	2004
Current Assets					
Cash	$53	$68	$148	$191	$237
Net accounts receivable	10	20	20	30	40
Inventory	30	35	50	50	60
Temporary investment	9	10	10	10	20
Prepaid expenses	10	10	15	20	20
Total Current Assets	$112	$143	$243	$301	$377
Fixed Assets					
Long-term investments	$30	$45	$80	$54	$65
Land					130
Buildings (net of depreciation)				150	170
Plant & equipment (net)	110	178	200	200	200
Furniture & fixtures (net)	10	10	10	20	20
Total Net Fixed Assets	$150	$233	$290	$424	$585
TOTAL ASSETS	$262	$376	$533	$725	$962
LIABILITIES					
Current Liabilities					
Accounts payable	$10	$10	$10	$10	$10
Short-term notes					
Current portion of long-term notes					
Accruals & other payables	3	3	3	3	3
Total Current Liabilities	$13	$13	$13	$13	$13
Long-Term Liabilities					
Mortgage					
Other long-term liabilities	60	40	30	20	10
Total Long-Term Liabilities	$60	$40	$30	$20	$10
Shareholders' Equity					
Capital stock	$80	$80	$80	$80	$80
Retained earnings	109	243	410	612	859
Total Shareholders' Equity	$189	$323	$490	$692	$939
TOTAL LIABILITIES & EQUITY	$262	$376	$533	$725	$962

CASH BUDGET—FIRST 12 MONTHS

For the Year 2000
(all numbers in $000)

	Jan	Feb	Mar	Apr	May	Jun	Jul	Aug	Sep	Oct	Nov	Dec
Beginning cash balance	$2	$22	$25	$26	$30	$34	$35	$39	$42	$45	$47	$51
Cash from operations	10	10	10	10	10	10	10	10	10	10	10	10
Total Available Cash	$12	$32	$35	$36	$40	$44	$45	$49	$52	$55	$57	$61
Less:												
Capital expenditures	$84											
Operating Expenses	$15	$6	$6	$5	$5	$6	$5	$6	$6	$5	$5	$5
Interest			2			2				2		2
Dividends												
Debt retirement	1	1	1	1	1	1	1	1	1	1	1	1
Other												
Total Disbursements	$100	$7	$9	$6	$6	$9	$6	$7	$7	$8	$6	$8
Cash Surplus (Deficit)	($88)	$25	$26	$30	$34	$35	$39	$42	$45	$47	$51	$53
Add:												
Short-term loans												
Long-term loans	75											
Capital stock issues	35											
Total Additions	$110	$0	$0	$0	$0	$0	$0	$0	$0	$0	$0	$0
Ending Cash Balance	**$22**	**$25**	**$26**	**$30**	**$34**	**$35**	**$39**	**$42**	**$45**	**$47**	**$51**	**$53**

CASH BUDGET ACTIVITY—FIRST 12 MONTHS (all numbers in $000)

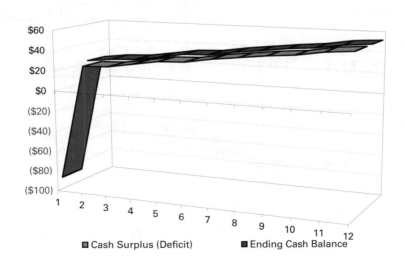

CASH BUDGET—YEARS ONE THROUGH FIVE

For the Years 2000 through 2004
(all numbers in $000)

	2000	2001	2002	2003	2004
Beginning cash balance	$2	$53	$68	$148	$191
Cash from operations	120	112	185	190	190
Total Available Cash	$122	$165	$253	$338	$381
Less:					
Capital expenditures	$84				
Operating Expenses	75	79	90	131	130
Interest	8	5	4	3	2
Dividends	0				
Debt retirement	12	13	11	13	12
Other	0				
Total Disbursements	$179	$97	$105	$147	$144
Cash Surplus (Deficit)	($57)	$68	$148	$191	$237
Add:					
Short-term loans	$0				
Long-term loans	75				
Capital stock issues	35				
Total Additions	$110	$0	$0	$0	$0
Ending Cash Balance	**$53**	**$68**	**$148**	**$191**	**$237**

CASH BUDGET ACTIVITY—FIVE YEARS (all numbers in $000)

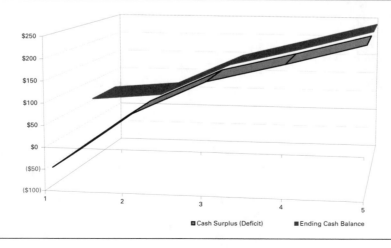

BREAKEVEN ANALYSIS

	Fixed Costs	Variable Costs
Product costs		
Average cost of product		$15.00
Monthly selling expenses		
Sales salaries & commissions	$1,000	
Advertising	$500	
Miscellaneous selling expense	$400	
Monthly general expenses		
Office salaries	$0	
Supplies	$1,000	
Miscellaneous general expense	$1,000	
Totals	$3,900	$15.00
Average selling price per unit		$60.00
Results		
Contribution margin per unit		$45.00
Monthly unit sales at break-even point		87
Monthly sales dollars at break-even point		$5,200

BREAKEVEN ANALYSIS (all numbers in $000)

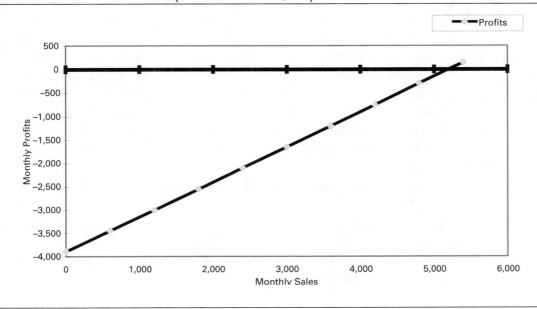

4 | *Obtaining the Financing You Need*

Business ownership can bring many new challenges to your life. Many of these challenges center on having enough money to help you stay afloat in down times and keep you riding high during times of profitability. As a start-up, you will need to obtain financing for many aspects of your venture. For instance, unless you are a home-based business, you will need to purchase a building or rent office space to operate your business. More than likely, you will need equipment or machinery—even if all you need is a computer and a fax machine. And, until your profits can carry your business, you will need working capital to sustain your business's life.

This chapter explores the world of financing and teaches you how to do the following:

- Understand the basic types of funding and learn which one might be best for you;
- Deal with your local bank;
- Approach the often elusive venture capital community; and
- Find out more about the numerous federal, state, and private loan programs available to small businesses.

You may be fortunate enough to have family members, friends, or local associates who can lend you money. You may even be able to rely completely on your personal savings. Most new and current small business owners, however, must obtain financing from outside sources.

Some Factors a Lender Will Consider

Obtaining financing for your small business will ultimately depend on two major factors:

1. The ability of your business to repay the loan, and
2. The ability of the principal owners or management team of the business.

Funding a new business venture from outside sources can be difficult to obtain for one overriding reason: a start-up business usually has no track record that will show its ability to repay a loan. The owners or managers may not have a proven track record either. Risks are very high for untested ideas and untested owners and managers. Just because you were a manager for a large corporation doesn't necessarily mean you can successfully run a small business. In fact, you may find it easier to obtain financing for an existing business than for one that you start from scratch.

The time to look for start-up or expansion funds from prospective lenders is when you have completed your business plan. As you read in the previous chapter, a business plan can make or break your business. This is especially true in securing financing.

The time to look for start-up or expansion funds from prospective lenders is when you have completed your business plan.

Basic Types of Funding

Before you approach a lender, make sure you understand the basic types of funding. The two most common types are:

1. Debt financing, usually asset-based loans, and
2. Venture (equity) financing.

Lenders will fund asset-based loans on the probability of obtaining repayment of the loan and the type and marketability of the collateral you have. Your collateral may be in the form of stocks or bonds, a home or automobile, or any other items that have a value and can be easily sold by the holder of the collateral if you fail to make your loan payments.

Equity financing usually does not require collateral, but the lender will probably put a performance requirement on your business. If your business does not meet the requirement, you may lose management say-so in the business and, in some cases, your stake in the venture.

Most equity funding is based on a participation in ownership of the business with the expectation of getting a multiple of the investment during a fixed period—usually five years. In contrast, with debt financing the lender makes no provision for participating in the business. The lender simply expects a payback of the amount borrowed, plus interest (or rent on the money), for the period of the loan. The loan can normally be paid in installments or a lump sum or a combination of both.

Most debt lenders want to rent money to you at a rate that is higher than what they can get by investing in safer investments, such as treasuries, municipal bonds, or other businesses. Most lenders do not want to risk their money—it is to get a good interest return on it, with a reasonable risk. They do not want to own your collateral and collect their money by selling the collateral; they want to receive payment on the scheduled dates with both interest and principal. Most lenders will require you to guarantee the loan with assets other than the collateral that you pledge for the loan. Therefore, your entire net worth may be at risk if your business fails.

> Most lenders will require you to guarantee the loan with assets other than the collateral that you pledge for the loan.

Alternative Types of Funding

In addition to the above traditional methods of funding, alternative types of financing exist, including:

- Lines of credit
- Letters of credit
- Factoring
- Floor planning

Take a moment to learn about these nontraditional forms of financing to see if one might apply to your business situation.

LINE OF CREDIT

If your business is in need of a quick infusion of cash to maintain a positive cash flow, you may want to consider using a line of credit. Most commercial banks will give revolving lines of credit: they make available a fixed amount and you are able to draw on funds up to that limit, repay the funds when you receive payment on invoices, and redraw the funds again when you need them. You can use this amount of credit to meet expected increases in inventory and receivables that may be caused by seasonal fluctuations.

Keep in mind: you need to pay a line of credit to a zero balance as soon as you have an inflow of cash from collecting receivables. Lines of credit are not to be used for long-term capital purposes or to fund a continuing operating deficit.

LETTER OF CREDIT

If you find yourself dealing with a new vendor who is not assured of your company's creditworthiness, you may want to look into a letter of credit. A letter of credit is a guarantee from a bank that it will honor a specific obligation if a borrower fails to pay. Because your bank knows you and your ability to pay—from cash, collateral, or some prearranged credit facility—it will put its own credit standing in place of your credit standing. A bank will normally charge a fee to grant a letter of credit.

FACTORING

You can acquire cash based on the value of your receivables, not in the form of a loan, but rather by selling your account to a lender. In this situation, the lender is called a factor and the factor (not you) is responsible for collecting on the account. As a result, your customers pay their bills directly to the factor. The factor will typically give the owner 50 to 70 percent of the face value of the invoices upfront and the balance on the collection date of the receivables.

FLOOR PLANNING

Floor planning is a relatively new financing tool that uses an asset-based approach to lending. In this situation, a company would finance its inventory and the purchased inventory would act as collateral until the sale is made. Floor planning is ideal for businesses that have large-ticket retail items, such as furniture, appliances, and automobiles. Floor planning allows these businesses to maintain a high level of inventory so their customers have many choices. As items are purchased, the business repays the inventory cost to the lender.

> Floor planning is a relatively new financing tool that uses an asset-based approach to lending.

Lending Sources

There are many sources of funding. Some possible sources of capital are banks, credit unions, loan companies, family, friends, credit cards, venture capitalists, private investors, small business loan consortia, and even government loans and grants. Start with your bank or local small business development center (SBDC).

Your Local Bank

Like all businesses, your venture will need banking services to maintain a checking account, conduct credit card transactions, and handle other specialized services. It is only natural to go to a local bank for business financing. Unfortunately, banks rarely finance new businesses because they have yet to establish their ability to repay, they have little collateral, and the owners or managers are often inexperienced.

Frequently, banks will not finance your business unless it has been established for several years and shows a history of clear profitability. Even then, very small businesses may have difficulty obtaining conventional financing. Banks notoriously shy away from funding ongoing operations; they prefer giving loans for expansion or improvements where significant collateral and a large safety margin play a big role.

Not all banks cater to small businesses. Some banks specialize in handling consumer accounts and generally avoid small businesses altogether. Fortunately, the reverse is also true and there is probably a bank in your area that is experienced in small business loans.

Select and Develop a Good Banking Relationship

To establish good banking relations, be honest and provide your banker with knowledge about your business and industry. A good banker will become interested in your business and keep abreast of your problems and successes. If you see your banker only when you need a loan, you are not developing a good relationship. Your banker is much like your attorney and accountant. He or she should be kept up-to-date about your business and is an integral part of helping you solve problems in your business.

It is extremely important that you understand your bank's lending philosophy. Most bankers require two sources of repayment. For instance, your bank may give you a loan as long as you agree to a lien on your accounts receivables, inventory, fixed assets, or real property. In addition to this, a bank will require your personal guarantee—a situation that fosters a psychological commitment to the success of your business. If you are not willing to personally sign and stand behind your business, your banker may hesitate to give you a loan.

Once you have established a relationship with your banker and have earned a reputation for fiscal responsibility, sound management, and trustworthiness, your banker will begin to consider you a valued customer. This distinction carries significant advantages to your small business, including easier financing in the future.

When you present your banker with a loan request and your business plan, your proposal undergoes an evaluation process. Your banker will look for the following information:

- The amount requested
- The purpose of the loan
- The source and ability of repayment
- Sources and type of collateral
- Management abilities

You can easily remember the loan evaluation process by learning the "five C method." Your bank will look at all five C's:

- *Conditions.* What is the current status of the economy and your industry?
- *Collateral.* What will be your secondary source of repayment?
- *Capacity.* Are you prepared for others to take a cold, hard look at your financial track record?
- *Capital.* Do you or your business have any equity?
- *Character.* A key to the lending process, do you have the ability to convey your trustworthiness and integrity?

If you've done your homework, your business plan will contain all of this information in a highly readable and readily understandable format.

Foster your banking relationship by avoiding some actions that will send red-flag danger signals.

- Don't request another loan after you have spent the money from your first loan.
- Don't change banks to get a better interest rate.
- Don't approach a bank if you are undercapitalized or have a history of bad management or serious profit losses.
- Above all, stay in close communication with your banker—presenting both the good and bad sides of your business.

Venture Capitalists

Whereas banks use past performance as primary criteria when evaluating a loan proposal, venture capitalists focus mainly on the future prospects of a company. A venture capital firm is a pool of capital, typically organized as a limited partnership, that invests in companies that offer the opportunity for a high rate of return, typically between five and ten times their investment, within five to eight years. In 2005, venture capitalists invested $21.7 billion in 2,939 deals, according to MoneyTreeTM Report.

If your business is part of an industry segment that is poised for rapid growth and exceptional profits, then you may want to pursue venture capital funding. Venture capitalists seek markets that are sufficiently large to achieve a value of $100 million or more. The primary goal of venture capitalists is rapid capital appreciation. This goal is usually achieved through a sale of a company to a strategic buyer or through an initial public stock offering (IPO). Keep in mind: sustained growth and profitability beyond a five-year horizon are essential for creating top value when the venture capitalist takes your company public or sells it.

> The primary goal of venture capitalists is rapid capital appreciation.

Most companies will not qualify for venture capital funding. As a rule, over 100 investment proposals are reviewed for every one company that receives venture funding. But if you think your idea has potential for funding, you should seek help in developing your plan to make presentations to venture capitalists.

If you decide to seek venture capital funding, be prepared to give up a portion of your ownership in your company's equity. Equity ownership will have a direct relationship to the amount a venture capitalist firm invests in your business and the risk that the firm assumes if your company fails. For example, suppose you want to start a business and have only 10 percent of the $100,000 you need to start the business. A venture capitalist may fund the other 90 percent, but you will probably be expected to turn over 90 percent of the ownership in your company as equity. This percentage ownership varies depending on the business type, business plan, competition, management expertise, projected profits, and overall investment risk. If this issue scares you, look into obtaining venture capital through small business investment companies (SBICs)—investors that use long-term debt guaranteed by the Small Business Administration (SBA) to supplement their private capital. (SBICs are discussed in detail later in this chapter.)

Finding a venture capitalist who may be interested in your business takes a lot of effort on your part. You will need to identify venture capitalists whose investment preferences match your needs and business profile. Look for firms that are looking for businesses like yours in terms of investment size, development stage, and industry and geographic location. Then, narrow your search to a manageable number of investor candidates, preferably six or less. After you have narrowed your search, you will need to write a well-documented financing proposal. There are several types of proposals you can use to raise venture capital and loans, including a private placement circular, a prospectus, and a limited partnership offering.

For sources of venture capital, check your library, ask your banker, and discuss your project with your local SBDC or the business department of a local college. Seek out resource guides that list venture capitalists, such as Pratt's Guide to Private Equity Sources (formerly Pratt's Guide to Venture Capital Sources) and the Directory of Venture Capital and Private Equity Firms.

You may want to check out the Active Capital (formerly Angel Capital Electronic Network, ACE-Net). This Internet-based listing service provides information to angel investors on small businesses that are seeking to raise $250,000 to $5 million in equity financing. (Angel investors are typically wealthy individuals with significant business experience who can provide invaluable advice to the companies in which they invest.) Only entrepreneurs who can sell security interest in their companies—corporations and limited liability companies—may participate in Active Capital; sole proprietorships and general or limited partnerships are not eligible. Entrepreneurs participate in Active Capital by answering a basic set of questions based on their business plans. Then, enrolled investors can anonymously view, online, executive summaries and additional investment information provided by the entrepreneurs. Thus, an investor in California and an entrepreneur in Maine can seem as close to each other as next door. To find out more, contact Active Capital through its Web site, activecapital.org.

> Angel investors are typically wealthy individuals with significant business experience who can provide invaluable advice to the companies in which they invest.

Private Loan Companies

In the past, most small businesses steered away from private loan companies because they were known for high interest rates and were the lenders of last resort. This situation changed during the 1970s. Thanks to the Small Business Administration (SBA), private loan companies, working as small business lending companies (SBLCs), have become one of the most important SBA loan sources today.

There are some advantages to using an SBLC rather than a traditional bank lender. First, an SBLC is regulated only by the SBA, whereas other lenders must report to other regulatory authorities as well. Second, SBLCs specialize in SBA-guaranteed loans. Therefore, your loan request is processed expeditiously and professionally.

Federal Government Programs

Although most small businesses are funded from private sources, there are numerous sources of state and federal help.

Most federal loan programs are processed by the SBA. In fact, up to one-third of all small business loans are guaranteed through the SBA. The SBA does not fund the loan but guarantees it through a bank or other institution. If a borrower defaults on a loan, then the SBA will reimburse the bank for a percentage of the loan loss. Thus, banks are more apt to make loans with the SBA's guarantee than they would otherwise.

To be eligible for an SBA loan, your business must meet the size standards established by the SBA for your industry type. Further, there are other loans for specific purposes, such as to assist the disabled or minority or economically disadvantaged individuals, provide incentives for energy savings, control pollution, or do business in a specific location.

> To be eligible for an SBA loan, your business must meet the size standards established by the SBA for your industry type.

SBA 7(a) Loan Guaranty Program

The 7(a) loan guaranty program is the SBA's primary business loan program. It provides loans to small businesses that are unable to secure financing on reasonable terms through normal lending channels.

The program operates through private-sector lenders that provide loans that are guaranteed by the SBA. The lenders, not the SBA, approve and service the loans and request the SBA guaranties. Lenders look favorably on the 7(a) loan guaranty program. The guaranties reduce the risks to the lenders, thus expanding their abilities to make small business loans.

For most SBA loans there is no legislated limit to the total amount that you may request from a lender. Generally, the SBA will guarantee up to $750,000. Under the program, the SBA can guarantee as much as 75 percent of a commercial loan. For instance, on a $50,000 loan, the SBA guarantees to repay the lender up to 75 percent of the unpaid balance if the borrower defaults. The lender's liability, then, is 25 percent, or $12,500. For its guaranty, the SBA will charge the lender a one-time guaranty fee of 2 percent of the guaranteed portion of the loan.

The interest rate on loans of more than seven years may not exceed 2.75 percent over *The Wall Street Journal*'s published prime lending rate; the interest rate on loans of under seven years may not exceed 2.25 percent over the prime lending rate.

The maximum SBA loan maturity is 25 years. However, your loan's maturity will be based on the cash flow and ability of your business to repay it without hardship. Generally, the maturity will vary according to the purpose of the loan and can be up to ten years for working capital and 25 years for fixed assets, the purchase of machinery or equipment, or the purchase or construction of plant facilities. You can use the proceeds of an SBA loan for most business purposes, including:

- Purchasing real estate to house your business operations;
- Funding construction, renovation, or leasehold improvements;
- Acquiring furniture, fixtures, machinery, and equipment;
- Purchasing inventory; or
- Financing receivables and augmenting working capital.

You can use the proceeds of an SBA loan for most business purposes.

You cannot use the proceeds of an SBA loan for any of the following:

- Financing floor plan needs;
- Purchasing real estate where the participant has issued a forward commitment to the builder/developer or where the real estate will be held primarily for investment purposes;
- Making payments to owners or paying delinquent withholding taxes;
- Paying an existing debt unless you can show that the refinancing will benefit your business and that the need to refinance is not a sign of bad management on your part.

Several loan programs under the 7(a) program address specific needs:

- *Low Documentation (LowDoc) Loan Program.* If your business needs a loan of $150,000 or less, applying for the loan under LowDoc could be as easy as completing a one-page SBA application.
- *CAPLines Loan Program.* In this program, loan proceeds generally will be advanced against a borrower's existing or anticipated inventory or accounts receivable to meet cyclical working capital needs.
- *Prequalification Loan Program.* This program uses intermediary organizations to help businesses develop loan application packages and secure loans. This program targets low-income borrowers, disabled business owners, new and emerging businesses, veterans, exporters, rural and specialized industries.
- *504 Certified Development Company Loan Program.* This program could allow you to get long-term, fixed-asset financing through certified development companies.

For details, visit *www.sba.gov/financing/sbaloan/7a.html.*

Small Business Investment Company (SBIC)

Licensed and regulated by the SBA, SBICs are privately owned and managed investment firms that invest capital in small businesses. They use their own funds plus funds obtained at favorable rates with an SBA guaranty or by selling their preferred stock to the SBA. In 2004 the SBIC Program invested more than $2.8 billion in small businesses

The SBIC program provides funding to all types of manufacturing and service industries. Some investment companies specialize in certain fields, while others seek out small businesses with new products or services because of the strong growth potential.

SBICs may invest only in qualifying small businesses. Your business is qualified for SBIC financing if it has a net worth of less than $18 million and average after-tax earnings of less than $6 million during the previous two years. If your business does not meet this test, it may still qualify as a small business under either an employment standard or an amount-of-annual-sales standard. Both of these standards vary from industry to industry.

Keep in mind: SBICs differ in size and investment philosophy. Each SBIC has a policy on the type of financing it prefers, size preferences, industry preferences, and geographic requirements.

If your business qualifies for the SBIC program, you may be able to receive equity capital, long-term loans, and expert management assistance. SBICs may not invest in:

- Other SBICs;
- Finance and investment companies or finance-type leasing companies;
- Unimproved real estate;
- Companies with less than one-half of their assets and operation in the United States;
- Passive or casual businesses (those not engaged in a regular and continuous business operation); or
- Companies that will use the proceeds to acquire farm land.

You should understand the differences between the two types of SBICs. You may encounter a "regular" SBIC or a firm that is known as a "specialized" small business investment company (SSBIC). SSBICs are specifically targeted toward the needs of entrepreneurs who have been denied the opportunity to own and operate a business because of social or economic disadvantage. To qualify, your business must be 51 percent owned by socially or economically disadvantaged persons. More than 100 SSBICs

> The SBIC program provides funding to all types of manufacturing and service industries.

operate in the United States. For a complete list of SBICs and SSBICs, contact the National Association of Small Business Investment Companies (NASBIC). The address and phone number of this agency is listed in Appendix C.

Microloan Program

One of the most difficult types of loans to obtain are for small amounts of debt. It has been very difficult to get loans of a few thousand dollars because they are not profitable for most lenders and generally are of a higher risk. In response to this issue, the SBA created the Microloan Program. Under this program, the SBA makes funds available to nonprofit intermediaries, which then make loans to eligible companies—start-up, newly established, or growing small businesses. The amounts of the microloans can range anywhere from $100 to $35,000. The average microloan is $10,500. The maximum term allowed for a microloan is six years.

One of the most difficult types of loans to obtain are of small amounts of debt.

Another advantage of the microloan is that a completed application can be processed by a nonprofit intermediary in less than one week. Although each lending organization has its own loan requirements, an intermediary is required to take as collateral any assets that you bought with the microloan. Further, your personal guarantee will be required.

Recently microloans have become more available through entrepreneur associations and some state agencies. Check with your chamber of commerce or small business development center if you are considering a business that needs a small amount of capital to get started. Often you will be required to have a mentor who is in business and possibly attend classes that discuss developing a plan and managing your prospective business.

SMALL BUSINESS INNOVATION RESEARCH (SBIR) PROGRAM

Since 1983, the SBA has used the Small Business Innovation Research (SBIR) Program, administered by the Office of Technology, to achieve the following objectives:

- Stimulate technological innovation;
- Fund projects initiated by high-tech small business to help meet federal research and development needs;
- Foster and encourage participation by minority and disadvantaged persons in technological innovation; and
- Increase the commercialization of innovations from federal research and development.

Each year, seven federal departments—Agriculture, Commerce, Defense, Education, Energy, Health and Human Services, and Transportation—and three agencies—the Environmental Protection Agency, the National Aeronautics and Space Administration, and the National Science Foundation—participate in the SBIR program. Under the program, these federal departments and agencies are required to reserve a portion of their R&D funds to award to small businesses. They request highly competitive proposals from small businesses in response to solicitations outlining their research and development needs. Awards are granted after an evaluation of the technical feasibility of the research and development concept. For more information, contact the Office of Technology as listed in Appendix B.

> The most important thing you can do in your attempts at getting an SBA loan is to be prepared.

CERTIFIED AND PREFERRED LENDERS

The SBA has streamlined its guarantee program, expediting loans through its Certified Lender Program (CLP) and Preferred Lender Program (PLP). These programs were designed to provide better response to borrowers, by placing additional responsibilities on the lenders for analysis, structuring, approval, servicing, and liquidation of loans, within SBA guidelines.

Only the most active and expert lenders qualify for this program. There are about 850 certified lenders, accounting for about 4 percent of all SBA loans. Some 450 lenders qualifiy as preferred lenders; these lenders process about 21 percent of SBA loans.

The SBA delegates partial authority to certified lenders, which allows the SBA to process an application in three business days. Preferred lenders have full lending authority; turnaround on completed loan applications can be one day. For faster approval of your loan application, make sure your bank is a certified or preferred lender.

TIPS FOR OBTAINING AN SBA LOAN

The most important thing you can do in your attempt to get an SBA loan is to be prepared. Your second most important task is to find the right lender. You must know your needs and have a ready explanation of the reasons for the amount you're requesting. Ideally, you will use your business plan to show the past, present, and future condition of your business.

As a reminder, make sure you include the financial history, management background, and monthly cash flow projections of your business. You will probably also be required to submit a personal financial statement and tax returns.

State Government Programs

Most states have economic development agencies that encourage the development of new businesses. The loans may be to encourage starting a business in a target area or expanding a business by building new facilities or adding equipment. Often the amount of the loan is tied to the number of new jobs to be created in the area.

Check Appendix D for a list of some state sources of funding. Funding of the programs often is insufficient to respond to a large percentage of applicants. However, it is well worth your time to check to see if there are loans for which your business qualifies.

Caution: You may hear of loans offered at very low rates of interest through federal or state agencies. If this information is available by buying a videotape or attending a seminar, beware. You will find that there are no such loans: the lending requirements are similar for all businesses. You may also be directed to companies that charge much higher rates of interest than banks if you have a high-risk venture. Beware of such loans because you will have to spend a much larger share of your business income to repay the loan and you will increase the chances that your business will fail.

Often the amount of the loan is tied to the number of new jobs to be created in the area.

Chapter Wrap-Up

One of the worst situations you can get into as a business owner is not having enough money to run your business. At the top of your priority list should be a clear picture of your business and personal financial needs before you make your first sale.

To start, estimate the money you will need to set up your business—from office setup expenses to production equipment needs; from utility deposits to insurance; from withholding taxes to licensing fees. Review Chapters 2, 3, and 4 and make a list of the fees for which you will be responsible—both in the short term and the long term.

Next, establish a business bank account. The key here is to find the right banker for your business's needs. Compare fees and credit card arrangements. Inquire about floor planning, factoring, lines of credit, and accounts receivable financing. Gain a thorough understanding of a bank's policies and procedures and the personalities of the major players before you choose to do business with it.

Last, but certainly not least, know which lenders to approach and which ones to avoid. Stay informed about the federal and state loan programs available to your small business. Lenders will notice how educated you are and respond with a greater respect and appreciation. Keep your financial records up to date. Be ready to show pro-forma (projected) financial statements for at least the next three years. Maintain easy access to your business's cash flow projections, balance sheets, and profit and loss (P&L) statements. (These and other critical finance and accounting terms are fully covered in the next chapter.) Show your prospective lenders that you mean business—be prepared with a completed business plan before you approach a lender. Make sure you use the tips for creating a smart business plan from the previous chapter.

> Last, but certainly not least, know which lenders to approach and which ones to avoid.

5 | *Essential Finance and Accounting Methods*

E very business owner will benefit from a better understanding of finance and accounting. Admittedly, these tasks are the last things most business owners care to spend time working on regularly. In fact, many feel that a once-a-year accounting at tax time provides sufficient financial information to guide them through the year. Unfortunately, this is unlikely to be true except for the smallest businesses.

Approximately one million businesses are started every year in the United States. Many of them will fail, leaving the owners and investors poorer, but wiser about how to operate a business successfully. One of the primary reasons for any business failure is insufficient financial resources.

Some start-up companies have enough money to operate for years without making a profit. Most businesses are not that fortunate and must generate enough revenue to pay creditors, employees (including the owners), and vendors. Some businesses are even so successful they grow faster than they can afford to—and go out of business because of too much success.

The secret to remaining in business is being able to monitor the lifeblood of the business—the cash flow. There are many indicators of the health of a business. They include the income statement, the balance sheet, the cash flow analysis, and a multitude of ratios and other calculations that monitor the daily, weekly, monthly, and annual success of a business.

A full understanding of basic finance and accounting could mean the difference for your business between success and failure. Even if you hire an accountant or bookkeeper to maintain your business accounts, you still need to understand the significance of the numbers he or she generates in order to manage your business.

Types of Accounting Systems

This chapter will introduce you to the main types of accounting methods:

- Cash-based accounting
- Accrual-based accounting
- Tax accounting
- Financial accounting
- Management accounting

You should understand each of these to get a full picture of your company's financial position. Also, you will learn some basic accounting documentation procedures and payment acceptance methods.

Cash-Based Accounting

> Cash-based accounting is the easiest and most popular method for sole proprietorships.

Cash-based accounting is the easiest and most popular method for sole proprietorships. Cash enters and leaves accounts as income and expense.

Cash-based accounting in its simplest form is similar to a checkbook ledger with a running balance. The balance gives you a snapshot view of the health of your business—the larger the balance at any given moment, the healthier your financial affairs.

However, a snapshot view such as this clearly has a limited value. A healthy balance now means nothing if you have to pay an expense tomorrow that is three times that amount. In addition, the ledger cannot show the value vested in inventory, equipment, or accounts receivable.

Cash-based accounting is used internally by smaller businesses to maintain the most accurate picture of their cash flow; however, the government requires you to report your yearly earnings using accrual-based accounting. You may want to use both methods.

Accrual-Based Accounting

Accrual-based accounting gives a more accurate picture of the state of your business's financial health. It also more closely conforms to generally accepted accounting practices.

Suppose you have a grounds maintenance business and you charge a flat fee of $600 for six months' work. Even though you collect and deposit your fee in April, a more accurate picture of your business is produced by amortizing—taking the monthly value of the fee and applying it to monthly income and expenses—rather than showing it as income in the month when you collect it. For example, if you collect the fee in April and apply it to your account at the rate of $100 per month, you will amortize the fee over six months.

Accrual accounting may cause an expense or a sale toward the end of a year to be booked in that year, even if the money actually goes out or comes in the following year. If you make a sale in December and don't receive the cash from it until the following year, the sale is recorded as occurring in the year you recorded it—not the year you received the cash. This can seriously affect your income tax if a large sale at the end of the year greatly increases your profit for that year.

Be aware of the accrual accounting rules—as well as the cash-based accounting rules—especially toward the end of a year, when you can dramatically affect your profit by delaying or accelerating a sale or expense.

> Accrual-based accounting gives a more accurate picture of the state of your business's financial health and more closely conforms to generally accepted accounting practices.

Tax Accounting

The IRS has developed its own set of rules for accounting. The information required to compile and pay your taxes differs from the information you need to manage your business. Further, the IRS rules you must follow may be different from the rules you choose to follow for your banker. While you may keep two sets of books—one for tax purposes and one for business operations—most small business owners simply maintain one set of books and comply with the IRS requirements.

For example, you may have a piece of equipment that you can depreciate according to IRS rules in five years. But the actual useful life of the equipment may be ten years. For tax purposes you would depreciate it as rapidly as the law allows, but for your own accounting you would know that it would not have to be replaced for ten years. Thus, for your internal calculations you would depreciate it over a longer period.

Most new business owners are confused by the rules and meaning of depreciation. If a machine is purchased with cash or a loan, it is paid for and most business owners would expect that they could deduct the cost of the machine from the current year's expenses. This is not the case when it comes to IRS requirements. Since there is a useful life to the machine, the IRS may require that you write it off over a period of years. The IRS groups equipment into categories for depreciation purposes. It is wise to consult with an accountant to be sure you select the correct depreciation period for equipment you purchase.

To better use the tax accounting method, you may want to look into a software program to get started. Some popular tax software comes close to achieving expert-level advice and works directly with files from your bookkeeping or current accounting software. These programs often include interactive video clips and sound files from top tax advisors. They can generate completed IRS forms for filing and then file your taxes electronically.

If you decide to use these tools, shop the market carefully. The software should meet these following minimum requirements:

- It should be updated annually.
- It should be able to use your current accounting program files.
- It should be endorsed by one of the "Big Four" accounting firms (Deloitte, KPMG, PricewaterhouseCoopers, or Ernst & Young).

As your business grows in both size and revenue, you will benefit more and more from the advice of a knowledgeable tax accountant.

Be cautious in relying on your computer and your wits in computing your taxes. While you are likely to file a return that meets the IRS requirements and expectations by using these methods, you are also likely to end up paying too much.

The IRS allows small businesses to deduct a certain amount of new capital purchases in a single year. Check the current IRS requirements to determine how much you can deduct.

Get Expert Help

As your business grows in both size and revenue, you will benefit more and more from the advice of a knowledgeable tax accountant. Tax law is complicated and changes yearly. Without expert help, you could end up paying thousands of dollars in excess taxes or be penalized for not paying sufficient taxes or taking deductions that are not acceptable to the IRS.

The IRS offers some help. As a new business owner, you can start with Publication 334, Tax Guide for Small Business, Publication 538, Accounting Periods and Methods, and Publication 583, Starting a Business and Keeping Records. The address and phone number of the nearest IRS taxpayer assistance center office are listed in Appendix B.

Financial Accounting

Financial accounting is the basis for all entry-level accounting classes and textbooks. It is used to prepare financial reports, such as income statements, balance sheets, and cash flow statements. Most often, these reports are generated using accrual-based methods, so that income is recorded as it is earned instead of as it is collected and expenses are recorded as they occur instead of as payment is made for them.

To better understand financial accounting, take a moment to become familiar with three essential financial reports. Samples of each of the statements are included in Appendix A.

Income Statement

An income statement is sometimes called a profit and loss (P&L) statement. It is used to determine current profitability and is based on the most current information available. It is the basis for determining income tax obligations and levels of supportable debt by lending institutions.

> An income statement provides detailed information about your expenses broken down into as many categories as you feel are necessary.

An income statement provides detailed information about your expenses broken down into as many categories as you feel are necessary. For example, you may choose to list a single utilities expense or you may choose to break utilities down into gas for heat, electricity for lighting, and water. The more information available to you, the more informed you are to make decisions about expenses in the future. Don't collect more information than you will use, however.

Income statements may also be used to track expenses against a budget. By comparing actual costs against projections, you can decide where you need to place more controls or where unexpected expenses occurred. This process will allow you to better plan your operating budget for the following year.

It is not unusual for an income statement to show a profit for a given period, any yet the bank account is much lower than the income statement indicates. This situation occurs because the company shows depreciation of equipment, which adds to the income but does not produce an equivalent amount of cash. The company may also be building inventory, using available cash, but the income statement will reflect the cost of what the company sold during the period, but will not add the additional inventory to the profit-or-loss situation.

You can see that while your income statement is useful for explaining how much profit you made relative to your cost of goods and other expenses, it does not describe accurately the state of your business. If you want a snapshot view of your business regarding its overall condition on a specific day, use a balance sheet.

Balance Sheet

Balance sheets are prepared periodically, usually monthly, quarterly, or yearly. They are used to summarize the net worth of your business, taking into account all assets, liabilities, and equity at a given moment.

Assets are everything the business owns—cash, accounts receivable, fixed assets, and inventory. Liabilities are everything the business owes—such as accounts payable, payroll, and tax liabilities. Total equity is equal to the sum of all assets minus the sum of all liabilities. If you operate your business as a corporation, then equity is the current value of all capital stock as well as the total profit or loss since the start of your corporation.

Balance sheets provide a numerical bottom line that is useful in evaluating business growth or decline and creditworthiness. By comparing a current period with previous periods, you can observe trends.

A cash flow statement will help you understand where cash has been used and where and why cash is short or in abundance.

Cash Flow Statement

While the income statement and balance sheet are the typical indicators of the condition of a business, the cash flow statement will explain why you do not have the cash in your bank account that you might expect. It will help you understand where cash has been used and where and why cash is short or in abundance.

A cash flow statement is basically an accounting of available cash, plus cash income minus cash disbursements, for each period forecast. When projected for the following months or years, it will help you plan for critical cash need periods if your business is seasonal or cyclical.

As you become more experienced in looking at your historical cash flow, you should project your cash flow for at least a year in advance. A projection will provide a clear picture of your ability to meet expenses over the forecast period. If you will need a loan in the future, start before the need is upon you; most lenders are suspicious of a business owner who suddenly realizes that there will be a cash shortage and must obtain a loan within the next week or two.

Compare your cash flow statement against actual performance during a forecast period. This comparison provides crucial feedback that will allow you to predict potential cash shortfalls and prevent them before they occur.

Comparing predicted performance with actual performance also allows you to adjust basic assumptions and thereby more accurately prepare future cash flow forecasts.

Management Accounting

Management accounting, also called cost accounting, is a specialized form of internal accounting that provides managers and owners with detailed operating information about production processes. This type of reporting is particularly useful in manufacturing businesses and may include such information as unit production cost, product line profitability breakdowns, and sales performance by region or by store.

The information produced by management accounting will give you timely, detailed feedback about your operations. This feedback will allow you to draw conclusions about efficiency, cost, inventory valuation, quality control, product turnover, return or repair rates, warranty issues, and the cost-effectiveness of design changes. Anything that can be measured will provide potential input for management accounting.

> The information produced by management accounting will give you timely, detailed feedback about your operations.

Management accounting can be complex and labor-intensive, depending on the amount and type of information gathered, so it is important to place controls on how much and how often management accounting is needed to adequately control your business.

Track Key Indicators

Your business may benefit from simply tracking a few key indicators instead of a wide array. Take the analysts of the U.S. economy as an example. They often rely on key economic indicators to predict how the economy is reacting to world events. They rely on these indicators instead of the numerous other factors that affect the economy. If they were to analyze all factors, their reports would be out-of-date and completely useless. Similarly, you can rely on key indicators to predict how your business will perform.

For instance, suppose you have a small retail business and are concerned about losses to shoplifting. So you start to collect information to compare profit against sales and inventory data on a monthly basis to determine the rate of losses incurred and to test the effectiveness of the control methods you use to deter shoplifters.

This same concept can be applied to other types of businesses. A manufacturer will measure quality control reject ratios to evaluate the effectiveness of its job training program. A service station will compare storage tank inventory data against sales figures to determine whether its underground tanks are leaking.

There are many internal sources of information that will tell you how your business is faring. Don't depend solely on the end of quarter or year accounting to provide you with the information you need to determine if your business has a problem.

Accounting Documentation

You need to know how to use standardized forms to document sales transactions.

All businesses need to develop ways to process and account for their purchases and sales. When you start your business, you may be able to remember what you have ordered and how much cash it will take when you receive it. As your business grows and you hire employees, you will need to develop procedures that track income and expenses. A paper trail of sales and expenses will help you better understand the true cost of doing business and your profit.

In addition, the IRS demands that you have documentation for the figures that you report in your income tax return for the business. It can make an IRS auditor happier, if you ever have the unpleasant experience of being audited.

The two simplest methods for documenting income and expenses involve using purchase orders and invoices.

Purchase Orders

Regardless of which method of accounting you use, you will need to have a means of collecting data. You need to know how to use standardized forms to document sales transactions. One of these standard forms is the purchase order.

A purchase order is used to place an order with a supplier or a manufacturer. It acts as official authorization for the supplier to ship the merchandise being ordered. Since it functions as a permanent record of a transaction, prepare a purchase order even when placing orders by telephone or by letter.

A purchase order is traditionally designed as a three-part form—that is, an original and two copies. The original is sent to the supplier as the transaction approval document. The first copy is forwarded to the accounting department for payment processing once an invoice is received. The second copy is retained by the purchasing department as a record that the required merchandise was ordered. An optional third copy, used in larger companies, is returned to the requisitioning department as documentation that purchasing action was taken. Very small businesses—fewer than five employees—may require only the original and a single file copy.

If your business ships merchandise, you will receive purchase orders from customers. These purchase orders will contain the same information as the purchase orders that you send to suppliers. These purchase orders are a promise to pay for goods shipped. They also provide the shipping department with an address and a phone number.

A well-designed purchase order is essential for accurate recordkeeping. At a minimum, the purchase orders you use should include the following information:

> If your business ships merchandise, you will receive purchase orders from customers as a normal part of business.

- Your company's name, address, phone number, fax number, and e-mail address
- A purchase order number to allow future tracking and filing of the purchase
- The supplier's address and a "ship to" address (which may be different from the address of the business)
- The date the purchase order was prepared
- The quantity, product code number, description, unit price, and extended price of the merchandise (unit price multiplied by quantity, less any discounts) being ordered
- A column listing the line item costs, applicable sales tax, shipping and handling costs, and final total for the purchase order
- Your internal accounting information that identifies which account the purchase is to be charged against
- An authorization signature line
- Any other information you may require, including conditions of the purchase and special instructions to the supplier

You will want your purchase orders to project the same degree of professionalism as all other paperwork that leaves your company.

Beyond their value as means of tracking and internal control, purchase orders are important legal documents. If you disagree with a supplier as to what was supplied or the terms under which the item was shipped or produced, a purchase order that spells out the exact details of the expected purchase can provide you with a legal document and probably help resolve any issue without involving attorneys.

Invoices

Another business form that you will use to collect accounting data is an invoice. An invoice is an itemized list of the merchandise shipped to you and an accounting of the costs associated with it. The supplier sends it to document merchandise shipped to you. As delivery is made, you will use the invoice to inventory what you receive and verify that everything that was shipped to you arrived in good condition. The invoice is then forwarded to the accounting department for approval and filing. The accounting department will routinely compare the invoices against the originating purchase orders to verify that no errors were made and that actual costs were in line with expected costs.

An invoice is an itemized list of the merchandise shipped to you and an accounting of the costs associated with it.

As a supplier, you will prepare a shipping invoice or packing list to send with the merchandise that you ship to your customers. Like a purchase order, an invoice will contain specific information about your company, such as your company name, address, and phone number. An invoice will reference a specific purchase order or purchase agreement and will list the goods shipped, the prices charged, any shipping and handling charges, and the total cost.

You send a copy of the invoice to your customer as a bill. A copy of the outgoing invoice is forwarded to the accounting department, where it is verified and filed. An outgoing invoice is filed as an account receivable, while an incoming invoice is filed as an account payable.

Standardized forms—like purchase orders and invoices—are available through mail order business supply companies, your local printer, or office supply stores. Another helpful resource is *Ultimate Small Business Advisor* by Andi Axman (Entrepreneur Press, 2003), which contains sample forms in the book and on CD that you can adapt to your business. Also, most of the popular business software programs include standardized templates that you can use. Merely fill in the blanks on your computer screen and the program will prepare completed purchase orders for you. For your convenience, a sample purchase order and a sample invoice are included in Appendix A.

Methods of Accepting Payment

Every business needs cash to operate. How you collect the cash will differ greatly according to your type of business and the custom within your industry. If you are in an industry that traditionally gives credit for 30 or 60 days, you will be at a disadvantage if you can't provide the same to your potential customers. If you don't offer to take checks or credit cards, but your competitors do, you can bet that many customers will buy your product or use your service only once.

There are risks with all types of payment options except cash—and even with cash, there is a greater chance that you will be robbed or that employees can siphon off some of the receipts.

You need to develop payment acceptance policies and procedures.

You need to develop payment acceptance policies and procedures. If you sell with the expectation of receiving payment within 30 days after billing, you will need to have a cash reserve to help you get through your initial months of business. Some companies do not pay from invoices—they expect to receive a statement at the end of the month that summarizes their account and then they will pay at the end of the month or sometime during the following month.

Take some time now to familiarize yourself with the various methods of accepting payment. Then, decide what will work best for you.

CHECKS

Accepting checks as payment for goods or services is a generally accepted practice, but it is unwise to accept checks indiscriminately, particularly from new or potentially unreliable customers. A check is basically a promise to pay; it is only as good as the word of the person or entity issuing it. Some problems that can occur when accepting a check are fraud, nonsufficient funds, and stop-payments.

- *Fraud.* This occurs when a customer intentionally writes a check against a dormant, empty, or closed account or against an account that the customer does not own. Frequently, the checks have been stolen or reproduced illegally. In all cases, the customer has no intention of ever making the check good.
- *Nonsufficient funds (NSF).* When a customer's check is returned marked "NSF," you should immediately call the issuing bank to see if the account might now have sufficient funds to cover the check. If so, immediately send the check through again or take it directly to the bank and cash it. If there are still insufficient funds, you will have to take steps to collect from the customer directly.
- *Stop-payments.* By law, your customers can put a stop-payment on their checks if they have good reason to do so, such as dissatisfaction with the product or the service. If you have an adjustment-and-returns policy in place, it will help you collect on the account if it comes into dispute.

You can protect yourself against bad checks through local and national services that verify checks as you accept them. They may also guarantee reimbursement if the check is bad. However, you may find that the cost of such a service is greater than any potential loss—if you take a few precautions.

A few basic precautions will reduce the chances that you'll get stuck with a bad check. The effort expended to verify a check before you accept it will pay off.

You can protect yourself against bad checks through local and national services that verify checks as you accept them.

- *Require proper identification.* Make sure the check is properly signed and that the signature matches the signature on the driver's license or other identification. The check should be made out to your business.
- *Compare the amounts.* The amount of the check should be written legibly in two places. Both figures should be the same.
- *Do not accept starter checks.* A starter check is a non-personalized check given to a person opening a checking account. Accept only checks that have a preprinted address and phone number.
- *Do not accept two-person checks.* A check that a customer wants to endorse over to you is susceptible to fraud because you cannot verify the identity of the originator of the check, only the recipient, and because the originator can stop payment.
- *Verify with the bank.* If the sale is especially large or you don't know the customer, call the bank to verify the check before providing the service or merchandise.
- *Require verification.* You can require customers paying by check to present a check verification card or you can subscribe to an electronic check-verification service that you access at the point of sale.
- *Wait.* If you have a mail-order business, you may decide to wait a certain period to allow checks to clear before shipping the ordered item. You will need to determine how long it will take for a check to reach the bank on which it was written and be returned if the check is bad.

CREDIT CARDS

There are significant advantages to accepting credit cards. But there are also downsides.

The first downside is the paperwork. You must take several basic steps before you can accept credit cards. You must establish merchant discount agreements with each major credit card you decide to accept. You must establish a working agreement with your bank to handle the transactions. And you must learn how to process credit vouchers.

Another downside is the expense. Merchant accounts generally charge for the equipment and then assess monthly fees or minimums.

Some private companies handle all parts of the credit card transaction for you by establishing agreements with the appropriate credit card companies, conducting the credit transactions, and verifying available credit electronically before completing the sale. However, the one-step convenience comes at the cost of considerably higher processing fees. As electronic transactions become more commonplace, fees for these services will drop considerably.

Credit card transactions are subject to many of the same problems as check transactions. Credit card fraud is a growing concern. If you accept a card that has been lost, stolen, altered, or counterfeited, you will lose any income from that sale as well as the cost of the merchandise.

> If you accept a card that has been lost, stolen, altered, or counterfeited, you will lose any income from that sale as well as the cost of the merchandise.

Even if the sale and the card are valid, a customer could return merchandise or dispute a charge, resulting in a chargeback to your account and a loss of income. You have rights regarding chargebacks, but you should clearly understand how the credit card company handles complaints and be certain to respond to the credit card company's inquiry about the chargeback within the time indicated by the credit card company.

You can avoid many of the problems associated with accepting credit cards by taking these few extra precautions at the time of the sale.

- Check the card against the list of invalid cards provided by the credit card company.
- Certify the card electronically through a card verification service.
- Verify the signature on the card against the signature on the driver's license or other valid identification.
- Record additional information on the credit card invoice, such as address, phone number, and driver's license number.
- Have the customer sign an adjustment-and-return agreement so you can collect on the account if a chargeback is made to your account.

DEBIT CARDS

Many banks are turning to a debit card as a means of controlling overdrafts on checking accounts. The debit card is similar to a credit card in appearance and use, but operates on an entirely different principle. Instead of drawing funds for the transaction against a line of credit, the debit card draws funds directly from the customer's checking or savings account.

This system provides significant advantages to the retailer. Funds are verified as being available at the point of sale, eliminating bounced checks and failed transactions. Also, a personal code, which must be entered electronically by the customer, virtually eliminates fraudulent use of the debit card. Since no cash changes hands, the opportunity for theft is reduced as is the amount that could be stolen. Finally, payment is faster: frequently the funds are transferred from the customer's account to your business account within one working day.

Paying by Check

One of the first financial actions you should take after deciding to get into business is to open a checking account under your business name. Many banks will not open an account unless you have documentation that a business has been formed legally.

Although you can operate a sole proprietorship from your personal checking account, it is advisable to have a separate checking account for all business transactions. If you form a corporation, it is imperative that you do not mix your personal funds with your business funds. Nothing raises a red flag quicker than lack of responsibility with your business finances and your personal finances. Having separate bank accounts will help you avoid accounting and accountability problems. Banks will probably demand some proof that you operate as a corporation and will expect to see documentation from a state authority that the corporation operates legally in your state.

Once an incoming invoice is received, verified, routed, and filed, all that remains is to pay for the transaction. By convention, most invoices are paid by check, allowing you to easily track expenditures and simplify bookkeeping tasks.

However, you will want to establish a petty cash account that will enable you to purchase some items with cash. It is important to keep track of the use of petty cash purchases. If you can't show they were used for business purposes, you will not be able to deduct the amounts as business expenses and so you may pay additional taxes because your profit will be higher.

Billing invoices generally indicate a specific due date; you will prepare payments based on that date. A check provides you with a record of payment: it should reference the purchase order number or invoice number on the memo line. Send the check to the supplier along with a copy of the invoice so your payment arrives on or just before the due date.

> Nothing raises a red flag quicker than lack of responsibility with your business finances and your personal finances.

When you receive your monthly bank statement, immediately compare the cleared checks against those you issued to be certain that the signatures match. Banks generally do not look to see if a check is signed or if the signature matches the one on the signature cards they require you to provide.

If you find a check with no signature—or a forged or improper signature—you have between 30 and 60 days to return the check to the bank and receive credit. The liability for forged checks is generally deemed the responsibility of the account holder if it is not presented to the bank within this time period. However, if you fail to notice an improper check, be aware that the account to which it was deposited may be closed by the bank before you can obtain a credit.

There are three helpful rules when it comes to protecting yourself from internal fraud. First, make sure that a person other than the person who writes the checks reconciles your checking account. Second, never accept a check reconciliation using a copy of the statement—always use the original. Third, consult with your accountant on additional methods for protecting your assets.

Chapter Wrap-Up

Now that you are familiar with the basic accounting methods, you may even be more convinced of your desire to steer clear of the books and let an accountant manage your finances. Hiring a financial professional is a wise management decision.

However, it's up to you to control your business's financial health—the difference between success and failure.

Work toward a personal involvement with your business's finances and educate yourself as much as possible so you can better understand the cash flow needs of your business. Establish internal controls—like purchase orders and invoices to help track income and expenses. In addition, establish procedures that apply to all customers. You may change your procedures as you learn more about your customers and customs within your industry. Also, it is essential to have procedures in writing if you hire employees, because they cannot guess what your procedures may be from customer to customer or from day to day.

Finally, get a firm grasp on which collection techniques your business will use. Collecting the cash that is owed you, either immediately upon sale or within 30 or 60 days, is what will make your business work successfully.

You may feel uneasy about calling customers to remind them that they have not paid a bill. But if you are unwilling to call and ask for payment if it is overdue, customers will take advantage of you. If you want to stay in business, you must be able to collect on your accounts receivable.

6 | *Effective Human Resources Management*

As federal, state, and local governments focus more on the rights of employees, no employer can afford to be unaware of the laws affecting selection, hiring, and dismissal. Chapter 11 will introduce you to the various responsibilities of an employer, including fair employment practices, paying at least minimum wage, reporting wages, and anti-discrimination practices.

This chapter gets into the nitty-gritty of managing your personnel program and establishing and enforcing company policies. In short, you get the basics of managing your human resources. From writing a job description to interviewing applicants, from conducting performance reviews to dealing with disciplinary issues, from establishing a benefits package for your business to developing a company policy handbook—this chapter gives you a beginner's look at the often elusive subject of human resources management. Even if you don't plan on hiring employees right away, make sure you know what laws pertain to you when and if you decide to hire.

Hiring

Eventually you will face the task of hiring employees. This important process will have an enormous impact on your business. Your employees represent your business, so it's natural to want to select the best candidate possible for each position. Select well and you will add an effective team member to your organization. Select poorly and you will lose valuable time and money attempting to correct your mistake.

> Your employees represent your business, so it's natural to want to select the best candidate possible for each position.

The most common method is to clearly define the job position by writing a job description (which we'll discuss next) and then publicize it and take applications. Yet even in this simple scenario there are pitfalls.

You must base any hiring decision strictly on each candidate's qualifications and suitability for the position. Failure to be aware of the laws regulating hiring practices and to obey them leaves you open to litigation. The Americans with Disabilities Act of 1990 (ADA) and the Civil Rights Act of 1964 (CRA) provide specific guidance for hiring. Both prohibit discrimination based on race, sex, national origin, color, religion, age, marital status, sexual preference, or physical or mental disabilities. Both apply to employers having 15 or more employees for 20 weeks or more per year. For more information, visit the Equal Employment Opportunity Commission (EEOC) Web site, www.eeoc.gov.

As guidance for complying with the ADA and the CRA, the EEOC and other federal agencies adopted the Uniform Guidelines on Employee Selection Procedures (1978). To learn more about these guidelines, visit the Department of Labor Web site, www.dol.gov.

Writing a Job Description

The key to hiring well is to start by defining the positions clearly in writing. Make sure your job descriptions include the following:

- job qualifications
- assigned duties
- responsibilities
- knowledge
- coordination and reporting requirements
- physical working conditions

In addition to being key to hiring well, good job descriptions will help your current employees understand what their jobs entail and what you expect from them. Good descriptions will also help you structure your operations. For a sample job description, see Appendix A.

Advertising a Job Position

Advertising a job position is the second step in the recruitment process. A good ad will draw a diverse group of applicants who meet the qualifications of the position. Before writing the ad copy, consider the requirements of the position you are filling. Will the position require interaction with the public, your customers, or both? Will it require a valid driver's license? Will it require any special skills or abilities? What level of experience are you seeking?

Review your ad for discriminatory language. Make sure the wording does not unintentionally exclude any segment of the population. Include a phone number and a physical address in the ad to avoid discriminating against hearing-impaired or visually impaired applicants. Select a closing date and time for the position and require that all applications be submitted before that deadline or specifically state in your ad that you will accept applications until you fill the position.

Place your ad in as many places as necessary to ensure that all potential applicants have the same opportunity to see it and apply for the position. Consider listing the position with the unemployment agency in your state to ensure that all potential applicants are aware of the opening.

> A good ad will draw a diverse group of applicants who meet the qualifications of the position.

The Job Application

A well-prepared application form is your first line of defense in preventing hiring discrimination lawsuits. It is also your best tool for reducing a large pool of applicants to a group of the best qualified. Use a standardized form, to ensure that you collect the same information for each applicant. Because it must conform to the requirements of the ADA and the CRA, the form serves as a guide to prevent collecting data that might become the basis for discrimination.

The application package should include a statement about being an equal opportunity employer, a privacy act statement, and a release allowing your business to investigate the accuracy of the application. Appendix A contains a sample application. You must ensure that all applicants understand these special provisions of the application and that the wording and layout of the application are not discriminatory. Extra fine print, for instance, discriminates against people with weak or impaired vision.

You may also choose to have applicants provide you with a resume along with a completed application. Other sources of information may be letters of recommendation and copies of awards, transcripts, and professional citations.

While these documents can be helpful in deciding between two equally qualified candidates, they are no substitute for a completed application form to protect you against claims of hiring discrimination.

The Screening Process

Review application packages as you receive them. Place those that do not meet the advertised qualifications in a separate pile from those that do meet the qualifications. Record which qualifications each applicant did not meet.

> Interview each applicant under the same conditions and in the same way.

When the closing date has passed, review the qualified applicants objectively. Select the five or six best to schedule for interviews. Record your reasons for not selecting each of the other applicants. Ensure that your reasoning is as objective as possible and based solely on the qualifications for the job. Do not discriminate, for example, against applicants who are from a town whose high school is the big rival of your high school's football team.

Once you have selected the applicants to interview, contact each of them to verify that he or she is still interested in the position and to set a date and time for their interviews. One or more of your chosen five or six applicants may withdraw for various reasons, but you should try to interview at least three to allow an objective comparison of each candidate's qualifications.

How to Conduct an Interview

Interview each applicant under the same conditions and in the same way. Conduct the interviews in a place where there will be no interruptions or distractions. Make sure the atmosphere is nonthreatening, to allow a free flow of communication. It is a good idea to have a third party present during the interview to prevent accusations of sexual harassment or misconduct. Use the job description as a guide through the interview process as you become familiar with the qualifications and strengths of each applicant relative to the job.

Prepare for the interviews by deciding what questions to ask and what types of information to elicit from each applicant. Determine exactly what you need to know and avoid asking forbidden questions that could become the basis for complaints of discrimination. Use a checklist, if necessary, to ensure that you stay focused during the interview. Ask each applicant the same general questions. You can use one of four basic types of interview—structured, informal, stress, or panel. Whichever you choose, use it with each applicant.

A structured interview relies on questions that you select in advance to ask of each applicant. It is quick and consistent, but lacks flexibility. It's suitable as an initial screening interview.

For an informal interview, the atmosphere is far more relaxed and can be nearly conversational. This type of interview requires more skill and usually takes much more time than a structured interview. You ask open-ended, non-judgmental questions, to establish a flow of information from your applicants about their expectations, qualifications, and abilities. In this type of interview, you can gain information from applicants that you cannot legally request.

Using a stress interview to screen applicants for jobs that require calm and composure under pressure is particularly desirable. Such an interview may be useful in eliminating candidates from consideration. The questions asked in a stress interview require the applicants to respond to hypothetical situations, describe past experiences, or discuss their relative strengths or weaknesses. It's usually necessary to do a follow-up interview with successful applicants to further determine their qualifications.

A panel interview is efficient when a hiring decision is the responsibility of a group or committee. The panel should be headed by a single individual who keeps the panel focused. All members of the hiring team have the opportunity to interview each applicant under similar conditions.

After you have finished an interview, take the time to record what happened. Using notes you took during the interview as a guide, record the applicant's responses to your questions as well as your observations about the applicant's demeanor and characteristics. Include an appraisal of that individual's qualifications for the position and suitability for employment with your company. Also note any negative characteristics.

Use a stress interview to screen applicants for jobs that require calm and composure under pressure.

Handling the Background Check

After the interview, do a background check. Early in the selection process, obtain permission from the applicant to contact past employers, educators, family members, and references. Most employers include an authorization statement in the application form. Refusal to grant permission for the employer to investigate can be reason to reject an application.

The best approach to verifying application information and checking references is to call past employers and references. Speaking with a person on the telephone usually results in more detailed information with less likelihood of misunderstanding. Restrict your questions to verifying information given on the application and to gaining impressions of the applicant's work habits and qualifications. Collect information only from sources authorized by the applicant. Take care to avoid questions relating to the applicant's physical or mental health.

Generally, references provided by past employers, educators, and coworkers are more useful than those obtained from friends, neighbors, and relatives. The former are more likely to have observed the applicant's work habits while the latter may simply be doing the applicant a favor rather than providing an objective appraisal.

Keep in mind: you assume liability for information that you receive during the background checks. Therefore, avoid basing your hiring decision solely on information gained during the verification process.

> Avoid basing your hiring decision solely on information gained during the verification process.

Testing a Job Applicant

Occasionally, it may be appropriate to include testing as part of the process for screening applicants. Some types of testing are aptitude, achievement, situational, personality, drug, polygraph, and honesty testing. You must consider carefully which types of testing you will conduct, if any. It is not always appropriate to test applicants. If you use testing, all applicants must take the same test under the same conditions.

Testing is sometimes useful and appropriate in filling certain positions. For instance, you may wish to test an applicant's typing speed if a specific typing proficiency is a job requirement. Drug testing is allowable provided the test cannot detect prescription medication. If it can, you must make an offer of employment before conducting the testing. You may require a test for HIV only when there is reasonable risk of an exchange of bodily fluids between employees. Remember that it is illegal to discriminate against persons with HIV. You may use paper-and-pencil honesty testing when prospective employees will handle money or have access to pilferable equipment or supplies.

Testing is always inappropriate when it results in hiring discrimination. You must always test fairly and use the results correctly and appropriately. Allow only qualified professionals to conduct testing. Ensure that all testing conforms to the 1978 Uniform Guidelines on Employee Selection Procedures as adopted by the EEOC.

Alternatives to Hiring Employees

There are alternatives to hiring through applications and interviews, including contracting to independent agents, using temporaries from an agency, or leasing employees. Each method offers advantages over conventional methods, including reducing paperwork and employee costs.

Using Independent Contractors

If the work can be done away from your business or outside normal business hours, an independent contractor may work best for you. For instance, suppose you need standard bookkeeping activities each week. A private bookkeeper can do this work at his or her place of business on a weekly basis, usually for a set fee. You save the expense of providing the bookkeeper with office space and equipment. The fee you pay is your only expense. The contractor is responsible for all overhead employee costs, such as federal, state, and Social Security taxes, and all the paperwork required to collect and deposit those taxes. You need only file IRS Form MISC-1099, Miscellaneous Income.

The distinction between employee and contractor is important and you are required to properly classify such workers.

The Fair Labor Standards Act (FLSA) defines employer-employee relationships. The distinction between employee and contractor is important and you are required to properly classify people who work for you. For instance, if you provide office space or equipment and set specific work hours, the IRS may consider the contractor to be an employee. You must then collect and file taxes for that person. A rule of thumb is that a contractor provides a service or a product while an employee provides labor in a structured way. Refer to Chapter 11 for more information on dealing with independent contractors in your state.

Temporary Agencies to the Rescue

Temporary agencies rent employees, typically for periods from half a day to several years. Temporary employees frequently possess characteristics not found in regular employees. They often have qualifications beyond their job description. They usually have a wide range of experience. They can be available on very short notice.

It may be wise to use temporary employees to conduct inventory for tax purposes, to handle sudden increases in business production, or to cover the temporary loss of a permanent employee due to illness, pregnancy, or military recall. The temporary agency will normally bill you on a weekly basis. The fee you pay to an agency usually covers all employee expenses.

Employee Leasing as an Option

Employee leasing, also called *contract staffing*, is a relatively new idea in business. An agency provides your business with all employees and handles all personnel management concerns from hiring to firing. You start to realize savings over the normal hiring process when you lease more than five employees. The benefit to employees is that the leasing agency typically manages a much larger workforce than your business would and is therefore able to provide a better, more diverse benefits package.

Withholding for Employees

When you hire an employee, give him or her a federal Form W-4, *Employee's Withholding Allowance Certificate*, which he or she must complete and return to you prior to receiving any pay. You may obtain forms from your IRS district office. You will receive copies of the forms and tax withholding tables and instructions from the IRS when you register with your state's employment office.

A sample of Form W-4 is included in Appendix A. Refer to Appendix B for the address and phone number of the IRS district office nearest you.

> Policy and procedures are predetermined responses to employee-related problems.

Your Company's Policies and Procedures

Policies and procedures are planned responses to situations that involve employees. It's wise to set company policies in writing before a problem occurs that requires a response. Your handbook of policies and procedures will help you do the following:

- Provide written guidance for handling employees.
- Communicate your business rules and expectations to your employees.
- Communicate your business approach and philosophy.
- Protect your business from litigation.
- Ensure that all problems are handled consistently.

The process of developing a cohesive set of policies and procedures for your business will lead you to firmly review your goals and business philosophy. This process will be particularly helpful if you haven't yet considered a set of policies. Some policies will be required by law. Others will be extensions of your personal approach to business. In either case, you will want to be certain that each policy is accurate and complete and reflects your best interests and those of your company.

Nearly any issue can be addressed as a matter of policy. However, there are a few that are basic to any policy manual or handbook. In most cases, these policies were developed in response to federal regulations, so it is prudent to use them as the foundation of your policy manual. Here are some of these basic policies:

- Equal employment opportunity
- Equal pay
- Sexual harassment
- Substance abuse
- Smoking
- Safety
- Termination
- Leaves of absence
- Use of company time, equipment, or resources

Equal Employment Opportunity

Equal employment opportunity is mandated by federal law under the Civil Rights Act of 1964 (CRA) and the Americans with Disabilities Act of 1990 (ADA), as well as other, clarifying legislation. These laws prohibit employment discrimination based on race, religion, color, national origin, age, gender, sexual orientation, or physical or mental disability. Your company policy should prohibit discriminatory practices in hiring, promoting, demoting, or firing employees. Your policy should also prohibit discrimination in pay, compensation, working conditions, and working assignments.

> Your company policy should prohibit discriminatory practices in hiring, promoting, demoting, or firing employees.

Equal Pay

The Equal Pay Act of 1963 is an amendment to the Fair Labor Standards Act of 1938 (FLSA). It prohibits unequal pay for equal work based on gender. For instance, paying a male supervisor more than a female supervisor when both possess similar skills, tenure, experience, and performance levels constitutes discrimination under this act. This is equally true of the reverse scenario.

When preparing company policy statements regarding equal pay and equal opportunity, seek advice from professional sources to ensure that you are complying with all federal, state, and local guidelines.

Sexual Harassment

There are two types of sexual harassment, quid pro quo and hostile environment.

Quid pro quo sexual harassment is when employment conditions oblige an employee to submit to sexual harassment or abuse. Employment conditions include promotions, demotions, hiring, firing, and preferential treatment in job assignments, opportunities, and perks.

Hostile environment sexual harassment includes behavior that is unwelcome to the recipient, which includes requests for sexual favors, exposure to sexually explicit jokes, and innuendoes, whether through telephone calls, faxes, e-mail, or other forms of visual, aural, or written communication. When these conditions are prevalent, the work environment may be considered hostile.

Sexual harassment is not gender-specific; both men and women can be victims of sexual harassment, usually by members of the opposite sex, but sometimes also by same-sex coworkers.

In the case of quid pro quo sexual harassment, the employer is held liable, regardless of whether or not he or she knew what was happening. Employers are usually not held liable for hostile environment sexual harassment unless it can be shown they knew or should have known that a hostile environment existed.

Your company policy should clearly state a zero tolerance for sexual harassment. You may want to specify punitive and corrective measures in the event of a claim of sexual harassment. Make a clear channel for reporting abuses to the appropriate management resource. Consider formal training for your employees during orientation and then periodically thereafter.

Office romances and flirtations do not constitute sexual harassment provided that they meet the following conditions:

- The romance is consensual,
- The romance does not enter into the work environment, and
- No quid pro quo condition can be inferred or implied.

Even meeting these conditions is no guarantee that accusations of sexual harassment will not be made if the relationship ends poorly. As an employer, any interference in the personal lives of your employees may be considered an invasion of privacy. Thus, word your policy to insist on professionalism and decorum in the workplace.

Substance Abuse

Drug or alcohol impairment results in lower performance levels, production losses, and higher rates of absenteeism. Employees who engage in substance abuse are four times more likely to have accidents and five times more likely to file workers' compensation claims.

If any employees are impaired on the job, they are a safety risk to themselves as well as to other employees. In addition, if they represent your com-

---

Your company policy should clearly state a zero tolerance for sexual harassment.

pany to the public or to customers, it hurts your image. Your company's personal liability insurance may not protect in the case of increased risks—and there's no insurance coverage to protect you from the image damage.

Company-sponsored events, such as picnics, dinners, and outings, may invite abuse, particularly if alcohol is served. Your policy must address these issues to protect your company from litigation. In addition, your policy must clearly define behavior that is unacceptable, such as:

- Drug or alcohol impairment while on the job,
- Possession or use of drugs or alcohol on the job, and
- Sale of drugs or alcohol on business property.

Clearly explain disciplinary actions for violations of your substance abuse policy. Be careful not to discipline an employee for addiction. Addiction is a medical condition beyond the employee's control that requires outside, professional assistance to correct.

Consider drug and alcohol awareness training for managers or for all employees as a method to prevent substance abuse. Require managers to be aware of indicators of substance abuse and to intervene when appropriate, even if substance abuse is not specifically suspected. You may even require that employees inform you when they are taking prescribed medication that may make them drowsy or interfere with their operation of machinery.

> If any employees are impaired on the job, they represents a safety risk to themselves as well as to other employees.

Smoking

Smoking reform laws have dramatically changed the way America works. Smoking on the job was once the norm, but now most companies prohibit it and require smokers to go outside or to a specially ventilated area to smoke. These policies were largely enacted in response to legislation, most based on clinical studies linking second-hand smoke to health risks for nonsmokers. But smoking also presents risks to smokers in the workplace beyond the health risk of smoking itself.

Smokers have a higher rate of absenteeism and get sick more often than nonsmokers. Smoking on the job diverts attention from the work activities, increasing the risk of accidents. Smoking takes time, resulting in a lower productivity rate than for nonsmokers. Smokers file proportionately more workers' compensation and health insurance claims than nonsmokers. Taken in aggregate, smokers represent a significantly higher expense than nonsmokers. Yet many states specifically prohibit discrimination against smokers.

In your company policy handbook, address smoking as a health risk that violates the rights of nonsmokers but also respect the rights of smokers. Use company policy to define the rights of each group. Ensure that designated smoking areas are adequately ventilated. Designate specific areas and times for smoking that do not interfere with productivity. Ensure that nonsmokers receive a comparable amount of time away from their workstations so that smoking is not perceived to be justification for a privilege.

> Address smoking as a health risk that violates the rights of nonsmokers but also respect the rights of smokers.

Safety

As an employer, you have a duty to provide a safe working environment for your employees. This duty has both an ethical and a legal basis. As will be discussed in Chapter 11, the Occupational Safety and Health Act and similar laws at the federal, state, and local level regulate many aspects of business safety and require reporting of workplace accidents and illnesses.

Your business may present specific risks to your employees that may result in physical dangers, hazardous or toxic materials, or environmental conditions such as excessive heat or noise. You must provide protective equipment and training to employees exposed to these risks.

Most risks can be identified through careful evaluation of the workplace by an objective individual. Professional evaluations are available at little or no cost. You can get assistance from your insurance carrier, state department of labor office, or even local Occupational Safety and Health Administration (OSHA) office. Further, the local office of the U.S. Small Business Administration (SBA) or a small business development center (SBDC) can provide you with referrals to safety professionals. Finally, professional safety consultants can be found in most metropolitan areas. Keep in mind, however, that hiring a consultant can be expensive. Refer to Appendix B and Appendix C to learn how you can contact your local SBA office or nearest SBDC.

You can word your safety policy so that unsafe practices by any employee are strictly prohibited. Accident report forms should be readily available to all employees and filled out promptly after each on-the-job accident. Your policy should also define disciplinary actions as well as provide a means for reporting unsafe conditions or practices.

Many companies have formed active safety committees to monitor safety, investigate accidents, and make recommendations for handling unsafe practices or conditions. Further, large companies are incorporating wellness topics into training programs to address such issues as alcoholism, smoking cessation, and stress reduction.

Termination

A well-written termination policy may save you from unnecessary litigation at the hands of a disgruntled former employee. Sadly, not all employees are models of perfection and, sooner or later, you will encounter an employee who is a frequent discipline problem.

Your termination policy should specify any behaviors that will result in immediate termination, such as:

- Theft of company property
- Crime on company property
- Violence against another employee

You might also want your company policy to include an employment-at-will clause. Employment-at-will means employment can be terminated at any time by either the employer or the employee for any reason.

Your termination policy should also address lesser infractions that could lead to termination if a behavior isn't corrected. This part of the policy must define procedures to be followed to correct inadequate or errant behavior. Then, strictly follow these procedures to protect your company from litigation.

There is a long list of unlawful reasons for terminating employment, most of which have developed from legal precedents. These include retaliatory discharge, breach of contract, discrimination, and bad faith. The National Labor Relations Act (NLRA) and numerous other pieces of legislation are increasingly protecting employees from wrongful discharge. You should consult with an attorney prior to terminating an employee whenever legal precedents are unclear.

Certain laws apply to terminated employees with some minor variations from state to state. You should pay a terminated employee up-to-date at the time of termination, including all money owed for accrued vacation time or sick time. Make sure to collect keys, identification cards, and company property.

> A well-written termination policy may save you from unnecessary litigation at the hands of a disgruntled former employee.

Leaves of Absence

Employees may encounter various reasons for requiring extended leaves of absence. You should consider any absence of ten days or less to be a personal leave rather than a leave of absence.

FAMILY LEAVE

The Family and Medical Leave Act of 1993 (FMLA) permits employees to take up to 12 weeks of unpaid leave each year for the birth or adoption of a child; to attend to a seriously ill child, spouse, or parent; or for serious personal illness. As an employer you must guarantee that your employees can return to their same jobs or comparable jobs and you must continue health care coverage, if you provide it, during the leave period.

This law is enforced by the Equal Employment Opportunity Commission (EEOC) and applies to employers with 50 or more employees within a 75-mile radius. The law does not apply to employees with less than one year on the job or who have not worked at least 1,250 hours or at least 25 hours per week in the past year. Workers who are on family leave are not eligible for unemployment benefits or other government compensation. To learn how your state handles family and medical leaves, refer to Chapter 11.

Workers who are on family leave are not eligible for unemployment benefits or other government compensation.

MILITARY LEAVE

The Uniformed Services Employment and Re-employment Rights Act of 1994 requires that military leave must be granted for up to five years. The employer must rehire the employee if that person was inducted into or voluntarily enlisted in the armed forces of the United States. The law also protects reservists and National Guard members who are called to active duty. See Appendix C for the address of the National Committee for Employer Support of the Guard and Reserve. This organization can either help you or direct you to a local representative who can answer questions about employer and employee rights and responsibilities.

Use of Company Time, Equipment, or Resources

The temptation to use company property or equipment for personal benefit is fairly understandable. Your business is likely to be able to afford equipment that is bigger, faster, stronger, or better than home equipment. However, the employee who types a garage sale flier and makes 50 copies during the lunch hour is imposing some degree of wear and tear on company equipment. Similarly, sending or receiving personal faxes, using the company phone for personal business, or borrowing a tool set to work on the family car constitutes misuse of company property for personal gain.

You may decide to take a no-harm-done approach to some of these abuses, but small abuses invite larger ones, and a thousand minor expenses add up to a significant loss over the course of a year. On the other hand, you don't want to impose a harsh, prohibitive atmosphere that makes employees feel uncomfortable working for you.

Your policy should make it clear that all equipment, supplies, and services were purchased for the benefit of the company and that even minor theft of services or supplies is not in the company's best interest. At your discretion, you may allow employees to check equipment out over night for personal use. However, such practices invite theft and make tax depreciation of eligible equipment difficult to determine.

Employee Orientation

Now that you have a good idea of the major issues to include in your company policy manual, you will want to ensure that your employees understand the importance of adhering to these procedures. One way to open up a clear line of communication is to formally acquaint each new employee on the day when he or she joins your business. As part of your orientation, make sure you discuss the following with your new employees:

- The driving force—overall vision and spirit—of your business;
- The structure and organization of your business, identifying the key players and major divisions;
- The various employee policies, with a focus on essentials like starting and quitting times, breaks, meal times, sick days, vacation days, and timecards; and
- The benefits package your business offers and the dates for becoming eligible to participate.

If you establish this open line of communication up front, your employees will feel more valued and will get a clear picture of where they fit in.

Monitoring Your Employees' Performance

A performance review and an improvement plan are valuable tools to ensure that employees stay on the job and remain productive for your company. Firing employees is costly. Your losses include the time and effort expended in hiring, in training, in making them part of your company, and in attempting to help them overcome their deficiencies. Finally, the time you spend when terminating an employee represents a significant loss.

The Importance of Performance Reviews

A performance review is a process used by managers or owners to evaluate and document an employee's job performance. To be effective, performance reviews must be fair and impartial. Administer them following the schedule set forth in your employee handbook or other company policy document.

> One way to open up a clear line of communication is to formally acquaint each new employee on the day when he or she joins your business.

Effective performance reviews, based on job requirements, provide a systematic record of an employee's job performance.

Effective performance reviews, based on job requirements, provide a systematic record of an employee's job performance. This continuous record gives the employee valuable feedback and encourages improvement. It provides fair documentation of strengths and weaknesses. It also simplifies management decisions regarding raises, promotions, transfers, demotions, and terminations. Complete records may even protect a company in the event of legal actions initiated by a discontented employee or former employee.

It's important to use standardized methods and formats for all performance reviews. You will want to rate all employees according to a set of consistent standards. The 1978 Uniform Guidelines on Employee Selection Procedures prohibit basing performance reviews on discriminatory practices or biases concerning race, ethnicity, religion, gender, or sexual orientation.

Most employers conduct performance reviews annually, usually during the anniversary month of the employee's start date, while a few prefer scheduling them semiannually. Schedule several reviews during the employee's initial probationary period and one at the end. These reviews provide feedback to the new employee on his or her conformance with job requirements as well as company policy, and serve to identify problem areas early in the employer-employee relationship. They also provide information on which to base a decision to terminate a new employee, if necessary, at the end of a probationary period.

Preventing Performance Review Problems

When administered properly and fairly, performance reviews are a valuable management tool. However, even a well-designed program is subject to problems resulting from human error. An awareness of these potential problems will allow you to take steps to prevent them and will help you keep your program consistent and fair.

MANAGERS RATE EMPLOYEES DIFFERENTLY

Managers will not rate employees in the same way. Some tend to see all employees in the most positive light, while others take a more negative approach. Ideally, you want everyone involved in rating employees to do so in a balanced, even-handed way that uniformly recognizes both strengths and weaknesses. Discuss the review process with your managers periodically. That's the best way to ensure fairness and objectivity in the performance review process. Some employers use a dual review method: the employee's supervisor and a supervisor from another area who is familiar with the employee's work each evaluate the employee separately.

UNCLEAR RATING STANDARDS

Unclear rating standards cause a performance review program to produce inconsistent results. When standards are defined poorly, it allows situations in which, for example, one manager defines good attendance as zero absenteeism and another manager defines good attendance as no more than three absences. Performance standards must be clear to supervisors and workers alike. Define all terms and avoid vague generalities when defining standards.

> Performance standards must be clear to supervisors and workers alike. Define all terms and avoid vague generalities when defining standards.

LAST IN, FIRST OUT

It's natural for reviewers to remember recent events best, so they tend to rate employee performance based on work accomplished during recent months rather than during the entire evaluation period. If employees significantly improve their performance as evaluation time approaches, that's a good indication that this problem exists in your review process. To prevent this problem, encourage supervisors to frequently notice performance trends and to collect performance data throughout the evaluation period. Examples of pertinent information include letters of recommendation or congratulation, voluntary participation on committees, taking on new leadership positions, and completing additional training. Also, make note of minor infractions, tardiness, and informal counseling.

THE HALO EFFECT

An employee who is neat, well-mannered, and cheerful seems to be brighter and more capable than a casually dressed, introverted employee. This "halo effect" hinders objective performance appraisal. Reviewers must be alert to this and be sure that they are evaluating real performance rather than perceived performance. Train your reviewers to be aware of the halo effect and provide them with clear-cut standards to use in appraising performance.

The Documentation Process

Document all performance reviews consistently using a standardized performance review report. The performance review report provides a permanent record of the performance review, its timeliness, and its fairness. It's best to use a standardized form for performance reviews. The form should be general enough to be used with all employees, yet specific enough to provide a clear appraisal that generates information that managers can use. Most forms combine a scaled rating system with space for amplifying comments. A sample performance review is located in Appendix A. For other formats, consider getting a copy of *The Complete Book of Business Forms* by Richard G. Stuart or *Ultimate Book of Business Forms* by Michael Spadaccini.

The employee and the supervisor fill out the performance review report through cooperative effort. The employee should sign the report to indicate that he or she has read it and understands its content. Signing does not necessarily indicate that the employee agrees with the report. After completing and signing the report, the supervisor forwards it to upper management for review, if applicable. After review, file the report in the employee's personnel record.

In cases where the employee disagrees with the content of the performance appraisal, you should have a procedure in place that allows fair rebuttal. Typically, an employee can rebut in written form to an upper manager. After review, the rebuttal becomes a part of the employee's personnel file.

Counseling—An Opportunity to Improve

Counseling is similar to the performance review, but differs in that it occurs as a result of a change in performance. Generally, employees view counseling as being negative because it most often occurs as a result of poor job performance. The manager's role when this happens is to help the employee understand how his or her performance is inadequate. Then, he or she can work with the employee to identify the source of the problem and recommend ways to correct it.

Ideally, both the manager and the employee will approach counseling as a means of improving rather than as a punitive measure. It is important to state the goal of the counseling at the beginning of the meeting. Remember that your employee is a valued asset who has contributed time and effort to your business. Your goal is to keep each of your employees productive and motivated.

Poor performance may be a result of poorly defined policy, personality conflict, politics, or environment. For example, an employee suffering from eye strain from his or her computer terminal may perceive that management is uncaring, particularly if the condition has persisted over time. Timely counseling in an open and supportive atmosphere will allow you to identify these problems and correct them.

Management will rarely intervene directly when degraded performance is the result of external problems, such as family difficulties, substance abuse, or financial woes. In these cases, refer the employee to an outside professional agency. A referral gives the employee the clear message that you value him or

> Generally, employees view counseling as being negative because it most often occurs as a result of poor job performance.

her. Arrange for a follow-up meeting to inquire about the employee's progress in coping with the problem and provide feedback on performance issues.

Your Disciplinary Action Policy

The time to decide how to handle a discipline problem comes long before it occurs. Disciplinary actions must follow a prescribed format in accordance with your company policy manual.

In matters of discipline, preparation will save you a great deal of trouble in the long run. Decide which behaviors you will consider as minor infractions and which ones you will consider to be grounds for immediate suspension or termination. Develop a policy for dealing with each of these two types of infraction.

Typical minor infractions include tardiness, waste of supplies, arguing with coworkers, or violating company policy. Your company policy manual is the basis for determining infractions, but you should leave room in your discipline policy for supervisors to use good judgment in determining when violations have occurred.

Your disciplinary action policy is a series of specific steps. Those steps include a verbal warning, counseling with a written warning, an improvement plan, a review, suspension, and termination. The process takes time, but when you consider the cost of hiring, training, and developing a new employee, it's worth the effort to save an employee with potential.

> In matters of discipline, preparation will save you a great deal of trouble in the long run.

Giving Warnings

As part of your disciplinary action policy, you need to decide the basis for giving warnings and the process. Warnings can come in a verbal or written form.

A verbal warning given when an infraction occurs will send a clear message to your employee that the specified behavior is inappropriate and unacceptable. Give verbal warnings in a friendly, yet firm manner. Most people want to do well and will respond immediately to friendly guidance. When a behavior ends with a verbal warning, place a note to that effect in the employee's personnel file.

A written warning is the next step in the process. It is a formal counseling session with the employee, documented on a standardized company form. The form will require a detailed explanation of the infraction and the expected behavior. It will provide space for the employee to explain extenuating or mitigating circumstances. It will suggest methods for the employee to correct the deficiency, set a time limit for improvement, and explain the consequences for failure to improve.

The supervisor or manager will discuss the written warning with the employee and clearly explain each part of the document and the process. At the conclusion of the counseling session, the employee should sign the warning to indicate that he or she completely understands it. Then, the supervisor or manager forwards the warning to upper management for review, if applicable, and it is filed in the employee's personnel record.

Handling Suspensions

When an employee does not respond to warnings, suspension should follow. Suspending an employee is a serious action and it's appropriate for only the most serious disciplinary problems. Suspension without pay conveys a clear message to the employee to change his or her problem behavior or risk termination. Your goal is to retain otherwise valuable employees by giving them every opportunity to change.

As with counseling and written warnings, it's important to keep detailed records of your personnel actions. Also keep in mind that the problem you're attempting to correct must be about performance and not personality. Detailed records will clearly show that you acted appropriately and dealt with the problem fairly and professionally. Use a formal suspension notice to record this action.

A suspension notice is a standardized form that the employee's supervisor should complete, date, and sign. A notice should include:

- A description of the suspension action,
- A statement of the reason for the suspension, and
- A list of the corrective actions required.

The form should include space for the employee to sign to acknowledge receiving and understanding the suspension notice. File the original in the employee's personnel folder and provide copies to the employee and the employee's supervisor.

A suspension is not a substitute for termination. You cannot suspend an employee indefinitely. So be certain that the description of the suspension action includes a specific ending point for the suspension period. Suspensions usually last from several days to several weeks. After the employee returns to work following suspension, any further infractions normally lead to termination.

> Suspending an employee is a serious action and it's appropriate for only the most serious disciplinary problems.

Take Caution with Disciplinary Terminations

The practice of employment-at-will and the right to terminate an employee for good or just cause are being increasingly challenged in the courts. There is a growing list of legal precedents for wrongful discharge of an employee. The list includes such concepts as retaliatory discharge, breach of written contract, breach of implied contract, and discrimination based on sex, age, or disability.

Your best defense is to ensure that your employee handbook and company policies make the employment-at-will doctrine perfectly clear. Further, ensure that the wording of these documents does not imply permanent employment.

Observe the following guidelines when terminating an employee.

- Terminate employees only for documented substandard performance or misconduct and only in accordance with established equal opportunity doctrine.
- Handle terminations discreetly, privately, and professionally.
- Ensure that terminated employees receive all pay earned to date.
- Make sure that all company policies are followed, when applicable, including performance review, counseling, grievance, and appeal policies.

Use a standardized company form to document the termination. Make sure the form includes the reason for termination and refers to supporting records and documents. Provide a checklist on the form to ensure that correct termination procedures are followed and that the employee's rights are observed.

Following these recommendations does not guarantee protection from wrongful discharge suits. The law is changing continuously and your best insurance is to consult with your attorney when you prepare your company policy manual. Stay abreast of changes in the law and keep your manual current with legislation.

Write a separate policy in your personnel manual for handling termination due to misconduct, such as theft or destruction of company property, fighting, criminal activity, or continuous unexcused absence. Carefully define those conditions that will result in either immediate termination or termination following suspension. When you terminate an employee for misconduct, take care to observe all the precautions and requirements of normal termination procedures. Fully document the termination decision and process, including

Terminate employees only for documented substandard performance or misconduct and only in accordance with established equal opportunity doctrine.

a description of the type of misconduct. Include documentation that proves or supports the determination of misconduct.

Other Types of Terminations

Termination also results from other actions, such as resignation and layoff due to restructuring or elimination of a position. These terminations follow the same basic procedures as other types of termination. Fully document the circumstances of the termination, treat the departing employee with dignity and professionalism, and provide the employee with all earned pay before he or she departs.

Require resigning employees to give notice of their intent to resign whenever possible. Sufficient notice allows you time to complete all administrative paperwork, verify pay and benefit requirements, conduct an exit interview, and start looking for a replacement. Generally, two weeks or ten working days is sufficient notice.

A departing employee frequently feels more free to express dissatisfaction with working conditions. Take advantage of this opportunity to learn more about your company. An exit interview is a valuable means of getting feedback about the company, the working environment, and management practices.

Layoffs result from a reduction in the workforce and elimination of positions through restructuring. Notify employees of an impending layoff and the reasons for it as far in advance as possible. Carefully consider which employees will be laid off, following established policy guidelines. Consider company needs, seniority issues, and the abilities of individual employees. When possible, consider reassigning individuals to other areas for which they are qualified.

> An exit interview is a valuable means of getting feedback about the company, the working environment, and management practices.

Benefits Packages

Benefits fall into two categories: those that are legally required and those at the discretion of the employer. Legally required benefits include payment of Social Security taxes, workers' compensation insurance, and unemployment insurance. Discretionary benefits include anything from medical insurance to free tickets to sporting events. Virtually anything of value that you provide or make available to your employees qualifies as a discretionary benefit. The only limitation is your imagination.

Keep in mind that employees expect a benefits package along with their salary or hourly wage. Typical benefits include medical insurance coverage, accidental death and disability coverage, and some form of retirement plan. The cost of these benefits increases each year, but you can generally expect to pay approximately 25 to 35 percent of each employee's salary or wages. This means that an employee who earns $7.50 per hour will represent an hourly expense of as much as $10.15. Generally, employees are not aware of the costs associated with providing benefits.

You may decide that the nature of your business does not support the cost of providing employee benefits. This is particularly true under the following conditions:

- Your employees are generally unskilled;
- All or most of your employees are part-time or temporary; or
- Your nearest competitors are not providing a benefits package.

However, as your business grows and you require more employees with more skills, a comprehensive benefits package will help to attract the best-qualified applicants.

If you decide to include a retirement plan as part of your employee benefits package, make sure it is in sync with the Employee Retirement Income Security Act (ERISA). This act governs how certain pension plans and welfare plans are administered. Pension plans include certain retirement plans, profit sharing, stock option plans, and individual retirement accounts (IRAs). Welfare plans include most types of employee insurance, such as health, disability, life, and accidental death coverage.

Recent shifts in cultural values are subtly changing the way employees view benefits. Tomorrow's employees are likely to value a clean and pleasant working environment, state-of-the-art equipment, and a four-day workweek over tickets to the next big game. So before planning a benefits package, take the time to survey the needs and desires of your employees.

> Before planning a benefits package, take the time to survey the needs and desires of your employees.

Chapter Wrap-Up

If your business will have employees, you will need to manage them carefully. Just like other critical investments, the time you take to hire and retain top-quality people is an investment that can pay huge dividends or seriously affect your ability to make a profit.

Effective human resources management is a multi-faceted process that requires you to stay informed and proactive:

- Develop thorough job descriptions before you announce an opening.
- Understand anti-discrimination laws, so you know which questions to avoid on application forms and during interviews.
- Know how to screen job applicants and track your evaluations after both formal and informal interviews.
- Properly acquaint and train new employees, so they know exactly what your business expects of them.
- Review and monitor your employees' performance to foster their existing skills and support their developing new ones.

A good human resources package means having well-defined policies and procedures. In short, create a company policy and procedures manual or an employee handbook and make sure each employee gets a copy. Document that employees have read your handbook by having them sign a paper indicating they understand all the policies and procedures outlined in the manual. In general, make sure your company policy manual covers the following:

- Benefits
- Career opportunities
- Company background
- Employee evaluation procedures
- Employee grievance procedures
- Employee safety
- Employee/management relations
- General policies and procedures
- Pay rates and schedules

Remember: the people who will work for you will communicate the character and quality of your business and its product or service. Build a team that will help you and your employees make the most of your enterprise. For specific state and federal government regulations related to your business, refer to Chapter 11.

7 | *Insurance Matters*

Getting into business is inherently a risk: there's no guarantee of success. However, you can improve your chances by making informed decisions that can reduce the possibility of losses due to risks, reduce or eliminate the chance of particular risks, or insure against losses due to risks.

The most common way to guard against many risks is by obtaining insurance. Insurance is a necessary business expense. You need insurance to protect yourself and your business from fire and other disasters, crime, general liability, and any interruption of business. If you have employees, you are required to purchase workers' compensation insurance and you may also choose to provide health, life, or disability benefits for your employees. This chapter discusses the numerous types of insurance coverage to help you make informed decisions.

For some risks, there is no insurance. For other risks, the cost of insurance is too high. In these cases, you will assume the risks and hope that you do not have a loss that is not covered.

Your first step in evaluating your need for insurance is to assess the risks that your business faces.

What Is Risk Assessment?

Risk assessment is the process of determining the risks to which your business is exposed and what you should do about them. You will have to strike a balance between the expense of being covered against every eventuality and the costs of risks associated with insufficient insurance coverage. By evaluating each aspect of your business critically and considering its relative importance to your business, you will lay the groundwork for determining your insurance needs. This will save you a great deal of time and money as you shop for the best coverage at the best price.

> Risk assessment is the process of determining the risks to which your business is exposed and what you should do about them.

To assess risks, you must determine where losses can occur by reviewing every aspect of your business to identify which people, property, or conditions you need in order to continue operating. Evaluate safety issues and concerns, your crime risk, and the potential for fire or other disaster. Evaluate the financial condition of your business and decide how much loss your business can absorb without risking failure. Consider temporary closures, downtime, inventory, cash flow, borrowing power, and other pertinent variables. Prioritize and categorize each potential loss based on its severity and potential frequency.

Four Ways to Handle Risks

You will handle risks in one of four ways:

- *Elimination.* This means that you decide to drop a product or service that exposes you to a particular risk. For example, you would eliminate the potential for delivery van accidents and potential damage to your vehicle, driver, other drivers, and other property if you no longer delivered your product or provided service only for items that customers would bring to your place of business.
- *Reduction.* This entails modifying a potential loss by changing an element of the risk in order to reduce the likelihood and/or the severity of a loss.
- *Retention.* You understand the potential for the risk, but because the likelihood of a loss is low enough and/or because the cost of insuring against the loss or changing your business are higher than you can afford or want to pay, you assume the full consequences of the potential loss.

- *Transference.* When you obtain insurance to cover a risk, you transfer the risk to the insurance company. The company is insuring many risks and thus spreading the cost of the consequences of a loss across many insured companies or individuals.

Each alternative imposes different levels of cost or potential cost. You must weigh the cost of each method against the potential risk to your business. The example below, while simplistic, clearly demonstrates the application of each method.

For example, suppose your business is a feed and grain store. You determine that one of your risks is loss of inventory due to spoilage from mice. If mice are a frequent and severe problem, you may choose to eliminate the risk by periodically hiring an exterminator. If mice are frequent visitors, but don't spoil much inventory, you may choose instead to reduce the risk by investing in cats. If infestation is infrequent and there's not spoilage, you will probably retain the risk and absorb the losses as part of the cost of doing business. you are concerned about a rare yet devastating invasion that would destroy your inventory completely, you might transfer the risk to an insurance carrier.

> You may have risks that are not insurable.

To better understand the four methods of handling risks, consider the following scenario.

You own a food processing company with more than 100 products. One of the products requires much more care in preparation than the others because of past problems with a fungus in the food. The product accounts for only 1 percent of your total sales and less than 1 percent of your profit. To solve the problem, you have four options:

- *Eliminate the risk.* Discontinue the product; thus, you eliminate the need for extra care that's required to offer a product that generates only a marginal profit.
- *Reduce the risk.* Install new equipment that's easier to maintain and monitor and more reliable than your current equipment.
- *Retain the risk.* Assume that with constant vigilance you will not have a problem with the product.
- *Transfer the risk.* Purchase a liability insurance policy that will cover the consequences if any of the product is bad food and makes any of your customers sick and causes you to recall the product.

In the above scenario, you have all four options for handling the risk. That's not always the case.

You may have risks that are not insurable. For example, your company may be located at the end of a road that floods sometimes make impassable. Although you may obtain flood insurance, the risk is not from damages, but rather from temporary inaccessibility. Although you may be able to obtain special insurance for such an eventuality, most insurance will not cover this risk.

You may also find that you can obtain insurance for certain risks, but the costs of insuring them may be more than the potential loss over a given period. For example, if you want to insure against theft and you believe that the greatest loss you would incur due to theft would be $10,000, you may find that insuring all items that could be stolen would cost $2,000 in premiums per year. If you have a losses of more than $10,000 more often than every five years, you would be financially ahead to insure the loss. However, if a loss might occur only once in ten years, you can cover the loss with what you save from not paying insurance premiums. Of course, you don't know how often a loss will occur. And you can be certain that if your business is prone to losses often, the insurance company will either cancel your policy or increase the premium.

> Insurance is very cost-effective if you can pay low premiums for potentially high losses, as with liability insurance.

Insurance is very cost-effective if you can pay low premiums for potentially high losses. as with liability insurance. However, the insurance companies will determine if your business has a high potential for liability claims and will charge on the basis of the industry experience for such claims—and may even refuse to write insurance because of the potential for high losses.

Other risks normally associated with running your business are not insurable, such as the loss of a major customer or an increase in the cost of raw materials after you've made a bid or set a price for an item you produce. In such cases, you need to determine the potential risks and include the costs of solutions in contracts or pricing policies.

Types of Insurance

To start, understand the unique characteristics involved with the two broad classes of insurance—property-casualty insurance and life insurance.

- *Property-casualty insurance.* This type includes property insurance for fire and other hazards and casualty insurance. Workers' compensation is a casualty insurance. This type of insurance also includes auto liability, general liability, credit insurance, bonds, boiler and machinery, crime, and other miscellaneous casualty.
- *Life insurance.* Both term and whole life policies are available. These types of insurance are used in business partnerships: each partner

takes out a policy on the other in order to be able to buy his or her share in the event that he or she dies.

Property Insurance

The chances are high that you will need some form of property insurance for your business. If you lease an office or warehouse, the lease will probably require you to obtain some type of fire policy. If your product is transported via truck or ship, you may want a policy to cover potential loss.

Fire insurance is generally considered to be property insurance. There are policies to cover direct losses due to fire; others cover consequential losses, such as being out of business for a couple of months due to fire.

There are many ways in which policies can be written and interpreted, but you must determine which of the following you want from your policy:

- Replacement cost (what it would cost to replace property that was damaged, with no deductions for depreciation);
- A stated loss amount; or
- Actual cash value (what you paid for property that was damaged, less an amount for depreciation).

There is also a provision in some insurance policies called coinsurance. If you do not insure for at least 80 percent (sometimes 90 or 100 percent) of your potential loss, the insurance will pay only the percentage that you have insured of the total potential loss. For example, you may insure a building that has a value of $1,000,000 for $500,000, taking the chance that you would not suffer a complete loss of the building in a fire. Then, if a fire caused $50,000 damage, the insurance company would not compensate you for the entire $50,000; it would pay only $25,000, since you insured only half the value of the building.

In addition, if your building appreciated in value while you occupied it and the value at the time of the fire was considerably greater than when you took out the insurance, the insurer may invoke the coinsurance provision based on the value of the building at the time of loss, not the value when the policy started. Therefore, you should review your policy for the values insured every time you renew it.

If you operate your business out of your home, your coverage for losses to your business will be limited with the usual homeowner's insurance. In addition, if you conduct part of your business from buildings other than your home, but on the same land as your home, the other buildings and their con-

> The chances are high that you will need some form of property insurance for your business.

tents will probably not be covered unless you have a separate business policy for them.

Casualty Insurance

Insurance that is not life insurance or property insurance is normally considered casualty insurance. As mentioned above, workers' compensation is a form of casualty insurance; we'll discuss it a little later in this chapter. Other forms of casualty insurance include automobile and liability insurance.

AUTOMOBILE INSURANCE

If you own or lease a vehicle for your business, you should be aware that there are different rules for a business policy than for your personal vehicles. Your personal insurance covers you ("the named insured") for whatever vehicle you drive, including rentals. Business insurance covers the vehicle for any drivers who have permission to use it.

There's also coverage called "drive-other-car endorsement" that you can add to your company policy to cover you when you are driving a vehicle not owned by your company if you do not have personal automobile insurance. As a part of automobile insurance, liability insurance pays for bodily injury or property damage to others due to the use of the vehicle.

Insurance to cover physical damage consists of two types: collision and comprehensive. Collision covers losses due to a collision of the vehicle with another object. Comprehensive covers almost all other losses, including vandalism, theft, broken windshields, damage to the car if it's stolen, and damage from fire or flood.

A third element of automobile insurance is for medical payments. It includes the occupants of either vehicle or both and normally covers medical, dental, surgical, ambulance, and funeral services.

In many states you can obtain uninsured motorist coverage to protect the company against loss if another driver causes an accident and does not have insurance.

Finally, there's hired auto coverage and non-owned coverage. The former protects you if someone from your company rents a vehicle in the company name and is involved in an accident. The latter protects you if an employee has an accident in his or her own vehicle while on company business.

LIABILITY INSURANCE

Liability for a situation occurs in one of three ways:

> Insurance that is not life insurance or property insurance is normally considered casualty

- Negligence
- Statutory law
- Assumption by contract

There are legal requirements for acts to be defined as negligent; a discussion of the requirements is beyond the scope of this book. Virtually every business has a potential for being sued for a negligent act. Therefore, you should carefully determine your potential exposure in this area and locate an insurance company that can insure against what might be devastating loss to your company. As an employer you can be held responsible for the actions of one of your employees, even though you have taken steps to prevent a situation.

Statutory law liability occurs when a law has been enacted that creates a legal obligation, such as the requirement to carry workers' compensation insurance or liability regarding products that may be inherently dangerous.

"Assumption by contract" refers to a hold-harmless agreement in a contract. For example, your lease agreement probably will contain a hold-harmless agreement that requires you to maintain liability insurance and hold the landlord harmless for any accident that may occur on the premises.

> There are several forms of liability insurance coverage; they may be combined into one policy or insured individually.

There are several forms of liability insurance coverage; they may be combined into one policy or insured individually. Check with your agent regarding potential liability that your company may have and see if the cost of insurance is reasonable for the level of coverage you will receive. If you have a home office and have a homeowner's policy with liability coverage, the policy may not cover liability for anyone hurt at your place of business. Check with your agent to see if you need a separate policy for your home office.

CRIME COVERAGE

Crime is a real threat to many businesses. Virtually all businesses must be aware of employee dishonesty, theft, bad checks, vandalism, and personal injury as possibilities. The potential for any of these crimes varies from business to business, so you should check among the different types of coverage to find those that meet your particular needs.

Coverage for loss of money by employees or others handling cash or accounts is most frequently provided through the use of bonds. There are various types of bonds available that protect against theft, embezzlement, loss of money on or off the premises, counterfeit money, and forging. The cost of coverage for such problems may exceed the value of the coverage to you, so you may go without.

Or you may decide to implement company policies to protect against such losses. For example, some retail establishments do not accept checks unless the customer has a check guarantee card or they may not accept checks at all. Many stores have a policy of a separate cash drawer for each cashier.

Even if you have a policy for theft, you many not be able to collect the amount of a loss. Policies will generally limit the circumstances under which you can make a claim against the policy. For example, you probably will not be able to collect on a theft policy if you find that your inventory is actually $10,000 lower than you expected according to your computerized inventory. You may suspect theft, but it is unlikely that the insurance company will pay for your loss.

Theft policies also have coinsurance provisions, described previously, so be careful that you are aware of the potential payoff if you need to make a claim.

Life Insurance

Life insurance is probably the best known of all insurance policies. There are two major types of life insurance: term and whole life. There are variations of the policies, but basically this insurance covers against death rather than against other hazards.

> Life insurance is probably the best known of all insurance policies.

Term insurance pays a benefit if an insured person dies during the term of the policy. If the person does not die, there is no remainder value of the policy. It is similar to other casualty policies that expire with no payment made if no claim arises. Term insurance is less expensive and the most widely used form of life insurance.

Whole life policies are designed to pay the beneficiary the face amount of the policy in case of death. If the insured decides to terminate the policy, there may be some cash value to the policy.

There are many variations of both types of policies. In business, life insurance policies are generally used for retirement, the purchase of partners' shares of the business (funding buy-sell agreements), or as protection against the financial impact of the loss of a key employee. In addition, business owners with whole life policies may borrow the cash value from the insurance company or use it as collateral for loans.

When You Have Employees

In addition to property-casualty and life insurance, you will need to explore other types of insurance if you have employees. You should know about the following:

- State-mandated workers' compensation
- Optional health, disability, and accidental death insurance

If you offer insurance as part of your employee compensation package, be aware of certain recent legislation that affects how you administer that insurance.

Workers' Compensation Insurance

You are required to purchase workers' compensation insurance if you have a certain number of employees. The requirements vary from state to state. Make sure you read Chapter 11 to understand the workers' compensation laws in your state. Workers' compensation coverage pays benefits for job-related illnesses, injuries, and death. Paid benefits may include medical expenses, death benefits, lost wages, and vocational rehabilitation. Failure to carry coverage for your employees could leave you liable for payment of all benefits and subject to fines.

To better understand your role in carrying workers' compensation insurance, make sure you know how your premium is calculated. Premiums are calculated by dividing an employee's annual payroll by 100 and multiplying the result by a factor based on the employee's classification rating. Classification ratings vary from occupation to occupation and from state to state. The insurance industry in your state has classified hundreds of occupations according to the risk of injury suggested by the occupations' loss histories. For instance, cashiers experience lower job-related injury risks than mill workers, so their rating factor is much lower and workers' compensation insurance coverage for a cashier is much less expensive than for a mill worker.

Premiums are further modified by an experience factor based on a business's claim history. For example, a business with a good workers' compensation claim history will have a lower experience modification factor—resulting in lower premiums. The reverse is also true. Thus, when you purchase workers' compensation insurance, you must ensure that all your employees are correctly classified and their claim histories have been considered in the final

> You are required to purchase workers' compensation insurance if you have a certain number of employees.

premium calculations. These simple checks could save you a considerable amount of money each year.

You can reduce your insurance costs in other ways. Purchase a type of policy called a participating policy, which pays dividends to companies with low loss records. Another good service to look for is loss control assistance. Your insurance company's loss control department can help you reduce or prevent claims by providing free published materials and guidance as well as evaluation and troubleshooting. Work environment and safety program evaluations are expensive to purchase independently, but your insurance company may provide them as a free service.

Investing in safety will usually produce a positive return on your investment. You can lower your compensation payments if claims are low. It usually takes three years to develop a rate, called an experience modification factor. This rating can be higher or lower than the standard rate, based on claims. If your rate goes up, you pay the increase on all employees based on their payroll for the entire year. Thus, a small increase or decrease in a rate can mean a substantial savings or additional payment at the end of the year.

Some states require companies to have employee committees that review workplace safety issues. Even if your state does not require it, it's a good idea to obtain ideas from employees regarding workplace safety. You can have a formal policy or a suggestion box. Employees are good at anticipating safety problems because they're most exposeed to potentially dangerous situations.

Not all industrial accidents involve heavy machinery. Employees may slip on the floor or trip over wires or obstacles. Lighting or seating can cause long-term problems that will cost you much more money than correcting the problem would cost. In addition, accidents cost you in terms of time due to an employee's absence. If an employee has an accident, you must either do without him or her or get a temporary, who will be less familiar with your business than your absent employee, and spend time training the new person.

If your business is home-based, you will find it helpful to obtain information from your workers' compensation company regarding how it handles injuries when workers are in your home. Your insurance company's policies may affect your policies regarding working at home.

Health Insurance

Employers are the major provider of health insurance for most people in the United States. There are two basic types of health insurance: disability insurance and medical insurance.

DISABILITY INSURANCE

A business can use disability insurance to help the owner hire a manager if the owner becomes disabled. In a partnership, it may also be used to pay off a partner if the other partner becomes disabled and is unlikely to be able to return to work.

Whatever kind of disability insurance you obtain, be certain to get the following information:

- The income per month that the policy will pay;
- The number of months payments will be made; and
- The other conditions necessary to receive payments, including the duration of the disability.

MEDICAL INSURANCE

Most people will identify their primary source of medical insurance as the place where they are employed. Whether you are the owner of a business or an employee, medical insurance will likely be one of the first and most important benefits derived from the business.

Check with your industry association to see if insurance is offered as part of its benefit plan.

If you incorporate, your corporation will be able to deduct the full cost of medical insurance premiums as a business expense. If you are a sole proprietor or a partner, only a portion of the expense will be deductible. If your business is not a corporation, be sure to check the changing percentages with your accountant.

There are two major elements of medical insurance: major medical and comprehensive coverage. Major medical is coverage for hospital and recuperation expenses. Comprehensive is used for hospital and outpatient treatment, office visits, testing, and other health treatment.

There are many ways to purchase medical insurance, depending on the benefits you want and the premiums you're willing and able to pay. The deductible is one of the factors that make the greatest difference in premiums. By having a higher deductible, thus insuring for major medical problems only, you can keep the cost per employee lower than if the deductible is lower.

Check with your industry association to see if it offers insurance as part of its benefit plan. You should also check with your insurance agent regarding the coverage period for a policy. If you change insurance companies and a claim is filed for the period when you were with the previous company, you may not be covered. It's best to know how you are covered, especially if there is a chance that a claim can occur after you switch to another insurance company.

Follow ERISA Guidelines

If you provide employees with insurance other than workers' compensation or if you give other benefits such as a profit sharing or retirement plans, you will need to comply with the Employment Retirement Income Security Act of 1974 (ERISA). ERISA requires that you have a summary plan description (SPD) for each welfare plan in effect. Then, you must distribute a copy of each SPD to all covered employees. Each SPD must include specific information as well as an ERISA rights statement as specified by U.S. Department of Labor regulations. Insurance companies will often supply you with an SPD for each plan as a part of their service.

If your company grows to 100 or more employees, ERISA requirements become much more complex, involving several annual reports to the U.S. Department of Labor and an annual report to all employees. You should consult an expert on these regulations. Most insurance and investment companies have experts available to help.

Consolidated Omnibus Budget Reconciliation Act (COBRA)

If you have 20 or more employees, make sure you understand your responsibilities under COBRA.

The Consolidated Omnibus Budget Reconciliation Act (COBRA), passed in 1986, requires businesses with 20 or more employees to offer the same group health benefits as for regular eligible employees to the following:

- Employees who have been terminated (for reasons other than gross misconduct) or laid off or who have resigned;
- Employees whose hours have been reduced;
- Widowed, divorced, or separated spouses of employees;
- Employees eligible for Medicare; and
- Employees' children who have lost dependent status.

Eligibility for this coverage begins as soon as a sponsoring employee becomes eligible for coverage under the group health plan. Then, that employee and his or her dependents are eligible for continued benefits for up to 36 months thereafter. Your company can charge the employee up to 100 percent of the coverage cost plus a 2 percent surcharge.

If you have 20 or more employees, make sure you understand your responsibilities under COBRA. Consult with a knowledgeable insurance specialist; most insurance companies can provide up-to-date information about COBRA.

If a company fails to comply with the requirements of this act, it cannot deduct health plan contributions from its taxes. Finally, note that COBRA does not prevent a company from terminating its group health care plan.

Shopping for Coverage

Becoming an expert on insurance matters is probably the last thing on your mind as you attempt to start your business. However, high on your priority list during start-up should be finding the best coverage for the best price.

Your best option is to find a reputable agent or broker you can trust. Finding an agent may not be as difficult as it sounds. Ask for referrals from friends, your lawyer, your accountant, or friendly competitors.

Once you have several referrals, your next step is to narrow your search by selecting agents who have earned Chartered Life Underwriter (CLU) or Chartered Property/Casualty Underwriter (CPCU) designations. These professionals are generally more experienced and capable than agents without one of these designations. The Certified Insurance Counselor (CIC) agent is a professional designation very popular among agents; there's an annual update to keep agents current.

If you cannot locate a suitable agent, you can choose instead to hire an insurance consultant. An insurance consultant is an expert who can provide an objective analysis of your risk management and insurance needs. Follow your consultant's advice carefully when selecting coverage from your agent or broker. The hourly fees for consultants are usually quite high, but the investment can result in significant savings in annual premiums. Be wary of consultants who attempt to pad their fees by offering extended services that you may not need or that you can get elsewhere for far less.

If you hire a consultant, make sure he or she is a member of the Society of Risk Management Consultants. Members of this society cannot sell insurance. This stipulation prevents potential conflicts of interest and reduces the risk of unethical behavior. To contact the society, use the address and phone number listed in Appendix C.

> An insurance consultant is an expert who can provide an objective analysis of your risk management and insurance needs.

Chapter Wrap-Up

A smart start for new entrepreneurs involves a close look at their business insurance needs. It might seem unusual to plan for a major loss or potential disaster while you're planning to open your doors for business. However, countless business owners—even of relatively new businesses—have benefited from a solid insurance package.

The tasks of getting insurance quotes and making contacts with agents, brokers, and insurance companies are not high on any business owner's list of favorite things to do. You can simplify the process by informing yourself on the various types of insurance available. Then, look at your business and assess the potential risks. Know how you want to handle these risks—whether you will transfer, reduce, retain, or eliminate—before you approach an insurance agent.

> The way you solve problems should include being prepared for emergencies.

To be able to get the best quote, you will need to decide which types of coverage are necessary for your type of business. If crime is a real threat, then you will need to consider some form of crime coverage. If potential negligence as a result of using your product or service is likely, then you will want to explore liability coverage.

Of course, as an employer you will have to comply with workers' compensation issues for the state in which you will operate. Also, you must evaluate the need to include disability and medical insurance as part of your employee benefits package.

One thing you can be sure of as you start your business: problems will surface regularly. The way you solve problems should include being prepared for emergencies. Risk assessment and insurance will protect your assets and help you stay in business.

8 | *Setting Up Your Office*

New business owners tend to view office work as something to be handled later, when they get the time. This is generally a mistake. The adage that "no job is finished until the paperwork is done" has been presented humorously, yet it is based on a fundamental truth. Somewhere amid the excitement of producing and selling a new product hides the simple fact that you are engaged in a business. Businesses are managed from an office setting.

To lessen the pain of dealing with records and paperwork, it's vital to be as organized as possible. This chapter will help you:

- Organize your incoming mail,
- Improve your telephone answering techniques,
- Establish a home-based office,
- Choose the right furniture and equipment, and
- Select the best location for your business.

The effort put into organizing will pay off a hundredfold as your business grows and demands more of your time and energy. This chapter offers suggestions for running your office until you can hire someone to do it for you.

Managing Your Incoming Mail

Handling mail and other correspondence is the nuts and bolts of office management. Mail procedures are fairly simple to put into place. It takes a little self-discipline to follow these procedures, but the payoff is a headache-free office.

> Handling mail and other correspondence is the nuts and bolts of office management.

The easiest way to handle incoming mail is by using the one-touch approach. With the one-touch approach, you handle each piece of mail in your incoming mailbox only once. You may handle some of it again later as you respond to it, but only once as it comes in. Scan your mail and put each piece in one of three places:

- The wastebasket
- The interesting mail basket
- The action mail basket

E-mail must also be handled efficiently. Each morning, go through the incoming e-mail and forward, answer, save, or delete each new message. Set aside ten to 15 minutes each morning to review and sort your e-mail correspondence.

Wastebasket Mail

When handling incoming mail, the wastebasket is your friend. By throwing away the mail that you don't need as soon as possible, you save yourself the time you would lose rereading junk mail and your desk stays clean and uncluttered.

One small business owner automatically throws bulk mail away without even opening it. Her feeling is that no important material will be sent out bulk rate. She may be right. Her business is thriving. On the other hand, junk mail is fun to read and can be a source of marketplace intelligence unavailable anywhere else. Either way, unless you can't live without whatever the piece of mail is selling, throw it out.

Interesting Mail

Occasionally, mail will arrive that might be useful at some future point, such as equipment catalogs for your type of business, trade magazines, and business propositions. Place this type of mail in the interesting mail basket.

Interesting mail always does one of two things with time: it becomes junk mail or it becomes invaluable. Sort through this basket every week or so as you get the time to find any pieces of value. Keep your wastebasket at hand for the rest of it.

Action Mail

Action mail requires a response of some sort on your part. Keep your action mail box as empty as possible. Write the type of response required and a due date on the outside of the envelope. Make a similar notation on your calendar or in your computer. (Computerized personal information managers—PIMs—can help you stay organized. To learn more about PIMs, see the discussion later in this chapter.) Respond to this type of mail as soon as possible, preferably long before the due date and definitely not after it. As a general rule, do not take more than one week to respond to action mail.

Set aside a time in your workweek to handle action mail. Use this time to pay bills, respond to inquiries, and schedule appointments. As you respond to each piece of action mail, try to handle it only once. Handling mail more than necessary can waste a lot of time.

Avoiding the Telephone Traffic Jam

The telephone has been called the lifeline of business. With it, you can reach the world, and the world can reach you. But as anyone starting out in business can tell you, the phone will always ring at the worst possible time and you can become so busy handling telephone calls that you never get anything done. But the telephone is basic to business.

Telephone technology has continued to advance rapidly in the wake of personal computer technology. "Smart phones" and associated phone company services perform a wide variety of functions, including:

- Call waiting
- Call forwarding
- Conference calls
- Voice mail
- Data and voice differentiation
- Full duplex speakerphone

These features combined allow small business owners unprecedented flexibility in handling telephone traffic. Recent innovations in computer

> "Smart phones" and associated phone company services perform a wide variety of functions.

technology allow you to handle many of these functions directly from your computer terminal.

With the help of a personal computer, you can eliminate most of the hassles associated with business phones, while maintaining many of the advantages. The technology has been declining steadily in cost and becoming more accessible to the average person starting out in business. Many people are beginning to place telephone handling features above word processing and bookkeeping as the number-one reason for purchasing a business computer.

Answering Machines and Voice Mail

If you have decided that a computer is not in your start-up budget, technology is still on your side. Telephones incorporate some of the features of computer-based phone technology—such as answering machines and voice mail—at a fraction of the cost. Spend your phone dollars on the quality of features rather than quantity, and test telephones and answering machines in the store before you buy. A bargain buy is not a bargain if it makes your voice sound odd or unintelligible.

You may be tempted to record a cute or humorous message on your answering machine. Resist the urge to do so unless you know your customers and potential customers very well. Your message should be short and straightforward; avoid extraneous or superfluous information. A good message includes a greeting, the name of your company, the hours you are available, and how to leave a message. Don't say that you're unable to answer the phone right now; the caller will have already figured that out. Including the hours you are open is especially effective for a retail business, as fully half of the incoming callers want to know how late the store is open.

An appropriate message might sound something like this:

Hello. Thank you for calling ABC Mousetraps. Our hours are from 8:00 A.M. to 5:00 P.M., Monday through Friday. Please leave a message after the tone.

Many people use their answering machine to screen calls so they can pick up only those that require an immediate response. This approach is far more appropriate in a private setting. Your personal telephone is in place largely for your convenience. In a business setting, it's different. You probably installed your business phone for the convenience of your customers, as well as for your own convenience. When customers take the time to call you, they generally deserve some of your time in return. So, in

> A good message includes a greeting, the name of your company, the hours you are available, and how to leave a message.

your business, screen out only those calls that don't have the potential to result in a sale.

Similarly, if you have a phone system, make sure it's as efficient and professional as possible. Give the same basic information and briefly describe the options available to the caller. Avoid, if at all possible, forcing the caller through a maze of multilayered menu options. Most customers will be annoyed at wasting time just to leave a message.

This example shows the basics of a good voice mail message:

> *Thank you for calling. This is the ABC Mousetraps' voice mail messaging system. You may enter the extension you wish to contact now, or leave a message for the marketing department by pressing one, a message for the production department by pressing two, or a message for management systems by pressing three. To listen to a general information message about ABC Mousetraps, press four. To speak to an operator, press zero.* [Delete this last sentence for the after-hours version of your message.]

This message format is effective for even the smallest business, to establish and maintain a professional line of communication with clients, vendors, and suppliers.

For those times when you are not available by phone, an answering machine or voice mail allows your customers to leave messages for you. Check your machine frequently for important calls and return them as soon as possible. Make note of who called, when, and from where.

The Home-Based Office

A home-based office presents many difficulties that you may have never considered in a structured work environment. The greatest risk is a complete loss of organization as paperwork slowly spreads from your desk to the floor and out into the next room and maybe even throughout the house. Before you decide to go out and lease space in a new office, learn how you can easily keep track of the growing mounds of paperwork. The suggestions that follow apply to a business office as well as a home office.

When setting up their home office, many people take a haphazard approach to selecting furniture, equipment, and location. If their business becomes successful, these people end up rebuilding their home office at great trouble and expense—or they enter contests to win prizes for being the most disorganized office.

For those times when you are not available by phone, an answering machine or voice mail allows your customers to leave messages for you.

The best time to set up your home office is before you hang out your shingle. The slightest care at this point will pay dividends later.

The most obvious benefit to careful setup is avoiding the back pain and muscle aches caused by improperly fitted furniture. Careless placement of keyboards, monitors, tables, and chairs can lead to a whole series of repetitive stress injuries, including the dreaded carpal tunnel syndrome and bursitis as the most well-known. There are dozens of these disorders. Some are permanently debilitating; all are painful—and preventable.

Setting up your home office need not be expensive. Unless you will be receiving customers in your office, consider used furniture and fixtures for your office. Create an environment that is cheerful and motivates you to produce. An office composed of gray metal desks, files, and cabinets from a military surplus depot, while undeniably cheap, may have a withering effect on your productivity.

Basement, Garage, or Spare Room?

Setting up your home office need not be expensive.

Where you decide to locate your office in your home may be dictated by available space. Hopefully, your home office isn't relegated to a corner of the dining room—although some successful home businesses are operated from such corners. It's more common, however, to use a separate room, such as a spare bedroom, the corner of a basement, a converted porch, or an attic loft or garret. Some home business owners convert a section of the garage or build an office over the garage. And a very few make their office from a garden cottage or gazebo.

If you have a choice of locations, there are a number of factors that you may want to consider before choosing one over the other. Some of these factors are practical, some are environmental, and some are merely a matter of personal taste.

PRACTICAL CONSIDERATIONS

A primary influence on choosing the location of your home office is accessibility. If customers or clients will be regularly coming to your office, it's wise to choose a location with or near an outside door away from the rest of the house. However, that may not be possible.

If clients must travel through your home to get to your office, it's important to keep that part of your house neat and orderly. Keeping areas of the home orderly can be especially difficult when there are very young or teenage children living there.

If at all possible, your home office should not be located in your bedroom. As many new business owners will attest, a start-up business demands a great deal of time, and sleep comes dearly enough as it is without unfinished details calling to you in the middle of the night. Also, if your bed is just a few steps away, you may be tempted to nap as your energy levels wane in the afternoon or as you face the dreaded tedium of bookkeeping or routine correspondence.

Locating your office away from the living area of your home provides specific psychological benefits. An office in the basement, attic, or garage allows you the feeling of working away from home, helping you to tune out the distraction of waiting chores, visiting neighbors, and personal calls. That advantage works in both directions: if your office is separate, you can more easily maintain the rest of your home as a refuge from the demands of your business.

> Locating your office away from the living area of your home provides specific psychological benefits.

ENVIRONMENTAL CONCERNS

"Environment" here refers to the office rather than the great outdoors. Creating a good working environment is a challenge to any home worker, but choosing the wrong office location can make that challenge far more difficult.

Consider the vivid images invoked by the following descriptions of home office locations:

- A dark, damp basement
- A hot, dusty attic
- A cold garage
- A cramped loft

These locations require special treatment to be effective workplaces. You will need to pay more attention to extra lighting and heating, cooling, and ventilation. More than other places in the home, these will benefit from the installation of natural light sources.

An office in the attic or over the garage will benefit greatly from skylights or large gable windows. That location will need extra cooling and ventilation when the weather is hot and a source of heat when temperatures drop. Basement offices will require improved ventilation and extra light to make up for the lack of natural light.

Noise is another environmental consideration. A typical home office is much quieter than its corporate counterpart, and many corporate refugees find the change disconcerting at first. Soft music in the background may help ease the transition. If music is a distraction in itself, consider buying a noise machine, an electronic device that produces white noises, such as static, ocean waves, running water, rustling leaves, or rainfall. Other noise producers include aquariums, small tabletop fountains, and wooden or bamboo wind chimes.

Some home office workers have complained of the opposite effect. Playing children, running lawn mowers, and the general hubbub of today's busy world seem to filter more easily through the walls of your home than through the walls of an office building. Simple fixes for this problem include acoustical tile ceilings, sound-absorbing materials on walls and floors, and double- or triple-glazed windows.

OTHER OFFICE LOCATION CONSIDERATIONS

> Consider those things unique to your home and personality that would result in the most distractions from your work.

Everything else considered, the decision on where to locate your home office may boil down to personal considerations. Consider the following:

- Would office work conflict with children watching television or vice versa?
- Would your office be so close to the refrigerator that you would indulge in excessive or frequent snacking?
- Would doorbells and telephone calls in the rest of the house intrude into the office?

In short, consider those things unique to your home and personality that would result in the most distractions from your work. Conversely, consider those things about working at home that you value the most, such as being in regular contact with your family and integrating your work life and your home life. Then select the location for your office with these factors in mind.

Office on a Budget

Many owners of start-up businesses are concerned about trimming costs wherever possible and balk at equipping a home office with expensive equipment and furnishings. A few succeed at creating a functional work environment that is efficient, productive, and inexpensive. In general, setting up an office on a budget requires more room and more work. Important ergonomic, comfort, and lighting characteristics can be shortchanged only at the expense of productivity, health, or well-being.

Setting Up Basic Furniture, Equipment, and Fixtures

Now that you have chosen the right location for your home office, take the time to choose the furnishings. Begin by considering the basic office furniture complement of desk, chair, and filing cabinet. Then, evaluate your needs for equipment and lighting. Arguably, the most important piece of office furniture is the office chair. But even the most perfectly fitted chair will be of little benefit if the desk is at the wrong height. So, when setting up your home office, be particularly sensitive to the various dimensions suggested and then adjust as necessary to suit your particular size and configuration.

THE OFFICE CHAIR

If your tendency is either to use whatever you have on hand, such as a spare kitchen chair, or to buy a used swivel chair, you may want to think twice. Many people even splurge on a new office chair. The decision to purchase office chairs is far more important than a matter of mere convenience. When you consider that you will spend as much as three-fourths of your workday sitting in your office chair, your personal comfort and efficiency take on meaningful proportions.

The best approach to selecting the proper chair for your office is to sit in it with a "Goldilocks" mindset. The chair cannot be too big, too small, too soft, or too hard. It must be just right. Often this feeling of being just right is the result of an intangible set of conditions, but there are characteristics to consider while trying out chairs.

- *Height of the seat.* Make sure your thighs are parallel to the floor and your feet rest flat on the floor. If the chair isn't naturally at this height, it should be fully adjustable and, ideally, you should be able to adjust the height while seated so that you can easily change it for different tasks. You may require an ergonomic footrest if your legs are too short to rest on the floor comfortably.
- *Comfort.* Your chair should have a firm cushion and be contoured so as not to cut into your legs. The chair back should extend from the lumbar region of your lower back to mid-shoulder blade, providing firm, adjustable support to your entire back while you're in a normal sitting position. The armrests, if any, should be positioned at or just below the point of your elbow.
- Stability. Make sure the chair is accident-proof. The base of the chair should extend beyond the dimensions of the seat for stability and, if

If your tendency is either to use whatever you have on hand, such as a spare kitchen chair, or to buy a used swivel chair, you may want to think twice.

it's on casters, it should be designed with five points to reduce the chances of tipping.

To meet these requirements, you can spend $1,000 or more for a fully adjustable, designer, ergonomic chair. Or, as one home office worker did, slightly modify a wooden kitchen chair for less than $20. In either case, be certain that the chair fits you and that you can spend six to ten or more hours each day sitting in it. Remember: even a perfect chair will become uncomfortable with time, so make sure your daily routine includes occasional breaks away from your chair to prevent stiffness and fatigue.

YOUR DESK

Different office tasks demand different heights for your working surfaces. For instance, the ideal writing surface height may be 30 inches, while the ideal height for a keyboard may be 26 inches. Actual heights will, of course, vary from individual to individual. Luckily, there are ready solutions to this varying height problem in most workstations on the market.

> Different office tasks demand different heights for your working surfaces.

Your best strategy in purchasing a workstation or desk is to test it out in the showroom first. This requires no small effort on your part as you must first locate a suitable chair and get it properly adjusted. Sit at the workstation and test the heights of the writing surface, the typing surface, and the reading surface for comfort. Ideally, each of these surfaces will be slightly adjustable to allow for differences between your body proportions and national averages. Many higher-quality workstations offer several work surfaces with adjustable heights and positions. Some workstations will even alert you if you have worked from one position too long for comfort!

Other considerations in addition to working height include depth and width of the desk. Obviously, it must fit in your available office space without overpowering it or making the remaining space awkward or cramped in function or appearance. Many mass-market manufacturers are cutting costs by making the desktop shorter and narrower. Frequently, the result is a computer monitor positioned so closely that eyestrain is inevitable and the desktop space on either side unusable for reading and writing tasks.

Finally, in selecting a desk or a workstation, consider the ease of shifting from one task to another. You should be able to easily shift from typing correspondence to answering the phone to checking your calendar; from writing a short memo to pulling a file and back again without making a series of trips about your office. The transition from task to task should be smooth and take the least effort possible.

FILING CABINETS

You will find that you can't stay in business for long without a filing system. Your system may be as simple as having stacks of paperwork organized into piles around your office or as complex as banks of filing cabinets lining the wall. If you're like most people, however, you're likely to end up with at least one filing cabinet to hold the paperwork you will accumulate as your business grows.

New, well-made filing cabinets are expensive. However, it pays to seek quality in this purchase. Inexpensive, poorly made filing cabinets constructed of lightweight materials will inevitably become inadequate for your needs. The drawer guides on cheaper filing cabinets can break or jam under heavy loads or repeated usage. A full file drawer can weigh 100 pounds or more. Inexpensive cabinets are not designed to handle such loads safely.

There are many variations on the standard filing cabinet design. The drawers can be of standard width or wide enough to accommodate legal-sized files. Lateral filing cabinets on wheels are growing in popularity, but don't make as efficient use of floor space as vertical cabinets. Finally, the number of drawers in each cabinet can vary from two to six. Most quality filing cabinets are lockable.

Equipment

Office automation has had a profound and positive impact on home offices. Tasks such as routine correspondence and bookkeeping, which used to require hiring at least a part-time office assistant, may now be accomplished by a sole proprietor as a part of the daily routine.

Office automation has had a profound and positive impact on home offices.

Fax machines, answering machines, copiers, and printers are being replaced by business computers with special features to handle faxes, voice mail, and routine paperwork tasks. While not yet inexpensive, the costs of these computer systems are rapidly falling and are already well below the cost of purchasing individual office equipment components.

Just a few years ago it cost upwards from $6,000 to equip an office with a copier, a fax machine, an answering machine, and a basic desktop computer for word processing and bookkeeping. Now a single business computer workstation can accomplish the same tasks for about half the expense and simultaneously. The personal computer has begun to fulfill early predictions of being an all-purpose office machine.

Personal Information Managers

If you use a personal computer in managing your business, there are dozens of programs on the market that will help you organize your time and efforts. These programs—personal information managers (PIMs)—track business contacts, suppliers, customers, phone numbers, appointments, action items, and to-do lists. Many of these programs perform additional functions that may or may not be useful to you. Several good PIMs are available as shareware, so you can try before deciding to buy. Choose one that's easy to use and you will soon depend upon it.

A personal computer will automate many tasks and help you produce consistently high-quality correspondence. For handling stock and production records, payroll, and general ledger bookkeeping, a desktop computer shines. However, in-baskets, out-baskets, paperweights, and rotary card files are still basic office tools that will do much to help with the initial paper glut.

Office automated technology is easy to use. Hardware components require little effort to use. Often the user can simply plug in a component and turn it on; the computer does the rest automatically, prompting you on what to do and how to do it. Much software has become similarly user-friendly, with automatic installation programs and interactive tutorials. There are even special uninstall routines if you want to remove the software from your computer at any time. Perhaps more important, most of the software now features a similar interface. Drop-down menus, toolbars, and mouse-driven pointers allow new users to rapidly learn the ins and outs of new programs.

One downside of all-in-one technology is the risk, however remote, of equipment failure. While a complete loss of function is rare, it's wise to purchase warranty plans and to have a qualified repair technician available should the need arise. Make sure you consider this as part of your risk assessment plans, as discussed in Chapter 7. Many insurance companies will provide a rider to your policy to cover your hardware and software against theft, fire, and accidental damage.

You can do other things to reduce the impact of any equipment failure:

- *Keep paper copies of all documents on file.* The paperless office predicted years ago is not yet a reality for most businesses. Relying on a single storage method for important business documents invites disaster.
- *Save work in progress frequently.* At least once every ten minutes is a good rule of thumb. Most quality software incorporates an autosave feature, for which you can set the time between saves as appropriate

> One downside of all-in-one technology is the risk, however remote, of equipment failure.

to your task. The best approach, however, remains to discipline yourself to save your work manually. An unexpected power outage just as you reach the end of two hours of work without saving will make a believer of you.

- *Make daily or weekly backup copies.* Include all data files on your computer. Computer operating systems incorporate a backup function that can be invoked manually or sometimes on a specified schedule. Options include backing up to floppy disks, magnetic tape cartridges, CD-RWs, DVDs, external hard drives, or small USB storage devices (flash drive, jump drive, thumb drive, keychain drive, pen drive).

- *Safety-proof your backups.* Keep backups of vital information in a fireproof safe or in an off-site location. Safes are available in office and business supply stores. Most safes provide protection to vital documents from temperatures of up to several thousand degrees Fahrenheit as well as some security against theft.

- *Get assistance.* Subscribe to a service that stores electronic files for your company off site. Check your phone directory for services near you.

- *Perform preventive maintenance.* Your equipment should be checked and cleaned on a regular basis. Dirt and dust are the primary causes of electronic equipment failure. Excessive heat is the second most common culprit.

- *Plan for contingencies.* Purchase an older computer for emergency use if your primary system fails. At about 10 percent of the cost of a new system, you will retain minimum capabilities during down time. Also, if it becomes necessary to use the older system, you will develop a new respect for the speed and versatility of your primary computer system.

Lighting

Adequate lighting for your office space is an important consideration. The quantity, quality, and efficiency of various light sources will affect your decisions. Also, different tasks require different qualities and intensities of light. Finally, age is a determining factor. Older workers require as much as 50 percent more light than younger workers for the same task.

Choosing the correct lighting is vital to preventing eyestrain and promoting maximum efficiency. The best source of light for all tasks is daylight. An open, airy office with lots of natural light is ideal for many businesses. Ready sources of daylight include windows, conventional skylights, and tube skylights that gather light through a collector on the roof and direct it wherever you need it.

Not all offices have the advantage of access to natural light, nor is daylight always available. The solution, then, is to use artificial light from incandescent, fluorescent, or halogen sources. The characteristics of each of these light sources are different.

Incandescent light is the most common. Bulbs are inexpensive and produce a soft, pale yellow light that is warm and localized. The localized nature of incandescent light bulbs makes them most suitable as task lights, for providing spot illumination for paperwork, reading, or other close, detailed work. Incandescent lights are energy-inefficient, however, producing a great deal of heat. The bulbs wear out after as little as several hundred hours of use.

Halogen light bulbs are similar to incandescent light bulbs, but produce a whiter light. Halogen bulbs cost several times as much as incandescent bulbs, but use about ten percent less electricity and last four to six times longer. They have the advantage of fitting into existing incandescent fixtures without modification. Also, you can easily adjust the output of both incandescent and halogen fixtures by installing a dimmer switch in the circuit.

> The best lighting conditions for your office will depend on the tasks that you perform there.

Fluorescent fixtures are the most energy-efficient, producing the same amount of light as incandescent fixtures for approximately half the electricity. Fluorescent light is also diffuse, making it suitable for lighting large areas, but unsuitable for illuminating tasks. Fixtures are expensive, the tubes can have a noticeable flicker, and the lights cannot be easily dimmed. However, numerous types of tubes are available, producing remarkably different qualities of light that are suitable for different purposes. If yours is a home-based business, a full-spectrum daylight tube will probably serve you best in your home office. Fluorescent tubes usually last a long time. Tubes are rated from 3,000 to 7,000 hours between failure.

The best lighting conditions for your office will depend on the tasks that you perform there. However, the following general guidelines apply to most workspaces:

- *Consistency.* Prevent eyestrain resulting from adjusting to varying light levels by maintaining all lighting in the room at or near the same intensity.
- *Glare.* Eliminate glare and reflections from shiny objects. Position fixtures so that the light doesn't shine directly in your eyes.
- *Shadows.* Illuminate computer workstations by reflecting light from the ceiling and walls. Reflected light is more diffuse and produces fewer shadows and reflections from monitor screens.

- *Fluorescent bulbs.* Illuminate the room with indirect fluorescent lighting. Illuminate tasks with direct light from an incandescent or halogen source.

Select the Best Location

Location! Location! Location! You have probably heard this phrase in discussions of real estate. But did you know that "location, location, location" applies even more when it comes to selecting a place from which to operate your business?

Location is the most important ingredient for success for any business that depends on customers getting there. You might have the highest-quality product or the most reliable service in your area. But if you don't locate your business appropriately, you will lose potential customers traveling on foot, by car, or by public transport.

The reasons to locate in a certain place vary depending on your type of business. For example, if you are going to open a restaurant or retail business, you want to locate ideally in an area where there is a lot of parking available, a good flow of walk-in and drive-by traffic, and little competition. If you are a manufacturer or a wholesaler, you will be more interested in a site that is close to major transportation services, has a large pool of skilled labor available, and has sufficient access to water, sewer, and other vital services. Lastly, if you are going to be one of the millions of people who are starting their businesses out of their homes, then your location considerations are basically concerned with knowing zoning and land use restrictions in your neighborhood. You will need to know what you can and cannot do in terms of shipping and receiving, signage, business activity, and remodeling in your particular residential area.

Selecting the best site for your business involves taking a serious look at four factors that will ultimately influence your business.

> Selecting the best site for your business involves taking a serious look at four factors that will ultimately influence your business.

Know the City

First, understand the dynamics of the city in which you wish to locate. This means familiarizing yourself with the relationship of the surrounding cities, the road system and configurations within the city, the traffic patterns of the people who live, work, play, and travel in the city, and what causes people to take specific routes. In short, you must understand the traffic patterns of your potential customers and what generates these traffic patterns.

Identify Your Trading Area

Decide whether your product or service is suited for the area in which you want to locate—whether it be downtown, urban, suburban, or rural. Study the ways the parts of the city connect and how these connections or lack thereof affect the size, shape, and density of your trading area. Believe it or not, you will learn a lot about your trading area and the people in it by studying the grocery stores in that area.

Essential Characteristics

Consider the top location characteristics—accessibility, visibility, convenience, and high density. How visible, accessible, and convenient is your site? The flow of traffic or lack of flow will affect your customers' decisions to visit your business. Also, your customers' perceptions of safety and availability of parking will influence their decisions to return to your business. How dense is the population? High density is ideal: the law of numbers will work in your favor.

Know Your Market Position

You have probably already done most of this research for your sales and marketing plan. However, the point cannot be overemphasized: have a thorough knowledge of your industry and your product or service, your customers, and your competitors. The first three location suggestions are worth nothing if you haven't clearly identified your market position.

Chapter Wrap-Up

Whether you start your business out of your home or you rent space or you purchase land to build a new office suite or production center, you will need to set up your business for maximum efficiency. This entails a thorough evaluation of your operations to find out what you need to maintain your business—for both administration and production. Among other things, seriously consider the following:

- *How to handle incoming mail and incoming phone calls.* What type of phone system will you need for the services you offer?
- *How to arrange your workspace and your employees' workspaces.* How many chairs and desks will you require? What type of lighting will

best suit your operation? Are there any special equipment requirements?

- *Which city or road is the best location for your business.* Which areas will provide maximum accessibility and visibility while at the same time be close enough to your target customers?

The key to setting up your operation is organization. The more organized you are in planning, the better you will be once your business is up and running.

Part Two

Operating in Colorado

9 | *Your Business Structure*

As a small business owner, one of the first major decisions you will make is to choose a legal form under which to operate your business. It is important, therefore, to understand the four basic legal forms—sole proprietorship, partnership, corporation, and limited liability company—and then weigh the advantages and disadvantages of each.

Variations of these four entities are available to most business owners in most states. These variations, such as the S corporation and the limited liability partnership, are discussed in greater detail in this chapter. Further, the major advantages and disadvantages of each entity are covered to help you better evaluate which one may be right for your situation. Consult your attorney or accountant, or both, to find out which form makes the most sense for your business's financial condition.

To get started, first consider the criteria you must take into account when making your decision.

Five Factors

Five critical factors will influence which way you decide to go:

1. *Legal liability*. Determine whether your business has potential liability and if you can afford that risk.
2. *Tax implications*. Look at your business goals and individual situation to find out how you can best minimize your tax burden.
3. *Cost of formation and recordkeeping*. If you choose a structure that offers more legal protection to you as an individual, you can bet on increased administrative time and costs to ensure that liability protection.
4. *Flexibility*. You want to choose a form that maximizes the flexibility of the ownership structure—achieving both short-term and long-term goals.
5. *Future needs*. Even during the start-up phase, you will need to look down the road to what will happen when you retire, die, or sell the business.

With these key factors fresh in your mind, you are ready to explore the pros and cons of each form. In addition, if you will hire employees, your responsibilities will significantly increase in scope. You must become knowledgeable in matters such as minimum wage, labor laws, unemployment insurance, workers' compensation, and fair employment practices. Chapter 11 is dedicated to helping you understand the additional requirements that come with being an employer. For a better understanding of tax considerations prior to starting your business, read *Top Tax Savings Ideas* by Thomas J. Stemmy (Entrepreneur Press, 2004).

Sole Proprietorship

As the owner of a sole proprietorship, you are personally responsible for all business debts and liabilities.

A sole proprietorship is the simplest, most common form of business organization. It is defined as a business that is owned by a single individual. It is the easiest and least costly means of getting into business.

As the owner of a sole proprietorship, you are personally responsible for all business debts and liabilities. All your business profits will be considered as income to you and will be taxed at the personal income level. Refer to the discussion below on tax situations for Colorado sole proprietors. Conversely, all personal assets and properties are at risk if a sole proprietorship incurs debts beyond its ability to pay.

Advantages of a Sole Proprietorship

- It is easy and inexpensive to establish.

- A sole proprietor has full control over all business decisions.
- There are minimal legal restrictions or requirements.
- A sole proprietor owns all profits and reaps all benefits of ownership.
- There is no requirement to pay unemployment taxes.
- There may be no requirement for the owners to purchase workers' compensation insurance for themselves.

Disadvantages of a Sole Proprietorship

- A sole proprietor is personally liable for all business debts.
- A sole proprietor may have difficulty obtaining long-term financing.
- The success of the business depends wholly on the efforts of the sole proprietor.
- Illness, injury, or death of the sole proprietor will directly threaten his or her business.
- There are no unemployment benefits if the business fails.

If you will operate your sole proprietorship under your own name, and the business in which you are engaged does not require any form of licensing or permits, you generally need not register your business with any state agency. However, make sure you contact the city or town clerk where your business is located to determine whether or not there are any registration requirements at the city or county level.

If you will operate your sole proprietorship under a name other than your own, you must register the business name or trade name (commonly known as "doing business as" or "d.b.a.") with the Colorado Secretary of State. To register, file a statement of trade name. For more information, refer to the discussion on naming your business in Chapter 10.

If you are the owner of a sole proprietorship in Colorado, your business profits and losses will be subject to your personal income tax. You will be required to report these earnings or losses on your individual income tax return (Form 104) and on Form 104AMT (*Colorado Alternative Minimum Tax Computation Schedule*) or Form 104CR (*Credits—for Individuals*). Also become familiar with the requirements for filing state or federal tax prepayments based upon your estimated income from your business. This is discussed further in Chapter 10.

For more information on sole proprietorships in Colorado, contact the Colorado Business Center. You can find this address in Appendix C.

> If you are the owner of a sole proprietorship in Colorado, your business profits and losses will be subject to your personal income tax.

General Partnership

A general partnership is the association of two or more persons who have agreed to operate a business. You can form a general partnership by a simple verbal agreement of the partners. However, it is in your best interest and the best interest of all parties that you have an attorney prepare, or at least review, a formal, written partnership agreement that addresses such issues as:

> In a general partnership, any partner may hire or fire employees, contract for services, commit to sales, or accomplish any activity required to operate the business.

- The amount, type, and valuation of property each partner will contribute;
- The method for disbursement of profits and liabilities among the partners;
- A plan for sharing any gains, losses, deductions, and credits;
- A provision for changing the conditions of the partnership; and
- A provision for dealing with the loss or death of one of the partners.

In a general partnership, any partner may hire or fire employees, contract for services, commit to sales, or accomplish any activity required to operate the business independently from the other partners. The actions of a single partner are binding upon all partners.

Advantages of a General Partnership

- A partnership is easy to establish.
- There is more than one person to shoulder the workload and responsibilities.
- Financing is easier to obtain than for a sole proprietorship.
- The partners share all profits and reap all benefits of ownership.

Disadvantages of a General Partnership

- A partnership may be more expensive to set up.
- The partners are exposed to unlimited liability for business expenses.
- Each partner is bound by the actions of the other partner.
- Decision-making authority is divided.
- The loss of one partner may dissolve the business.
- The partnership may be difficult to end.

If your Colorado partnership owns real property, your written partnership agreement should be filed with the office where real estate records are kept in the county where the property is located. Otherwise, there is no requirement to file the agreement with any other state or federal agency. If your partnership is operating under a name other than the legal names of the owners, your business name must be registered as a trade name with the Colorado Secretary of State. Use the statement of trade name (previously mentioned in the "Sole Proprietorships" section) to register your trade name.

A general partnership does not, as a separate business entity, pay state or federal taxes. The partners, however, are required to report income and expenses of the partnership on federal and state information returns. Your Colorado partnership will need to file Form 1065, *Partners' Share of Income, Credits, Losses, etc.*, for federal reporting, and Form 106, *Colorado Partnership or S Corporation Return of Income*, for state reporting purposes.

Limited Partnership

If a partnership sounds appealing to you but you fear the liability issues associated with a general partnership, you may want to consider a limited partnership. A limited partnership is similar to a general partnership and has most of the same advantages and disadvantages. However, be aware of a few significant differences between the roles of limited and general partners. In a limited partnership, you must always have at least one general and one limited partner. If you are a limited partner, you will invest assets into the business and your risk will be typically limited to the amount of capital you have invested. As a limited partner, you will not be otherwise involved in the management of the business and, therefore, will not share in liability for its debts or losses.

A limited partnership is similar to a general partnership and has most of the same advantages and disadvantages.

If you are an operating or general partner in a business, you are responsible for the liability and operation of the business. You assume responsibility for all management decisions and debts. As in a general partnership, as an operating partner your personal assets are not protected from the creditors of the business.

Advantages of a Limited Partnership

- A limited partnership is relatively easy to establish.
- There is more than one person to share in start-up expenses.
- It is easier for a partnership to get financing than it is for a sole proprietorship.
- The partners share all profits and reap all benefits of ownership.
- A limited partner's personal assets are not at risk from creditors.

Disadvantages of a Limited Partnership

- A partnership is more expensive to set up, due to the requirement for a written agreement.

- An operating (general) partner is exposed to unlimited liability for business expenses.
- The loss of one partner may dissolve the business.
- A partnership may be difficult to end.

As the owner of a limited partnership in Colorado, you are required to file two signed copies of a Certificate of Limited Partnership with the Secretary of State. Further, you are required by law to draft a formal, written agreement when setting up a limited partnership. If it becomes necessary to amend the Certificate of Limited Partnership or cancel the certificate, this is also done at the Secretary of State's office. As a limited partnership in Colorado, you will also need to file Form 106, *Colorado Partnership or S Corporation Return of Income*, for income tax purposes.

Another Colorado business option is the registered limited liability limited partnership. This entity is discussed in more detail in this chapter under "Limited Liability Partnerships."

Corporations

A corporation is the most complex type of business organization. It is formed by law as a separate legal entity, fully distinct from its owners—also called stockholders or shareholders. As such, it exists independently from its owners and endures as a legal entity even at the death, retirement, or resignation of a stockholder. Thus, the corporation, not the individuals, handles the responsibilities of the organization. The corporation is taxed and can be held legally liable for its actions. Any person or group of people operating a business of any size may incorporate. Similarly, any group engaged in religious, civil, nonprofit, or charitable endeavors may incorporate and enjoy the legal and financial benefits of incorporation.

> A corporation is the most complex type of business organization. It is formed by law as a separate legal entity, fully distinct from its owners.

You may find that incorporating offers your business a number of benefits. For example, your corporation may be able to more easily raise capital through the sale of stock. Also, as an owner of stock you do not have to be publicly listed, affording you and other stockholders a degree of anonymity. Further, the costs of fringe benefits such as life and health insurance, travel expenses, and retirement plans are tax-deductible.

Until recently, only corporations were allowed to deduct health insurance costs, which provided significant financial incentive to incorporate. However, as of 2003, a congressional amendment to the tax law allows all business forms to deduct health insurance costs.

Corporations can take on several forms, depending on the individual business situation. For the most part, if you decide to incorporate your business, you will need to know the differences among the following forms:

- General (C) corporation—also known as a domestic corporation,
- S corporation,
- Foreign corporation,
- Professional corporation, and
- Not-for-profit corporation—also called a nonprofit corporation.

General (C) Corporation

A general business corporation is the most formalized type of business structure and is usually formed for profit-making organizations. A general corporation is the most common type of corporation. In a general corporation, the owners are stockholders and ownership is based on shares of stock. There is no limitation to the number of stockholders. Since the corporation operates as a separate entity, each stockholder's personal assets are protected from attachment by creditors of the corporation. Thus, as a stockholder, your liability is limited to the capital that you have invested in the purchase of stock.

> A general business corporation is the most formalized type of business structure and is usually formed for profit-making organizations.

Advantages of a General Corporation

- A corporation has a lifespan independent from its owners (stockholders).
- Fringe benefit costs are tax-deductible.
- Personal assets are protected from business liability.
- Ownership can be transferred through the sale of stock.
- It may be easy to raise operating capital through the sale of stock.
- Ownership of a corporation can change without affecting its day-to-day management.

Disadvantages of a General Corporation

- Incorporating involves considerable start-up expenses.
- Corporations are subject to more state and federal legislation.
- Profits are subject to dual taxation—as profits and again as dividends.
- Many legal formalities exist when filing and trying to maintain corporate status.
- Activities are limited to those defined in the corporate charter.

The basics of registering and operating your general corporation are presented later in this chapter under "Handling Corporate Formalities."

S Corporation

The S corporation is a form of the general corporation that has a special tax status with the IRS and many states. The most attractive benefit of an S corporation is the avoidance of double taxation. You have learned that if a dividend is declared, then shareholders must declare that dividend as income and it is taxed again—hence, double taxation. S corporations avoid this dual taxation because all losses and profits are "passed through" the corporation to the shareholders and are declared only once to the IRS, as part of each shareholder's income.

> The most attractive benefit of an S corporation is the avoidance of double taxation.

As in other forms of incorporation, each shareholder's personal assets are protected from the business's debts. There is, however, a downside to the S corporation when it comes to tax time for the corporation's shareholders. If the corporation makes a profit, each shareholder is required to pay taxes on his or her proportionate share of that profit—regardless of whether the corporation distributes the profit to its shareholders or not. Even if the profit is not distributed to the shareholders, the IRS still considers it part of each individual shareholder's income and taxes it at the appropriate rate.

If there is a disagreement with the IRS about who should pay the tax, the IRS can obtain payment from the assets of individual shareholders, thereby going around the protection from confiscation by the IRS if the tax is not paid. This can result in a big surprise for a shareholder who helps fund the business but doesn't get payments for the profits, either because the corporation is not liquid enough to pay the share of profit to a shareholder or because the managers want to use the profits to build the business and keep the profit in the corporation. Even if the S corporation distributes its profits to shareholders, the additional income for a shareholder may result in a higher tax rate—depending on his or her other income.

On the other hand, if the S corporation loses money, there may be a significant tax benefit to its shareholders. The loss is passed on to each shareholder, proportionate to his or her stock ownership. This loss can then be applied to the shareholder's overall income and potentially lower his or her tax liability. As in other forms of incorporation, each shareholder's personal assets are protected from the business's debts. Because of this duality of benefit vs. liability when it comes to S corporations, you should check with your accountant or attorney to determine which corporation is the best form for you.

If you want to form as an S corporation, your general corporation must meet specific requirements before applying for or being granted S corporation status by the IRS. To qualify for federal S corporation status, your business must:

- Already exist as a corporation;
- Have no more than 75 shareholders;
- Count beneficiaries and shareholders of a small business trust toward the maximum 75 shareholders;
- Be headquartered in the United States;
- Issue only one class of stock;
- Not have shareholders who are nonresident aliens;
- Not be a financial institution that takes deposits or makes loans, an insurance company taxed under subchapter L, or a Domestic International Sales Corporation (DISC);
- Not take a tax credit for doing business in a U.S. possession; and
- Not have more than 25% of the corporation's gross receipts from passive sources, such as interest, dividends, rent, royalties, or proceeds from the sale of securities. This provision has several conditions, so be sure to clearly understand how it may affect you if your company expects income from these sources.

If your corporation meets the above criteria, you may then apply for S corporation status if all shareholders consent to the election of S corporation status and your business files IRS Form 2553, *Election by a Small Business Corporation*. A copy of this form is located in Appendix A.

Keeping S Corporation Status

S corporation status is subject to many IRS regulations and qualifications. The special tax advantages of S corporation status will be lost if your corporation fails to maintain eligibility. Once S corporation status is terminated, it cannot be reactivated for five years. Your S corporation status can be terminated if your corporation:

- Exceeds 75 shareholders;
- Transfers S corporation stock to a corporation, partnership, ineligible trust, or nonresident alien;
- Creates a second class of stock;
- Acquires an operational subsidiary; or
- Loses corporate status.

The special tax advantages of S corporation status will be lost if your corporation fails to maintain eligibility.

Colorado recognizes the federal S corporation provision. To qualify as an S corporation in Colorado, you must complete Form 2553 and file it with the IRS within 75 days of incorporating or, for the status to be effective for the new tax year, by March 15. Contact the Business Center of the Colorado Secretary of State listed in Appendix C for more information.

Take a big-picture perspective when considering S corporation status for your business. You will avoid double taxation, yet there may be advantages to the general (C) corporation. For more information about S corporations, get a copy of IRS Publication 589, *Tax Information on S Corporations*, from your accountant, local IRS office, or the Internet at www.irs.gov.

Foreign Corporation

When your corporation does business outside the state in which it was incorporated, it is considered a foreign corporation. For instance, suppose you originally incorporate in the state of Maryland but later find you want to do business in Colorado. Your company, a domestic corporation in Maryland, will become a foreign corporation in Colorado. If your business will operate as a foreign corporation, it will be subject to potential liabilities, penalties, and problems unless it is qualified to operate in Colorado. If your business fails to qualify, you may be subject to corporate fines, criminal charges, or a lack of legal recognition in a court of law.

To qualify as a foreign corporation in Colorado, you must register with the Colorado Secretary of State by filing a Statement of Foreign Entity Authority with a filing fee. A certificate of good standing from the state in which your corporation was incorporated is also required. You must also maintain a registered agent and registered office. A registered agent is an individual or another corporation that represents your business and the agent must have a physical address, which may or may not be your corporation's place of business.

Contact the Colorado Secretary of State, Business Center, to obtain the necessary forms and filing procedures or visit the Web site. The address, phone, and URL number are provided in Appendix C.

Professional Corporation

Professional corporations are for individuals whose service requires a professional license. Examples of these professionals include doctors, lawyers, and accountants, but may include others, depending on individual state law.

Licensed professionals who incorporate enjoy tax benefits for the costs associated with fringe benefits. However, the shareholders of a professional corporation are personally liable to their clients. Liability spreads to all shareholders even if only one was negligent or accused of wrongdoing.

> To qualify as a foreign corporation in Colorado, you must register with the Colorado Secretary of State by filing a Statement of Foreign Entity Authority with a filing fee.

Advantages of a Professional Corporation

- Personal assets are protected from business debts.
- There are certain tax breaks or deferments for the cost of fringe benefits.

Disadvantages of a Professional Corporation

- The corporation is limited to a single profession.
- Only licensed professionals may be shareholders.
- Shares may only be sold to a licensed member of the same profession.
- Shareholders are liable to their clients as a group.

Colorado allows the formation of professional corporations, but only members of the same profession may be shareholders. To obtain the form for filing as a professional corporation, contact the Colorado Secretary of State, Business Center.

Make sure to contact your lawyer or accountant to understand the tax law changes that will affect your business. Further, compare the pros and cons of the professional corporation with those of the limited liability partnership (LLP)—akin to the limited liability company (LLC). LLCs and LLPs are discussed in greater detail later in this chapter.

> Colorado allows the formation of professional corporations, but only members of the same profession may be shareholders.

Not-for-Profit Corporation

Not-for-profit corporations, also called nonprofit organizations, are usually formed by religious, civil, or social groups. Profits cannot be distributed to members, officers, or directors of a corporation, but instead must be disbursed in support of the beneficial purposes outlined in its articles of incorporation.

A nonprofit corporation does not issue stock, and all activities are controlled by a self-perpetuating board of directors. If your business will operate as a nonprofit corporation, clearly spell out all business operations in your articles of incorporation.

A tax-exempt organization is closely related to a nonprofit organization. Most nonprofit organizations try to qualify as tax-exempt under Section 501(c)(3) of the Internal Revenue Code. To qualify as a tax-exempt organization, your business must be formed for:

- Religious, charitable, scientific, literary, or educational purposes,
- The testing of public safety,

- Fostering amateur sports competition, or
- The prevention of cruelty to animals or children.

Advantages of a Nonprofit Corporation

- A nonprofit organization can benefit from tax-exempt status because all contributions are tax-exempt.
- There is some flexibility in operations of the business.

Disadvantages of a Nonprofit Corporation

- All income must go to the not-for-profit purpose.
- Members, officers, or directors cannot benefit from dissolution of the corporation.
- A nonprofit corporation cannot merge with another corporation unless it is also classified as nonprofit.

For more information on tax-exempt organizations, contact your local IRS office or Web site for a copy of Publication 557, *Tax-Exempt Status for Your Organization.*

Handling Corporate Formalities

You have heard about the major benefit of incorporation—personal asset protection. Now consider some of the responsibilities of corporations to maintain their corporate status. So that the IRS will not find good cause to pierce your corporate veil, your corporation must do the following:

- Draft, approve, and file articles of incorporation. You file your articles with Colorado Secretary of State along with a fee.
- File reports every other year by the anniversary date of your incorporation with the Secretary of State.
- Pay corporate taxes on the biennial year by the anniversary date of your incorporation. Taxes are based on the income of the corporation.
- Keep bylaws and minutes.
- Issue official stock certificates.
- Maintain an official corporate seal.
- Maintain distinct and separate financial records and accounts.
- Designate an official registered agent.

Although time-consuming, incorporating your business is a simple process. In fact, the trend for many small business owners is do-it-yourself incorporation. You may want to consult with your accountant regarding the tax consequences of switching from sole proprietor to corporation.

Two resources help your do-it-yourself incorporation efforts. The first is *Ultimate Guide to Incorporating in Any State* by Michael Spadaccini (Entrepreneur Press, 2004). This user-friendly guide offers a simple method to incorporate and includes sample documents. *The Essential Corporation Handbook* by Carl R. J. Sniffen (Entrepreneur Press, 2001) is a nuts-and-bolts guide with checklists that will help you keep track of the numerous formalities.

Limited Liability Company (LLC)

A limited liability company (LLC) is a relatively new and highly touted business entity. Limited liability companies have been adopted into legislation in all 50 states and the District of Columbia.

The LLC is a hybrid business form that draws advantageous characteristics from both corporations and partnerships. It is similar to an S corporation without its restrictions. Like a partnership, an LLC's existence rests with its owners—in an LLC, owners are referred to as members. The loss of a member through death, retirement, or resignation can result in the dissolution of the business. However, like a corporation, a limited liability company offers some protection for personal assets from business creditors. Due to its dual qualities—corporate protection and partnership tax treatment—many feel the LLC could replace general partnerships, limited partnerships, and even S corporations as the future entity of choice.

> The LLC is a hybrid business form that draws advantageous characteristics from both corporations and partnerships.

An interesting LLC characteristic is the lack of limitation on the number and nature of its members. In the past, most states required at least two members to form an LLC. All 50 states now allow single-member LLCs. Members may be foreign persons or nonresidents, or even partnerships, corporations, trusts, estates, or other limited liability companies. An LLC is a good choice for real estate ventures that involve corporations, trusts, or foreign investors, or for new business ventures that involve existing corporations. Also, an LLC is an excellent estate planning vehicle for investment for you and your family corporation, trust, or partnership.

Advantages of a Limited Liability Company

- Profits and losses pass through the company to its owners for tax purposes.
- Personal assets are protected from business liability.

- There is no limitation on the number or nature of owners.
- An LLC is simpler to operate than a corporation.
- LLCs are not subject to corporate formalities.
- Owners may participate in management of the business.
- Some tax advantages result from business losses or high profits.

Disadvantages of a Limited Liability Company

- An LLC may be recognized differently in different states.
- Limits of liability have not been extensively tested in litigation.
- Legal assistance is needed to properly set up and structure an LLC.
- Professionals, such as lawyers, accountants, and doctors, are prohibited from registering as an LLC.

Simplicity and great flexibility are the hallmarks of the LLC. An LLC can be formed by a single person or any number of people. To start an LLC, you must file two original copies of your articles of organization with the Colorado Secretary of State.

The articles of organization must include the following six items:

- Name of the LLC;
- Principal mailing and street address for the LLC;
- Name and address of the registered agent in Colorado;
- A statement indicating whether or not the LLC will employ managers to operate the company;
- The names and business addresses of any managers that will be employed by the LLC; and
- The names and addresses of members that will be involved in the operation of the company.

There is a filing fee for an LLC and a name reservation fee to reserve your LLC's name for a period of 120 days. See Chapter 10 for more on naming your business.

Also, as an owner—or member—of an LLC in Colorado, you will need to draft an operating agreement. Similar to a corporation's bylaws, this agreement will define the rights, powers, and duties of members and managers. For example, you would want to spell out how investments in the entity—or contributions—can be made. Consult with your accountant and lawyer to determine if an LLC is beneficial for your situation.

Because an LLC is a relatively new entity, little legal precedent for it exists. Even though the IRS has ruled the LLC will qualify as a partnership

> Simplicity and great flexibility are the hallmarks of the LLC. An LLC can be formed by a single person or any number of people.

or a sole proprietorship for tax purposes, the Congress has yet to pass any tax legislation to that effect. A 1997 decision by the IRS allows sole proprietorships to change to LLC status without any negative tax ramifications. This "check-the-box" legislation allows LLCs to be treated as corporations, partnerships, or sole proprietorships for tax purposes. All existing LLCs must do is file Form 8832, *Entity Classification Election*, with the IRS and check which box applies to them. If no box is checked, the IRS will automatically treat the LLC as a partnership. Discuss the issues around LLC selection with your accountant or lawyer to determine what is best for your situation.

For more information about limited liability companies, consider getting a copy of *Entrepreneur Magazine's Ultimate Guide to Forming an LLC in Any State* by Michael Spadaccini (Entrepreneur Press, 2004).

Limited Liability Partnership

Yet another new entity, the limited liability partnership (LLP), is now available to small business owners in all 50 states. In an LLP, partners are afforded the same limited liability protection as in professional corporations. A limited liability partnership is a general partnership that provides professional services and is registered as a limited liability partnership under the laws of Colorado or any other jurisdiction.

> In an LLP, partners are afforded the same limited liability protection as in professional corporations.

Advantages of an LLP

- A partner in an LLP can enjoy the advantage of flow-through tax treatment.
- An LLP is not subject to the numerous limitations regarding ownership, capital structure, and division of profits.
- It is simple and familiar for an existing partnership to elect to become an LLP.

Disadvantages of an LLP

- A sole owner cannot set up an LLP because, as a partnership, an LLP must have at least two partners to exist.
- It is a relatively new legal form, so little legal precedent has been set.

Colorado allows the formation of LLPs. Two additional business structures recognized in Colorado since 1995 are the *limited liability limited partnership* (LLLP) and the *limited partnership association* (LPA).

The LLLP limits partners' personal liability to their personal investment in the business, similar to an LLP, except in areas related to their personal professional conduct. The general partner of a limited liability limited partnership limits his or her personal liability in the same way as a partner in a general partnership that is registered as a limited liability partnership. All remaining aspects of limited partnership law remain in effect. Other than the issue of the personal liability of the general partner, the underlying limited partnership agreement remains in effect. The LLLP is created by filing a statement ocf registration with the Colorado Secretary of State. Pending review by the IRS, LLPs and LLLPs are usually taxed as partnerships, but may elect to be taxed as corporations.

> The limited partnership association is different from a partnership or LLP in that the limited partnership association has an indefinite life.

The limited partnership association is different from a partnership or LLP in that the limited partnership association has an indefinite life—it does not terminate upon death, resignation, or bankruptcy of any of its partners. Its existence terminates when all of its members vote to terminate or as otherwise provided in the bylaws and by filing articles of dissolution with the Colorado Secretary of State. The LPA is an unincorporated business association created by filing articles of association with the Colorado Secretary of State.

As you decide on the legal structure of your business, carefully evaluate your present and future needs. You might also wish to seek the advice of an attorney who specializes in business formations and structures.

Chapter Wrap-Up

Choosing the legal form for your business is the first of many decisions you will make as you start your Colorado business. As you begin to make sense of the various legal forms, determine which of the five important factors—legal liability, tax implications, formation costs and recordkeeping requirements, ownership flexibility, and future goals—are the most critical for your business needs.

Are you most concerned with protecting your personal assets from your business's creditors? Then you may want to avoid forming a sole proprietorship and set up a corporation or limited liability company (LLC). What about the tax situation for your business? You may be interested in forming a corporation, but unless you form as an S corporation or LLC you will suffer the dreaded double taxation. You may have an excellent opportunity to start a partnership with an associate whom you respect. Do you know the differences between a general partnership and a limited partnership and how the advantages and disadvantages of these legal forms affect your ownership flexibility and future needs? And although the LLC and S corporation remain the most talked about legal forms, make sure you understand the potentially overwhelming recordkeeping rules and formation costs associated with starting your business as either of these two entities. Finally, consider the two other business structures allowed in Colorado—the limited liability limited partnership (LLLP) and the limited partnership association (LPA).

Keep this chapter handy as you weigh the pros and cons of each legal form. Make sure your decision involves a consultation with your attorney or accountant, or both. Also, contact the Colorado Secretary of State's office for any published material that will give you advice on structuring your business in Colorado.

Legal Form Checklist

❏ If you will operate as a sole proprietorship or a general partnership under a name other than your own, you will need to register your trade name with the Colorado Secretary of State. There is an initial registration fee.

❏ If you will operate as a limited partnership, write a limited partnership agreement (required by law) and file a certificate of limited partnership with the Colorado Secretary of State.

❏ If your business will be a corporation, file your articles of incorporation with the Colorado Secretary of State and pay a fee.

❏ If you will do business as a foreign corporation, make sure you file a *Statement of Foreign Entity Authority* with the Colorado Secretary of State and pay a fee.

❏ If you will file as a limited liability company (LLC), then draft your business's operating agreement, file with the Colorado Secretary of State, and pay a fee.

❏ If you will do business as a limited liability partnership (LLP), limited liability limited partnership (LLLP), or a limited partnership association (LPA), you will have to register with the Colorado Secretary of State.

10 | *Business Start-up Details*

Your decision regarding the legal form for your business is the first of many decisions you will make as you begin your enterprise. Now it's time to tackle the maze of business start-up details that face the approximately ten million people in the United States who are actively pursuing starting their own businesses.

You are responsible for a number of start-up activities that center around licensing and registrations and may include:

- Naming your business, possibly under a fictitious business name;
- Applying for a trade name, trademark, or service mark;
- Contacting the business assistance or business information centers in the state in which you will do business;
- Obtaining the necessary state and local licenses and permits to get your business running; and
- Learning which taxes your business will be responsible to pay.

This chapter will guide you through the bureaucratic snarls that entangle many start-ups. In short, this information will give you the confidence you need to approach the various state and federal agencies and the know-how to effectively deal with the mounds of paperwork you may encounter. In addition, once you have completed these start-up tasks, your business will become more of a reality—giving you a sense of being an official business owner.

Once you have survived this phase of startup, and you know that you will have employees, then look to the following chapter to learn about your duties as an employer.

Naming Your Business

The name you choose for your business is another important step you will take as a business owner. Many entrepreneurs underestimate the significance of naming their businesses. In choosing a name, you may want to consider the following tips.

> The name you choose for your business is another important step you will take as a business owner.

- Select a name that is easy to understand, spell, pronounce, and remember.
- Create a name that can be easily located in a telephone directory.
- Ensure that it portrays the image you want for your business. For example, if quick turnaround and quality service are part of your marketing strategy, then choose identifiers that will convey these aspects.
- Stay away from individual letters or acronyms that may confuse the potential customer trying to locate your business in the telephone directory.
- Steer clear of names that are similar or identical to those used by another business.
- Avoid unusual spellings that may cause your customer difficulty in finding your business name or listing.

If you need assistance with selecting a name for your business, consult a public relations, advertising, or marketing consultant.

Assumed Business Name

Any business entity can operate under an assumed business name, a trade name. If you will operate your business under your actual name, you need not file an assumed business name statement—also called "d.b.a." or "doing business as." In fact, many sole proprietors operate under their own actual names. However, if you operate your business under any other name, or your business name contains the words "Co.," "Son," or "Company," you are required to register your business name. To register, use Form DR 0592, Trade

Name Registration. Submit the form to the Colorado Secretary of State along with a filing fee. You can find the address in Appendix C.

Many businesses operate under a trade name, often referred to as a "fictitious business name" or an "assumed business name." For example, The Book Nook may be the name of a local bookstore, but this name does not reveal anything about the ownership of the business. It may be owned by a sole proprietor, a partner, a corporation, or a limited liability company. (If it is a corporation, it may contain the word "Inc." in its name.) To operate the store as The Book Nook, the corporation, Books, Inc. will have to file with county recorder in the store's county of residence, or file an assumed business name statement with the Corporations Section of the Colorado Secretary of State so the public can determine the true ownership of the store. Anyone wanting to serve legal papers to the business would need to determine the true owners and, in this case, the address and officers of Books, Inc.

Trademarks or Service Marks

You can protect your business name by registering it as a trademark, trade name, or service mark. Trade name or trademark protection is usually good for a specified period of time, usually five to ten years. Once that time period has elapsed, you will be responsible for reregistering your business.

You can protect your business name by registering it as a trademark, trade name, or service mark.

In Colorado, you must use your trademark or trade name in your business prior to registering it with the Colorado Secretary of State. The registration period is valid for a renewable ten-year period. Sole proprietorships or general partnerships are granted limited trade name and trademark protection under Colorado law.

If you will do business in other states, it may be to your benefit to obtain a federal trademark registration. Your trademark will distinguish your product or service from those of others that offer similar products or services. To find out more about federal trademark registration, obtain the free booklet *Basic Facts About Trademarks*. To order this booklet, use the address and phone number in Appendix B. You can also download it from *www.uspto.gov/web/offices/tac/doc/basic* formats.html or check the Q&A "Basic Facts About Trademarks" at *www.uspto.gov/web/offices/tac/doc/basic*.

For a closer look at trademarks and service marks, consider getting a copy of *Develop and Market Your Creative Ideas* by Dale A. Davis (Oasis, 1996). For an in-depth discussion, get *The Entrepreneur's Guide to Managing Intellectual Property* by Paul E. Schaafsma (Oasis, 2002).

Name Reservation for Corporations and LLCs

If you have decided to incorporate your business or to operate as an LLC, you may reserve your business's name. Most states charge a minimal fee to reserve a name for a specific period of time, usually 60 to 180 days. Colorado corporations and LLCs file a Statement of Reservation of Name and pay a fee of $25 (if filing electronically) or $125 (if filing paper) to reserve the name for 120 days. For more information, contact the Colorado Secretary of State.

One-Stop Center

Many states have formed centralized business assistance offices to help business owners who are starting, expanding, or relocating to their state. Referred to as a "one-stop center" or "business assistance center," this office works in coordination with the numerous other state agencies that will regulate your business.

Colorado has a one-stop center where you can obtain all the information you will need to keep your business legally operating in Colorado. Contact information for the Colorado Secretary of State Business Center is provided in Appendix C.

Once the state agencies are aware of your business, they will usually contact you regarding any filing requirement. However, be aware of their reporting requirements, because you may not be excused from reporting even though you were not sent reporting forms.

State Licenses

Many businesses and professions require special licenses to operate their specific types of businesses. A license is always needed for professionals such as doctors, lawyers, and dentists. A license is usually necessary for occupations such as cosmetologists, morticians, and contractors. A license may be granted by a state, county, or city agency. Some of the more frequently licensed occupations in Colorado are:

> Many businesses and professions require special licenses to operate their specific types of businesses.

- Accountants
- Acupuncturists
- Architects
- Barbers and cosmetologists
- Chiropractors
- Dentists and dental hygenists

- Electricians
- Engineers
- Guides and outfitters
- Insurance agents and companies
- Land surveyors
- Marriage and family therapists
- Nurses
- Nursing home administrators
- Optometrists
- Pharmacists and pharmacies
- Physical therapists
- Plumbers
- Podiatrists
- Professional counselors
- Psychiatrists and psychologists
- Real estate brokers and appraisers
- Social workers
- Veterinarians

This is not an inclusive list, but if you are in a profession that is licensed, you probably already know about that requirement. If you are uncertain of the status of licensing requirements for your Colorado business, visit www.colorado.gov/colorado/permits.html or contact the Department of Regulatory Agencies. (Contact information is in Appendix C.) The licensing agency may require some form of annual licensing renewal.

It is unlikely that your small business will need a federal license to operate. Licenses from the federal government generally are required for businesses that deal with securities, firearms, and use of the airwaves to transmit information, such as television and radio. If you deal with firearms or ammunition, the consumption or sale of alcoholic beverages or tobacco, or transportation by taxi or bus service, be sure to know the licensing requirements.

Local, County, and City Permits

If you plan to operate a retail or manufacturing business, you will probably be required to get permits, either for construction or to open your particular type of business. There are often requirements or restrictions regarding signage, parking, or the type of business allowed in a particular area. Check with the local city and county governments regarding any special zoning ordinances.

If you plan to operate a retail or manufacturing business you will probably be required to get permits either for construction or to open your particular type of business.

To assist you in determining if you will need a city, county, or state permit, contact the Business Center. (Contact information is in Appendix C.)

Environmental Permits

Permits often are required to conduct a business that may be regulated by a local or state government. Some federal agencies, such as the Environmental Protection Agency (EPA) or the Occupational Safety and Health Administration (OSHA), have state equivalents.

The regional EPA office is located in Denver. The Colorado Department of Public Health and Environment is the state agency that enforces state and federal environmental regulations. The regional EPA office is located in Denver.

Colorado does not have a state equivalent of OSHA, but it has a state-funded OSHA consultation program through the Colorado State University Occupational Health and Safety Section of the Environmental and Radiological Health Sciences. The program is designed to help you understand and comply with safety and health requirements. In addition, the U.S. Department of Labor OSHA regional office is also located in Denver. Contact information for these resources is given in Appendix B (for federal agencies) and Appendix C (for state agencies).

Do not assume that since you are a new or small business you will have little or no contact with these agencies. Due to the requirements of the Clean Air Act of 1991, local, federal, and state laws and regulations affect even one-person operations. You may find that new regulations are put into effect after you start your business, so you must be aware of changes in the laws for which these agencies are responsible.

If your business will use any solvent or substance that could become airborne or get into the water in the form of seepage or runoff, you will have reason to contact these agencies. Even if you don't operate a business that may release controlled substances, you may sell equipment that has a harmful effect on the environment. So it is best to know what the rules are when you represent your product or service.

Also, if you are buying a business, make sure you thoroughly investigate any potential environmental liabilities. It is not uncommon for the buyer of a business to be held liable for environmental problems caused by the business's previous owners. You are encouraged to contact a licensed environmental professional to perform an environmental assessment of the business. This assessment will show you any liabilities before it is too late.

> Once you've obtained the necessary licenses and permits, you must pay taxes—federal, state, and local.

Registering to Pay Taxes

Once you have obtained the necessary licenses and permits for your business, you will be responsible for notifying the IRS. In many cases, you can simply contact a central tax agency, which in turn will get you started with the appropriate forms and filing requirements. Once your business is listed in the agency database, you may receive periodic inquiries about your business or forms that you must complete to comply with state or federal laws or both. The main taxes you will need to be aware of include:

- Estimated federal and state individual income taxes
- Estimated federal and state corporate income taxes
- A sales and use tax
- Property taxes

Often, there may be a single form or tax application that will get you registered with several agencies for several taxes. If your Colorado business will have sales or employees or both, the Colorado Secretary of State has a single form, CR 0100, *Colorado Business Registration*, that will register your trade name as well as open your sales tax license, state wage withholding, and unemployment insurance accounts.

Get an Employer Identification Number

You must obtain an employer identification number (EIN), even if you do not have employees, unless you form a sole proprietorship and have no employees. The first registration you should make is to file Form SS-4, *Application for Employer Identification Number*, with the federal government. You will receive an employer identification number that you will need in many cases to complete other registrations. It is similar to your personal Social Security number, only for your business.

You can obtain Form SS-4 from your local IRS office or your accountant. A copy of this form is included in Appendix A, for information only. Obtain an official form from the IRS, *www.irs.gov/pub/irs-pdf/fss4.pdf*. (You can fill it out online.) Once you have the form, you can apply for an EIN either by mail or by telephone. If you want an EIN immediately, call the Tele-TIN phone number for the service center for Colorado. The Tele-TIN phone and address are located in Appendix B. If you are not in a hurry, you can apply for your EIN through the mail. You will need to complete Form SS-4 at least four to five weeks before you will need your EIN.

> You must obtain an employer identification number (EIN), even if you do not have employees, unless you form a sole proprietorship and have no employees.

After you receive your EIN, you will need to register with the Colorado Department of Revenue. See Chapter 11 for more information on filing employee taxes.

Estimated Income Tax

As a small business owner in Colorado, you will need to estimate the amount of money your business has made and pay taxes on these estimates. Regardless of the form of business you have chosen, you will be responsible for paying estimated income taxes several times throughout the year—usually quarterly. And, if you have underpaid, you will be required to pay underpayment penalties at the end of the year. Make sure you calculate these amounts or any underpayment penalties in your monthly cash flow projections. Your accountant may be able to advise you on how best to plan for paying estimated income taxes.

Individual Federal Income Tax

When you are a sole proprietor, a partner, or a shareholder in an S corporation, you are considered self-employed. Since there is no employer to deduct federal income tax from your wages, you must make quarterly advance payments against your estimated federal income tax. You must report this business income even if it wasn't actually distributed to you. File your payments along with IRS Form 1040-ES. You will then file Form 1040 at the end of the year along with Schedule C-which itemizes your business expenses for the year. Check with your accountant to make sure you know how to estimate, file, and pay correctly.

> When you are a sole proprietor, a partner, or a shareholder in an S corporation, you are considered self-employed.

Federal Self-Employment Tax

In addition to estimated tax payments you must pay a self-employment tax, which is your contribution to Social Security and Medicare. This tax is paid quarterly and is included in your estimated tax payment. Since you are self-employed, you are responsible for the full amount of the contribution, rather than the 50 percent you would pay as an employee. One-half of the self-employment tax is deductible as a business expense on federal Form 1040. See Chapter 11 for more information on FICA (Federal Insurance Contributions Act), SSI (Supplemental Security Income), and Medicare.

Individual State Income Tax

In Colorado, you must pay against your personal estimated state income tax if you are the owner of a sole proprietorship, partnership, LLC, LLP, or S corporation. You must file Form 104 EP, Estimated Tax Vouchers for Individuals, with the Colorado Department of Revenue by April 15, June 15, September 15, and January 15. Further, partnerships, LLCs, and S corporations must file Form 106, Colorado Partnership or S Corporation Return of Income, at the end of the year to show how profits were distributed. The necessary tax forms will probably come automatically after the first year of paying taxes; however, if not, you are still required to file and pay on time.

As a business owner, it is your responsibility to remain informed of these requirements. Contact your local Small Business Administration (SBA) office, the Small Business Development Center (SBDC), or the Colorado Department of Revenue for more information. The addresses and phone numbers of these resources are listed in Appendix B and Appendix C.

Corporate Income Tax

If your business is a corporation, you will be required to submit a separate business tax form with your personal tax report.

If your business is a corporation, you will be required to submit a separate business tax form with your personal tax report. In Colorado, corporate income taxes are imposed at the state level and administered by the Colorado Department of Revenue. If your corporation's tax liability is more than $5,000, plus estimated credits, you must pay estimated taxes during the year, using Form 112 EP, *Estimated Tax Vouchers for Corporations*. At the end of the year, you will file your state corporate income tax on Form 112, *Colorado State C Corporation Income Tax Return*.

Your corporation will be required to make quarterly federal payments based on its estimated tax using Form 1120-W, *Estimated Tax for Corporations*. The installments generally are due by the 15th day of the fourth, sixth, ninth, and 12th months of the tax year. That would be April 15, June 15, September 15, and December 15, unless your corporation operates on a different fiscal year.

Sales and Use Tax

Colorado imposes a sales tax on merchandise sold within the state. If you operate a retail business, you will be required to collect and pay this sales tax to the Colorado Department of Revenue. A retail sale is taxable unless what is bought is to be resold or used to manufacture a resalable item. A state sales tax is imposed on goods that are not to be resold.

You are required to obtain a sales tax license from the Colorado Department of Revenue, which will register your firm as a retail business that is authorized to collect sales tax. To obtain your sales tax license, complete Form CR 100, *Colorado Business Registration*. There is a fee for the license. You will be required to pay a refundable deposit if your business is new. When you remit $50 in sales tax, your deposit will be refunded.

Sales tax is also collected on rentals and leases of products and short-term accommodations of less than 30 days. Wholesale distributors must also have a wholesale license. In most cases you will not be required to pay sales taxes to wholesalers and distributors if you provide them with resale certificates on the goods you purchase. In like manner, if you are a wholesaler, a distributor, or a manufacturer, you will not be required to collect sales tax on the goods you sell, provided the buyer is a retailer purchasing those goods for resale and provides you with resale certificates at the time of sale. For example, if you sell exclusively to other resellers or if your primary business is mail order, you may be required to collect the tax only for items sold and delivered within the state. However, this area of the law is being challenged, so you will find it wise to stay informed about how any changes affect you.

> Sales tax is also collected on rentals and leases of products and short-term accommodations of less than 30 days.

You will be assessed additional taxes on certain types of goods provided for resale. The federal government and most states assess pass-through taxes on certain goods, such as gasoline, tobacco, and alcohol. As a retailer, you will pay taxes on these goods at the time of purchase and pass the tax through to the consumer. In the case of these taxes, you do not have to pay them separately to the state. The manufacturer, wholesaler, or distributor does this for you. However, you will still be required to maintain thorough records on all sales.

You are required to keep detailed records of your gross receipts regardless of whether those receipts are taxable or not. These receipts will justify the taxes you pay and the deductions you take on gross sales throughout the year. You will be required to file Form DR 0100, *Colorado Retail Sales Tax Return*, indicating that you know how much you sold was taxable and how much was not taxable. This form is due on the 20th day of the month of your reporting period.

The reporting periods vary based on the amount of tax you remit. You will file your reports annually or quarterly until your monthly tax liability reaches $300, at which time you must make monthly payments. Send your report and payments to the Colorado Department of Revenue.

Be careful to report on a timely basis. Colorado should send copies of reporting forms in advance of the due date. A late or incorrect form can result in heavy penalties or fines. If you don't receive your forms, don't assume that you have no tax liability. You are responsible for getting the forms, filing them, and paying the tax.

Also, contact the Colorado Department of Revenue to learn about its free seminars on collecting and filing sales and use taxes.

City Occupational Privilege Tax

Some cities in Colorado—including Denver, Aurora, Sheridan, and Greenwood Village—also impose an occupational privilege tax for which employees and employers share the liability. Contact the appropriate city office where your business is located to ascertain if such a tax is imposed in that city and, if so, how to register and file tax payments.

Property Tax

Property taxes are assessed to pay the operating expenses of your locality, pay for bonds, and provide for special projects at the county and community levels. Taxes are usually paid annually to the county treasurer. In most cases the county tax assessor will automatically bill you as the owner of record, so you will not need to contact this office when purchasing property for your business.

In Colorado, property taxes are assessed on any real or personal property that directly or indirectly produces income within your business. As a new business owner, you should contact the local county assessor's office to determine the amount of taxes you must pay. Taxes must be paid by April 15 unless you have been granted an extension.

Chapter Wrap-Up

As you will soon find out, the details of running a small business can be overwhelming. You'll need to educate yourself about the many requirements placed on your new Colorado business.

This chapter has introduced you to most of the start-up details that today's small businesses face. Some of these details are related to federal laws that affect businesses in all 50 states and Washington, DC. However, many of these details will vary according to Colorado state laws-and, in some cases, are superseded by state laws. In addition, you will need to be aware of the city and county rules and regulations that govern your small business. From choosing a name for your business to applying for a trademark or trade name;

from getting state permits and licenses to registering to pay taxes, as a business owner you will be responsible for making sure your business is "official."

To help you stay educated and informed of the latest rules and regulations that affect your Colorado business, stay in close communication with your state's one-stop center—the Colorado Business Center. This office may be able to put you on its mailing list for updates regarding issues that relate to not only starting but also operating a small business in Colorado. Also, if you have Internet access, visit the Web sites of your state and its economic development or trade and commerce agencies for the most current information. Refer to Chapter 12 for more information on the role of the Colorado Office of Business Development.

Start-Up Details Checklist

❏ All business entities must contact the Colorado Secretary of State to register their business name as a trade name.

❏ Register any trademark, trade name, or service mark you feel is necessary with the Colorado Secretary of State.

❏ Contact the Colorado Business Center to find out if it can help you register your business or it can send you a start-up packet.

❏ Contact the Colorado Business Center, visit *www.colorado.gov/colorado/permits.html*, or contact the Department of Regulatory Agencies to find out whether your business or profession is subject to any special state licensing requirements.

❏ Find out whether your business will be required to obtain a city sales or local occupational privilege license.

❏ Make sure your operations are consistent with current zoning and environmental regulations.

❏ Get a local certificate of occupancy, if applicable.

❏ Obtain a federal employer identification number (EIN) by completing Form SS-4 from the Internal Revenue Service.

❏ Contact the Taxpayer Service Division of the Colorado Department of Revenue for information on how and when to pay your federal and state estimated taxes.

❏ If you will operate as a corporation, determine your corporate income tax obligations.

❏ Use Form CR 100, *Colorado Business Registration*, to register with the

Secretary of State to pay the state sales and use tax to the Department of Revenue. Determine how and when you will pay the tax.

❏ Obtain a retail sales tax license and display it at your place of business.

❏ Find out your property tax (city and county) obligations and make sure you project these figures into your monthly cash flow statements.

11 | *Your Duties As an Employer*

Minimum wage. Affirmative action. ADA. Immigration. FUTA. FICA. OSHA. No, you won't have to completely learn a new language, but you will need to add more than a few dozen acronyms, buzzwords, and phrases to your vocabulary. Welcome to the world of employment.

Your duties as an entrepreneur will seem like a walk in the park compared with your responsibilities as an employer. In fact, your ability to conquer the multifaceted job of employer can cause your business to sink or stay afloat in both lean and profitable times. Your best course of action is to thoroughly understand and meet the numerous requirements of being an employer in Colorado. You will be responsible for complying with federal and state laws that govern fair employment, anti-discrimination, withholding taxes, workers' compensation, and safety in the workplace. The responsibilities that lie ahead include:

- The minimum amount you will pay your employees, the amount you will pay if they work in excess of a certain timeframe, and if you will employ minors;
- How you will report these wages and, in so doing, which taxes you will withhold;
- The anti-discriminatory manner in which to hire, promote, and retain your employees;
- Your obligations to grant various types of employee leave requests and how to accommodate individuals with disabilities;
- How to properly hire and use independent contractors for your business; and
- The safety and health programs that you must implement to comply with the multitude of regulations.

Much of what you need to understand about being an employer is contained in this chapter. And, to help you further, there is a checklist at the end of the chapter to help you remember your duties.

Fair Employment Practices

One of the first things you must do as an employer in Colorado—and that means before you hire employees—is to understand both the federal and state laws that govern fair employment practices. Many of these fair practices center around the laws that cover payment of wages and working conditions, including number of hours worked.

A good place to start is to understand the origin of fair employment practices. Drastic changes to employment standards came about in 1938 as a result of a law passed during the Great Depression, known as the Fair Labor Standards Act (FLSA), this federal law requires overtime for hours worked in excess of 40 hours in a week and sets minimum wages. In addition, the law includes child labor and recordkeeping provisions. In August 1996, the Fair Labor Standards Act was amended to provide a two-step increase in the minimum wage and a subminimum rate for youth during their first 90 days of employment. The amendments also:

- Changed certain provisions of the FLSA with respect to the tip credit that can be claimed by employers of "tipped employees";
- Provided an exemption for certain computer professionals; and
- Redefined home-to-work travel time in employer-provided vehicles.

> One of the first things you must do as an employer in Colorado is to understand both the federal and state laws that govern fair employment practices.

Every employer of employees subject to the Fair Labor Standards Act's age-hour provisions must post, and keep posted, a notice explaining the act in a conspicuous place in all of their establishments to permit employees to easily read it. The content of the notice is prescribed by the Wage and Hour Division of the U.S. Department of Labor. An approved copy of the minimum wage poster is available for informational purposes or for employers to use as posters via the Internet. For more information, contact www.dol.org.

Colorado is an "employment at will" state. This means that either the employer or the employee may terminate the employment without any requirement to provide an explanation or advance notice. Actions that are discriminatory are exceptions. Additionally, Colorado statutes do not require or prohibit the following:

- Severance or sick pay
- Paid holidays, vacation, or other fringe benefits
- Advance notice of work or duty schedule changes
- Release of information regarding reasons for selection or non-selection for employment
- Access to personnel records or providing copies
- Pay raises, promotion, or bonuses
- Premium pay for weekend, holiday, or night work
- Character references, recommendations, or release of employment information to other employers
- Mandatory overtime
- Drug or alcohol testing
- Polygraph examinations as a condition of employment or continued employment (federal law may apply in this situation)
- Involuntary weekend, holiday, or night work

Minimum Wage

The federal government has a minimum wage law. Pursuant to the Minimum Wage Increase Act of 1996, the federal minimum wage increased to $5.15 per hour as of September 1, 1997. Colorado has its own minimum wage law. The minimum wage in Colorado is $5.15 per hour, the same as the federal minimum wage rate.

Generally, the state minimum wage law relates to employees who work in companies that are exempt from the federal minimum wage law or those that primarily involve intrastate commerce. To find out if your business can

Colorado has its own minimum wage law. The minimum wage in Colorado is $5.15 per hour, the same as the federal minimum wage rate.

be categorized as involving interstate or intrastate commerce, contact the Colorado Department of Labor and Employment, Labor Standards Unit, to be certain which minimum wage amount applies to your business. You can find the address and phone number for this agency in Appendix C.

Colorado law and the U.S. Department of Labor require certain posters to be displayed in your employees' work area pertaining to minimum wage. Contact the Division of Labor, Colorado Department of Labor and Employment (see Appendix C), and the U.S. Department of Labor (see Appendix B) to determine if a minimum wage poster is required in your place of business.

Overtime Pay

Be aware that in addition to minimum wage, there are federal and state laws that govern overtime pay. If you pay your employees hourly, you are probably required to pay overtime. However, executive, administrative, and professional employees who are paid on a salaried basis are not covered by the Fair Labor Standards Act. To determine if your employees fall within one of these categories, consider the following:

- "Executive" means your employee spends a majority of time in management activities, exercises some discretion and independent judgment, and supervises at least two full-time employees.
- "Administrative" means your employee exercises some discretion and independent judgment in performing nonclerical office work directly related to management policies or business operations.
- "Professional" means your employee exercises discretion and independent judgment in a position requiring knowledge of an advanced type in a field of science or learning, or the employee works in a position requiring invention, imagination, or talent in a recognized field of artistic endeavor.

If an employee works in excess of 40 hours in a week, the additional hours must be paid at one and one-half times that employee's normal rate.

Generally, you should compute pay on a weekly basis to determine if overtime pay is payable to an employee. An employee may work more than eight hours in a day without earning overtime pay. However, if an employee works in excess of 40 hours in a week, the additional hours must be paid at one and one-half times that employee's normal rate. Even if you reduce an employee's hours in the previous or following week so as to average 40 hours over two or more weeks, you must pay overtime pay for the week when more than 40 hours of work was conducted. There are different requirements for exempt and nonexempt employees. You do not have to pay overtime for exempt employees, but you should be aware of the definition of an exempt employee. The above requirements apply to nonexempt employees. Retain payroll records in the event someone claims that overtime pay was not paid.

Colorado requires overtime to be paid at the rate of one and one-half times an employee's regular rate of pay for hours worked in excess of 40 in a workweek as well as for any work in excess of 12 hours in a workday. There is an exception for hospital and nursing home employees that requires overtime to be paid if they work more than 80 hours in 14 consecutive days or more than eight hours in a day.

Employees exempt from minimum wage provisions are exempt from overtime. Also exempt from overtime are some salespersons, parts persons, and mechanics employed by automobile, truck, or farm implement (retail) dealers. Employees of the ski industry and medical transportation industry also have special requirements for minimum wage. Contact the Colorado Department of Labor and Employment for complete information if you are in one of these industries. See Appendix C for contact information.

Equal Pay

A part of the Fair Labor Standards Act, the Equal Pay Act requires equal pay to men and women doing substantially the same work with similar skill levels, responsibilities, and effort under similar working conditions. It applies to all local, state, and federal agencies and to any business engaged in interstate commerce. It is regulated by the Wage and Hour Division of the U.S. Department of Labor. If you don't comply with equal pay statutes, you may receive a claim based on wage or sex discrimination. If you are found liable, you may be forced to pay back wages or fines up to $10,000 and may possibly face imprisonment.

Employment of Minors

Both federal and state agencies regulate the employment of children. These laws usually define the type of work done, the maximum number of hours and days worked, and other conditions that may affect a minor's ability to complete his or her education.

In general, federal law allows anyone 18 years or older to perform any job, whether hazardous or not, for unlimited hours. Youths 16 or 17 years old may perform any non-hazardous job for unlimited hours; and 14- or 15-year-olds

> A part of the Fair Labor Standards Act, the Equal Pay Act requires equal pay to men and women doing substantially the same work with similar skill levels, responsibilities, and effort under similar working conditions.

may work outside school hours in various nonmanufacturing, nonmining, nonhazardous job, but they cannot work more than three hours on a school day, 18 hours per week in a school week, more than eight hours per day on a nonschool day or more than 40 hours per week when school is not in session.

If you plan to employ anyone under the age of 18, be sure to contact the Division of Labor of the Colorado Department of Labor and Employment for the rules and exceptions that apply to your business. The type of work a minor will perform is a major determinant in whether or not you can employ that individual. There are some exemptions for work such as delivering newspapers. Other exceptions include:

- Children nine years of age or older may deliver handbills, shine shoes, participate in casual work around the home, and work in the yard or assist with snow removal that does not involve the use of power-driven vehicles.
- Children who are 12 years old or older may participate in door-to-door sales, baby-sitting, and work with approved power-driven vehicles in tasks such as gardening or lawn care.
- Children who are 14 years old or older may work in nonhazardous manufacturing, messenger services, warehousing and storage, nonhazardous construction and repair work, retail food service, and gas station work—to name a few of the possibilities.

Reporting Wages

You are required to provide each employee who worked for your business during the previous year a completed IRS Form W-2, *Annual Wage and Tax Statement*. The W-2 is the form that the employee files with his or her state and federal tax returns to show the amount earned at your business. It also shows the state and federal withholdings. More on withholding taxes is located at the end of this chapter.

All W-2 forms and a summary form (W-3) must be sent to the IRS no later than February 28 of each year. When you apply for your employer identification number (EIN) on Form SS-4, *Application for Employer Identification Number*, you will receive the appropriate documents and instructions on how to properly report yearly wages. (See Chapter 10 for details on applying for an EIN and Appendix A for a copy of the form.) There are strict regulations for sending W-2s to your employees, so be sure to read and understand the information provided by the IRS.

You are required to provide each employee who worked for your business during the previous year a completed IRS Form W-2, Annual Wage and Tax Statement.

Anti-Discrimination Laws

The last century brought much change to the ways employers can treat their employees and prospective employees. Legislation that prevents discriminatory practices now pervades the day-to-day operations of U.S. businesses— touching the practices of both big and small businesses. It is critical that you know the various anti-discrimination laws that affect your business, which may include one or more of the following:

- The Civil Rights Act of 1964
- The Civil Rights Act of 1991
- Affirmative Action
- The Rehabilitation Act of 1973
- The Equal Pay Act of 1963
- The Age Discrimination in Employment Act of 1967
- The Americans with Disabilities Act of 1990
- The Immigration and Reform Act of 1986
- The Family and Medical Leave Act of 1993
- The Uniformed Services Employment and Re-employment Rights Act of 1994
- The National Labor Relations Act of 1935
- The Immigration Reform and Control Act of 1986

Don't let the lengthy titles scare you. Compliance with all of these laws is simple to understand and even simpler to achieve.

The Civil Rights Act of 1964

The Civil Rights Act of 1964 (CRA) is the principal federal legislation governing employment discrimination. The CRA protects individuals attempting to exercise equal employment opportunity rights from discriminatory practices. Title VII of the CRA prohibits employers from discriminating against employees and job applicants based on race, religion, sex, color, or national origin. In addition, it prohibits discrimination in recruiting, hiring, job advertising, testing, pre-hire investigations, pay and compensation, benefits plans, promotion, seniority, and retirement.

The Civil Rights Act of 1964 (CRA) is the principal federal legislation governing employment discrimination.

The CRA is regulated by the Equal Employment Opportunity Commission (EEOC). The act applies to:

- Public and private employers with 15 or more employees,
- Public and private employment agencies, and
- Hiring halls or labor unions with 15 or more members.

Employers that fail to comply with the CRA face severe penalties including court-decreed affirmative action programs and court-ordered back pay to the victim.

Sexual harassment is prohibited under Title VII of the Civil Rights Act of 1964. Unwelcome sexual advances, requests for sexual favors, or verbal or physical conduct of a sexual nature are all forms of sexual harassment. Specifically, these behaviors cannot be present as a condition of employment or as the basis for employment decisions, nor can they create an environment that is hostile, intimidating, or offensive.

The Civil Rights Act of 1991

The Civil Rights Act of 1991 extends punitive actions and jury trials to victims of employment discrimination based on the employee's sex, religion, disability, and race. Under previous legislation (the Civil Rights Act of 1964), employees could only seek back pay. The new act is regulated by the EEOC and applies to all businesses with 15 or more employees. Punitive damage awards are limited to $50,000 for businesses with 100 or fewer employees; $100,000 for businesses with 101 to 500 employees; and $300,000 for businesses with more than 500 employees.

> The Civil Rights Act of 1991 extends punitive actions and jury trials to victims of employment discrimination based on the employee's sex, religion, disability, and race.

Affirmative Action

The concept of affirmative action was born when, in 1965, President Lyndon B. Johnson signed an executive order that placed strict requirements on companies that provided goods or services to the federal government. This legislation made all employers practice affirmative action by actively recruiting and promoting qualified veterans, minorities, women, and individuals with disabilities. The law requires these companies to achieve and maintain an equitable distribution of each group within their workplaces.

Affirmative action is regulated by the Office of Federal Contract Compliance Programs (OFCCP) and the Civil Service Commission. It applies to companies with federal contracts of $10,000 or more per year as well as all federal agencies and the U.S. Postal Service. Companies with more than $50,000 per year in federal contracts must additionally file a written affirmative action plan with the OFCCP. Failure to comply with these requirements could result in cancellation of the company's federal contracts.

The Rehabilitation Act of 1973

Similar to President Johnson's executive order requiring affirmative action, this act requires firms providing goods and services to the federal government to hire and promote qualified individuals with disabilities. This act is regulated by the OFCCP and the Civil Service Commission and applies to companies with more than $2,500 per year in federal contracts. Failure to comply with these requirements could result in cancellation of your company's federal contracts.

The Equal Pay Act of 1963

The Equal Pay Act of 1963 (EPA), an amendment to the Fair Labor Standards Act, requires that male and female workers receive equal pay for work requiring equal skills, effort, and responsibility and performed under similar working conditions.

Wage differentials are permitted only if they are based on factors other than sex, such as a seniority system, a merit system, or a system by which pay is based on quantity or quality of work.

The EPA applies to all employers that engage in interstate commerce, regardless of the number of employees. Employees filing complaints under this law are not required to show that the employer intended to discriminate against them. The EPA specifically prohibits labor unions from causing or attempting to cause an employer to discriminate in wages on the basis of sex.

The responsibility of enforcing the EPA falls under the jurisdiction of the Equal Employment Opportunity Commission (EEOC).

The Age Discrimination in Employment Act of 1967

This act prohibits employers from age discrimination when hiring, retaining, and promoting employees who are 40 years of age or older. It encourages the hiring of older persons based on ability rather than age and it provides a basis for resolving age-related employment problems. The Age Discrimination in Employment Act is regulated by the EEOC and applies to all

- Government employers,
- Private employers of 20 or more persons, or
- Employment agencies or unions with 25 or more members.

Employers who don't comply may face court-ordered affirmative action programs, court-ordered back pay, fines of up to $10,000, and possible imprisonment.

This act prohibits employers from age discrimination when hiring, retaining, and promoting employees who are 40 years of age or older.

The Americans with Disabilities Act (ADA) of 1990

The Americans with Disabilities Act (ADA) prohibits discrimination against qualified employees and job applicants with disabilities regarding job application procedures, hiring, firing, advancement, compensation, job training, discharge, retirement, and other benefits or terms of employment. The ADA is enforced by the Equal Employment Opportunity Commission and applies to all employers with 15 or more employees during 20 weeks of any calendar year. Penalties for noncompliance can include administrative enforcement, back pay, and injunctive relief.

The ADA is a very complex act and can be costly if you don't understand it. Unfortunately, not even attorneys can provide definitive information about the act. It was written to help disabled workers find employment, but has been broadened to cover many physical and mental problems of potential employees. Some restrictions include:

- Employers must make reasonable accommodation for modifying a position to employ a disabled person. The term "reasonable accommodation" has not been well defined and is the source of much confusion and potential employer liability.
- Employers may not ask job applicants about the existence, nature, or severity of a disability.
- The act does not apply to employees or potential employees with temporary disabilities.
- The act protects persons with AIDS and HIV from discrimination.
- It provides limited protection for recovering drug addicts and alcoholics.

There are also tax benefits for making changes in your company to accommodate the disabled. To find out how to receive tax breaks for accommodating employees with disabilities, contact the IRS. To learn more about your responsibilities relative to the ADA, contact the Equal Employment Opportunity Commission. See Appendix B for contact information for these two agencies.

The Immigration Reform and Control Act of 1986

The Immigration Reform and Control Act of 1986 (IRCA) is legislation designed to prevent illegal immigrants from easily finding employment in the United States. The law protects your right to hire legal immigrants and prohibits the hiring of illegal immigrants. You are subject to fines up to $20,000 for each illegal alien that you hire.

The Immigration Reform and Control Act of 1986 (IRCA) is legislation designed to prevent illegal immigrants from easily finding employment in the United States.

To comply with the law you should request identification from everyone you hire and have each employee complete a Form I-9, *Employment Eligibility Verification*, from the Department of Homeland Security, U.S. Citizenship and Immigration Service (USCIS), prior to hiring. Form I-9 was developed to help you verify an employee's right to work in the United States. A copy of this form is in Appendix A.

Although you may not refuse to hire anyone because you think the person may be an illegal alien, you must obtain identification that is specified on Form I-9. Overall, as an employer you must:

- Have new employees fill out Part I of Form I-9 within three days of being hired;
- Have new employees present documents that prove eligibility to work in the United States (specified on the I-9, *uscis.gov/graphics/formsfee/ forms/files/i-9.pdf*);
- Complete Part II of Form I-9;
- Retain Form I-9 on file for each employee for at least three years, or for at least one year after the employee is terminated, whichever is longer;
- Present Form I-9 upon request to an officer of the U.S. Citizenship and Immigration Services or the U.S. Department of Labor. You will get at least three days notice before being required to do so; and
- Employers can use Form I-766, *Employment Authorization Document*, to verify employment as of January 1997. This form is used by aliens who are approved by the USCIS to work in the United States.

Detailed instructions are printed on Form I-9. For further information refer to the 17-page booklet entitled *Handbook for Employers: Instructions for Completing Form I-9*, which is available from the USCIS. Use Appendix B to find contact information for the USCIS employer relations officer closest to you.

The Family and Medical Leave Act of 1993

The U.S. Department of Labor's Employment Standards Administration, Wage and Hour Division, administers and enforces the Family and Medical Leave Act (FMLA) for all private, state, and local government employees, and some federal employees. FMLA became effective on August 5, 1993, for most employers.

The act permits employees to take up to 12 weeks of unpaid leave each year:

- For the birth of a son or daughter, and to care for the newborn child;
- For the placement with the employee of a child for adoption or foster care, and to care for the newly placed child;
- To care for an immediate family member (spouse, child, or parent, but not a parent "in-law") with a serious health condition; or
- When the employee is unable to work because of a serious health condition.

As an employer you must guarantee that your employee can return to the same job or a comparable job and you must continue health care coverage, if provided, during the leave period.

This law is regulated by the EEOC and applies to employers with 50 or more employees within a 75-mile radius. The law does not apply to employees with less than one year on the job or to employees who have not worked at least 1,250 hours or at least 25 hours per week in the past year. Workers who are on family leave are not eligible for unemployment benefits or other government compensation.

Be sure you understand all the provisions of the act before you disallow a request by an employee who wants to take advantage of the provisions of the act.

The Family and Medical Leave Act can be another source of problems for the unwary employer. Be sure you understand all the provisions of the act before you disallow a request by an employee who wants to take advantage of the provisions of the act.

Colorado has a family leave law that applies only to state employees; private employees are covered by the federal act. In addition, Colorado has a pregnancy leave act independent of the federal law: it allows employees a leave of absence for family or medical purposes, such as the birth or adoption of a child or a serious health condition of the employee, spouse, child, or parent.

All covered employers are required to display and keep displayed a poster prepared by the U.S. Department of Labor that summarizes the major provisions of the FMLA and tells employees how to file a complaint. The poster must be displayed in a conspicuous place where employees and applicants for employment can see it. A poster must be displayed at all locations even if there are no eligible employees. You can download a copy of this poster via the Internet. For more information, go to www.dol.gov.

To learn more about family and medical leave in Colorado, contact the Equal Employment Opportunity Commission (EEOC) if you employ 15 or more employees or the Colorado Department of Regulatory Agencies, Division of Civil Rights, if you employ fewer than 15 employees. Contact information is included in Appendix B for the EEOC and Appendix C for the Department of Regulatory Agencies.

The Uniformed Services Employment and Re-employment Rights Act of 1994

The Uniformed Services Employment and Re-employment Rights Act of 1994 requires that military leave must be granted for up to five years. Thus, as an employer you must rehire an employee if that person was inducted into or voluntarily enlisted in the armed forces of the United States. The law also protects reservists who are called to active duty.

The law also grants insurance benefits if your company provides company insurance. Further, it applies to voluntary as well as involuntary military service—in peacetime as well as wartime. However, it does not apply to a state activation of the National Guard for disaster relief or riots. The protection for such duty must be provided by the laws of the state involved.

If you have questions regarding employer, Guard, or reservist rights and responsibilities concerning military leave, you can obtain additional information from a volunteer organization called the National Committee for Employer Support of the Guard and Reserve. This organization also provides assistance to employers on a local basis if problems develop between a guardsman or reservist and the employer. See Appendix B for contact information.

The National Labor Relations Act of 1935

The National Labor Relations Act of 1935, also known as the Wagner Act, established a national policy that encourages collective bargaining and guarantees certain employee rights. This legislation was amended by the Labor Management Relations (Taft-Hartley) Act of 1947 and the Labor Management Reporting and Disclosure (Landrum-Griffin) Act of 1959. Together these laws establish a balance between management and union power to protect public interest and provide regulations for internal union affairs.

These laws apply to all private employers and unions and are governed by the National Labor Relations Board (NLRB). The NLRB has the power to investigate, dismiss charges, hold hearings, issue cease and desist orders, or pursue cases via the Circuit Court of Appeals or the U.S. Supreme Court.

> The National Labor Relations Act of 1935, also known as the Wagner Act, established a national policy that encourages collective bargaining and guarantees certain employee rights.

Right-to-Work Laws

Many states have right-to-work laws that prohibit employers from denying employment to individuals who have refused to join a union. These laws also make it illegal for an employer to force mandatory payment of union dues by nonunion workers so as to keep their jobs.

Colorado does not have a right-to-work law and allows companies and unions to enter into "union shop" or "agency shop" agreements. A union shop agreement would allow you to hire employees who don't belong to a union with the stipulation that those employees join the union within a certain timeframe—usually 30 days. An agency shop agreement would not make it necessary for an employee to join the union but would stipulate that the employee must pay union dues in order to retain employment.

Independent Contractors

Many small business owners use independent contractors to complete certain tasks necessary for their businesses rather than go through the process of hiring additional employees. There are several advantages to contracting an independent worker. First, instead of paying the significant overhead costs for an employee—including taxes, benefits, and insurance—you pay a contractor only for the end result. Second, hiring a contractor involves a much smaller administrative workload. You need only file IRS Form MISC-1099, as opposed to handling the numerous forms and deductions required for a regular employee.

> When using an independent contractor, it is crucial that you don't treat that individual as an employee.

When using an independent contractor, it is crucial that you don't treat that individual as an employee. Be cautious that the contractor meets the definition of contract labor in the Fair Labor Standards Act (FLSA).

The Supreme Court has said that there is no definition that solves all problems relating to the employer-employee relationship under the FLSA. The Court has also said that determination of the relation cannot be based on isolated factors or upon a single characteristic, but depends upon the circumstances of the whole activity. The goal of the analysis is to determine the underlying economic reality of the situation and whether the individual is economically dependent on the supposed employer. In general, an employee, as distinguished from an independent contractor who is engaged in a business of his own, is one who "follows the usual path of an employee" and is dependent on the business she serves. The following are factors the Supreme Court has considered significant, although no single one is regarded as controlling:

- The extent to which the worker's services are an integral part of the employer's business (examples: Does the worker play an integral role in the business by performing the primary type of work that the employer performs for his customers or clients? Does the worker perform a discrete job that is one part of the business's overall process of production? Does the worker supervise any of the company's employees?)

- The permanency of the relationship (example: How long has the worker worked for the same company?)
- The amount of the worker's investment in facilities and equipment. Examples: Is the worker reimbursed for any purchases or materials, supplies, etc? Does the worker use his or her own tools or equipment?
- The nature and degree of control by the principal. Examples: Who decides on what hours to be worked? Who is responsible for quality control? Does the worker work for any other company(s)? Who sets the pay rate?
- The worker's opportunities for profit and loss. Examples: Did the worker make any investments such as insurance or bonding? Can the worker earn a profit by performing the job more efficiently or exercising managerial skill or suffer a loss of capital investment?
- The level of skill required in performing the job and the amount of initiative, judgment, or foresight in open market competition with others required for the success of the claimed independent enterprise. (Examples: Does the worker perform routine tasks requiring little training? Does the worker advertise independently via yellow pages, business cards, etc.? Does the worker have a separate business site?)

The penalties for incorrectly labeling a worker as a contractor can be expensive. You are liable for the employer taxes that you failed to withhold as well as a portion of the employees' taxes that were not paid. You must file MISC-1099 for each contractor that you paid in excess of $600 during the year. Failure to file could double your percentage of the employee taxes you may owe should the IRS determine that your contractor was actually an employee. In like manner, contractors will report the income on Schedule C or Schedule F along with their personal income tax returns.

A written agreement with any independent contractor you will use will help to define your relationship with the contractor for the IRS. The agreement should define the work being accomplished and clearly state that the contractor is responsible for paying self-employment taxes. Further, the agreement can do the following:

- Determine start and stop dates but not working hours;
- Make payment dependent on results, not the amount of time spent to

> A written agreement with any independent contractor you will use will help to define your relationship with the contractor for the IRS.

get them; and

- Make the working relationship clear and base it strictly on a given result

You can get an opinion from the IRS as to whether a relationship is that of a contract or employee by submitting Form SS-8 to the IRS. You can get a copy of the form from the IRS Web site or by contacting the IRS. See Appendix B for contact information.

Withholding Taxes

When your business has employees, you must withhold federal income tax from their wages. In addition, you must contribute to Social Security, Medicare, and unemployment funds. Requirements for submitting withheld funds are somewhat complex, so be sure to clearly understand what is expected for your business. Contact the IRS for information relating to remitting withholding taxes; start with Publication 15 (Circular E), *Employer's Tax Guide*.

Federal Unemployment Taxes (FUTA)

Unemployment benefits are paid from state unemployment taxes and unemployment insurance. The cost of administering the unemployment program is paid from Federal Unemployment Tax Act (FUTA) funds.

The federal unemployment tax is your company's contribution to the unemployment insurance fund. You are required to pay 6.2 percent on the first $7,000 of each employee's annual pay. The actual rate you pay is normally 0.8 percent because you receive a 5.4 percent credit for the state unemployment taxes you pay.

You will be required to pay FUTA if you employ one or more persons (not farm or household workers) for at least one day in each of 20 calendar weeks (not necessarily consecutive) and if you pay wages of $1,500 or more during the year. You may be required to pay federal unemployment tax even if you are exempt from paying state taxes. If your FUTA liability is more than $100 in any quarter, you are required to make a federal tax deposit for the amount owing.

FUTA tax is reported annually on Form 940, *Employer's Annual Federal Unemployment Tax Return*, which is due by January 31 of the next calendar year. If you have made timely deposits, however, you have until February 10 to file. In addition, if at the end of any calendar quarter you owe more than $100 FUTA tax for the year, you must make a deposit by the end of the next month.

> The federal unemployment tax is your company's contribution to the unemployment insurance fund.

Some employers can qualify to file a simplified FUTA return. To be eligible to file Form 940-EZ, you must:

- Pay unemployment tax to only one state;
- Pay state unemployment taxes by the due date on Form 940-EZ; and
- Pay wages that are subject to FUTA and are also taxable for state unemployment tax purposes.

To find out more about this simplified filing, obtain copies of:

- Publication 334, *Tax Guide for Small Business*,
- Publication 15, Circular E, *Employer's Tax Guide*, and
- Publication 509, *Tax Calendar and Checklist*.

The locations and phone numbers of IRS taxpayer assistance centers are listed in Appendix B.

State Unemployment Taxes

As an employer in Colorado, you are responsible for paying unemployment tax at the state level if you employ one or more persons performing services.

Although the tax is on your employees' covered wages, you are not allowed to deduct this tax from their wages. The burden of paying the state unemployment tax lies on your shoulders as the employer.

If you operate as a sole proprietor or A partner, you won't be required to pay unemployment tax because you will not be considered an actual employee of your business. Also, in Colorado your sole proprietorship is exempt from paying state unemployment tax on your spouse or children under 21 years of age if they are employees of your business. However, if you fire them or lay them off, they will not be eligible to collect unemployment benefits.

To register to pay unemployment tax in Colorado, you will need to file Form CR 100, *Colorado Business Registration*, with the Colorado Department of Labor and Employment. The Division of Employment and Training offers the *Employer's Handbook* to help you better understand the filing process. See Appendix C for contact information.

Tax Experience Rating

The unemployment tax rate for your business is related to the overall experience your company has had with benefits claims over a certain number of years; hence, the name "tax experience rating." For example, if you have had many employees who have claimed benefits, your business will probably

> The unemployment tax rate for your business is related to the overall experience your company has had with benefits claims over a certain number of years; hence, the name "tax experience rating."

have a higher experience rating. On the flip side, if you have had few employees claiming benefits in the past, you will have a lower experience rating.

Colorado assigns each new employer a standard rate. Your experience with unemployment claims and benefits from the point you start your business or purchase a business will dictate whether your rate will increase or decrease. If you bought the business and the seller has an excellent rating, talk to the Colorado Department of Labor and Employment's Division of Employment and Training to learn how you can take over that rate.

As a precautionary measure, if you are buying a business, make sure the seller is current and has filed all necessary unemployment taxes and reports. If you don't, you may be held responsible for unpaid taxes. You are encouraged to get an unemployment tax release from the Division of Employment and Training. Discuss this important aspect of the sale with your attorney. If you do find unemployment taxes owing, make sure this amount is negotiated in the sale price of the business.

Social Security and Medicare (FICA)

The Federal Insurance Contribution Act (FICA) was passed into law by Congress in 1935. It requires all employers to pay Social Security taxes to the government to provide for old age, survivor, and disability benefits as well as hospital insurance (Medicare). Payments are made in equal amounts by an employee and his or her employer, with collection responsibilities falling on the employer.

The rate in 2006 is 7.65 percent for the employer and each employee, which includes 6.2 percent for Social Security and 1.45 percent for Medicare. You need to pay the Social Security rate of 6.2 percent for the first $94,200 of wages. This amount normally increases annually, so check for the maximum amount you have to pay for Social Security. There is no limit for the Medicare tax. Refer to IRS Publication 15, Circular E, *Employer's Tax Guide* (*www.irs.gov/pub/irs-pdf/p15.pdf*), for updates and more information.

Federal Income Tax Withholding

You must withhold federal income tax from the wages of any employee who meets threshold wage levels. This requirement applies to all employees who do not claim an exemption from withholding. The amount withheld is recomputed each pay period. Federal income tax is based on gross wages before deductions for FICA, retirement funds, or insurance. Most employers base income tax withholding on percentage or wage brackets. Refer to IRS

You must withhold federal income tax from the wages of any employee who meets threshold wage levels.

Publication 15, *Employer's Tax Guide*, for detailed descriptions of these withholding methods.

State Income Tax Withholding

You must also withhold a portion of an employee's wages for the state income tax. Again, this requirement applies to all employees who do not claim an exemption from withholding. You are required to have a Colorado withholding tax account number by filing a Form CR 0100, *Colorado Business Registration*, with the Colorado Department of Revenue or the Department of Labor and Employment. Contact either agency for the appropriate form and filing procedures.

> You must withhold a portion of an employee's wages for the state income tax.

New Hire Reporting

In compliance with the federal Personal Responsibility and Work Opportunity Reconciliation Act of 1996, enacted to expedite child support collections, all Colorado employers must report each newly hired employee to the Colorado State Directory of New Hires.

You have 20 calendar days from the hiring date to report the name, address, Social Security number, and hire date of each new hire, as well as the name, address, and federal employer identification number (EIN) of your business. Employees who are rehired after a layoff or other break in service of more than 26 consecutive weeks are considered as new hires. Your report may be a copy of the federal Form W-4, *Employee's Withholding Allowance Certificate*.

There is a penalty for not filing the required information, which will be raised substantially if there is conspiracy between employer and employee.

For more information on new hire reporting requirements, contact the Colorado State Directory of New Hires. You can report online, by fax, or by mail. You can find the contact information in Appendix C.

Workers' Compensation

Before 1911, if an employee was injured on the job, that employee was forced to take legal action against the employer to collect compensation. This led to a high risk of lawsuits against employers. But, in 1911, Wisconsin passed the first workers' compensation laws—paving the way for complex yet beneficial state-by-state workers' compensation laws.

Although the general trend is to expand coverage to protect as many workers as possible, each state's mandated coverage is based on the perceived risks of employees. For instance, manufacturing-based states have more comprehensive coverage whereas agricultural-based states are not as comprehensive. Because of these variations, workers' compensation laws don't cover all occupations in all states.

If you have three or more employees or had one or more workers for 35 or more hours per week for 13 or more weeks during the previous calendar year in your Colorado business, you are required to obtain workers' compensation insurance. This type of insurance pays the benefits for covered employees for job-related illnesses, injuries, and deaths. Benefits include medical expenses, death benefits, lost wages, and vocational rehabilitation. If you fail to carry workers' compensation coverage, you will be vulnerable to paying all of the benefits and possible fines.

Workers' compensation is offered in most states in one of three ways.

1. A wholly state-owned insurance company—or monopoly state fund—is the only insurance available.
2. A wholly state-owned insurance company—or state fund—competes with other insurance companies to provide coverage.
3. No state-owned insurance company offers coverage, only private insurance companies.

You can obtain workers' compensation insurance from an independent insurance agent or Pinnacol Assurance. Pinnacol is not a state agency, but is a quasi-independent, nonprofit insurance company established by state law that sells workers' compensation insurance at cost. See Appendix C for contact information.

> You cannot substitute workers' compensation insurance with other types of insurance, like general liability and health and accident insurance.

You cannot substitute workers' compensation insurance with other types of insurance, like general liability and health and accident insurance. Also, if you are a sole proprietor or a partner in a partnership, you are not required by law to obtain coverage for yourself. For more information on the workers' compensation requirements for Colorado, contact the Colorado Department of Labor and Employment, as referenced in Appendix C. Chapter 7 provides more in-depth information about workers' compensation as well as information on how you can reduce your costs.

To more fully understand the ins and outs of workers' compensation, obtain a copy of *Ultimate Guide to Workers' Compensation Insurance: Secrets of Reducing Workers' Compensation Costs* by Edward J. Priz (Entrepreneur Press, 2005).

Safety and Health Regulations

As part of the U.S. Department of Labor, the Occupational Safety and Health Administration (OSHA) creates regulations and enforcement practices to render the nation's workplaces safe and healthy for employees. Basically, any business engaging in interstate commerce that has one or more employees is responsible for complying with OSHA standards.

Some of businesses are exempt from OSHA compliance and include:

- Self-employed persons;
- Farms on which only immediate members of the farm employer's family are employed; and
- Working conditions regulated by other federal agencies under other federal statutes.

Since many of the OSHA standards are specific to certain types of industry, equipment, substances, environments, or conditions, it is important to have a clear understanding of OSHA regulations that apply to your business. The administration has established and is continually upgrading legally enforceable standards that fall into four major industry categories—general industry, maritime, construction, and agriculture. To help you better understand the federal OSHA standards that may apply to your business, consider hiring a professional safety consultant or refer to a comprehensive reference on workplace safety programs. Your local OSHA division of the U.S. Department of Labor can provide you with two helpful publications:

> Since many of the OSHA standards are specific to certain types of industry, equipment, substances, environments, or conditions, it is important to have a clear understanding of OSHA regulations

- *All About OSHA*, OSHA 2056
- *Employer Rights and Responsibilities Following an OSHA Inspection*, OSHA 3000

Check Appendix B to find out how you can contact the OSHA office nearest you. Both of these publications are also available online.

One requirement that you should be aware of is the need to keep a record of industrial injuries and illnesses. All employers with 11 or more employees are required to maintain specified records of all occupational injuries and illnesses as they occur on OSHA Form 300, *Log of Work-Related Injuries and Illnesses*, and OSHA Form 300A, *Summary of Work-Related Injuries and Illnesses*. However, this recordkeeping is not required for employers in retail trade, finance, insurance, real estate, and service industries. Further, employers must complete a detailed report for each occupational death, injury, or illness on OSHA Form 301, *Injury and Illness Incident Report*. The OSHA

Recordkeeping Handbook is available online (Appendix B). Recordkeeping Requirements for the Occupational Injuries and Illnesses, from the U.S. Department of Labor. Although you will not be required to send the reports to the government, you should have them available in case OSHA inspects your business.

Some states have their own occupational health and safety programs. Colorado is not one of these states. Your Colorado business must comply with federal OSHA standards as regulated by the state. The OSHA requirements include:

- Posting specific notices in your employees' work area pertaining to safety and health on the job,
- Keeping accurate records of all job-related injuries or illnesses, and
- Reporting the injuries or illnesses to the appropriate agencies.

Through a state-funded program at Colorado State University, your business can receive free consultation. You will get guidance on identifying or correcting any safety or health issues. To learn more about OSHA rules, contact the U.S. Department of Labor/OSHA (Appendix B) or the Colorado State University program (Appendix C).

Environmental Regulations

If your business handles hazardous materials, uses natural resources, or expels anything to air, water or land, you could be subject to dozens of federal, state, and local laws

Environmental protection is one of the fastest-growing areas of legislation relating to small business today. If your business handles hazardous materials, uses natural resources, or expels anything to air, water, or land, you could be subject to dozens of federal, state, and local laws that will regulate how you do business. You should become familiar with the laws that may affect your business regarding clean air and water.

Just as important, conserving, recycling, reducing waste, and being environmentally friendly will save you hundreds to thousands of dollars each year. These "green" policies will establish your reputation with your customers as a socially responsible, environmentally sound business.

The Environmental Protection Agency (EPA) is the federal agency that enforces environmental laws and regulations. Colorado has a state agency, the Colorado Department of Public Health and Environment, that represents the EPA. Contact this department or the EPA regional office in Denver and request information about services, permits, and publications. See Appendix B and Appendix C for contact information.

Further, the Colorado Small Business Ombudsman may help you stay informed about potential problems you may encounter because of the federal or state legislation regarding the environment. Contact information is in Appendix C.

Chapter Wrap-Up

To get a jump-start on your duties as an employer means to understand what lies ahead before you post your first job opening. As an employer in Colorado, you will be subject to numerous state and federal laws that govern employment. Although it probably wasn't part of your original job description, you must function as a personnel manager until your business grows to a size that warrants hiring such an individual. There are a multitude of state and federal agencies that can assist you with personnel management information.

Your main concerns will center on what is dubbed as fair employment practices. Fair employment means that you will comply with both federal and state laws regarding things like minimum wage, overtime pay, equal pay, employing minors, and wage reporting. In addition to these practices, you will be required to have a basic knowledge of what are known as anti-discrimination laws. The various acts described in this chapter—dealing with affirmative action, ADA, immigration, and family leave, to name a few—just scratch the surface. However, as you get to know these common federal laws, you will gain a bigger picture perspective that will help you better understand the sometimes elusive phrase "personnel management."

Further, as an employer in Colorado, you must withhold payments for Social Security and Medicare (FICA) and federal and state income taxes from the wages you pay to all covered employees. To protect your business and your employees, you must also comply with state workers' compensation requirements.

Of course, as a new business you may not need to hire anyone for a while. However, if you do need employees to get your business running, it is essential that you understand what it means to be an employer in Colorado. Use this chapter as a quick reference for future employment issues. Also, refer to Chapter 6 for a more detailed discussion of human resources management.

Employer Duties Checklist

- ❏ Register with the Colorado Department of Revenue to withhold state and federal income taxes from the compensation paid to your employees and learn the requirements for submitting reports.
- ❏ Contact the Colorado Department of Revenue to register to pay state taxes and Colorado Department of Labor and Employment to submit quarterly reports for the unemployment coverage for your employees.
- ❏ File with the Internal Revenue Service to pay federal unemployment taxes and submit quarterly reports.
- ❏ Determine your obligations to carry workers' compensation insurance coverage.
- ❏ Review state and federal labor laws to determine the personnel-related policies your business will follow.
- ❏ Check with the Environmental Protection Agency and the Colorado Department of Public Health and Environment to identify the environmental regulations your business must follow regarding all air, water, and solid waste standards.
- ❏ Check with the regional office of the U.S. Department of Labor/ OSHA to identify the safety and health regulations your business must comply with if you have employees.

12 | *Sources of Business Assistance*

A s you've learned so far, starting a business is hard work. You can make your life easier by getting to know the resources available to you and by learning how to use them effectively in your start-up. In fact, at the heart of your venture are knowledge and know-how—and these amount to power.

If you want the power to successfully start your business, you will seek help from qualified business experts. For today's burgeoning entrepreneur, this help is closer than you think.

Numerous federal, state, and private agencies and organizations are available to assist you. This chapter introduces you to the most important and most helpful organizations. Take the time to familiarize yourself with each resource—you will double your investment in time once you know how and where to get the answers you need to start and grow your business.

Federal Resources

Your biggest source of help comes from the federal government. Your government watches out for small businesses and wants to see them grow and prosper in the 21st century.

For every federal regulation and legal requirement that the federal government places on America's small businesses, there exists at least one federal agency that will go the extra mile to help business owners get their businesses started on the right track. Thus, your first points of contact should be one or more of the following agencies:

- The U.S. Small Business Administration (SBA), which includes the Service Corps of Retired Executives (SCORE), small business development centers, and small business incubators;
- The U.S. Department of Commerce, which includes numerous bureaus and administrations like the Census Bureau and the Economic Development Administration;
- The Internal Revenue Service (IRS); and
- The Equal Employment Opportunity Commission (EEOC).

You will find that many of these agencies offer state-specific business assistance and have state-level offices to better serve your business needs. See Appendix B for further information.

U.S. Small Business Administration

Formed in 1953, the U.S. Small Business Administration (SBA) provides assistance to entrepreneurs who are starting and expanding their own businesses. Many of the SBA programs and services are free of charge and include:

- Financial assistance through numerous loan and loan guarantee programs;
- Assistance with government procurement of small business products and services;
- Minority business assistance programs;
- Counseling on a variety of topics from marketing your products and services, to managing your business, to developing a business plan; and
- Educating entrepreneurs about international trade, technology, and research.

The SBA is easy to reach and is praised by numerous business owners as being one of the easiest government agencies to deal with. Colorado has a regional office and a district office to serve your needs; see Appendix B for addresses and phone numbers. Also, you can quickly access a warehouse of information by using one of the SBA's telephone hotline or online services.

A computerized telephone message system is available from SBA Answer Desk and can be accessed 24 hours a day, seven days a week. This toll-free number will put you in touch with operators who will answer your start-up questions and give you guidance on how to get additional assistance. Operators are available Monday through Friday, from 9:00 a.m. to 5:00 p.m. (eastern standard time).

Another way to get help from the SBA is by using the SBA Online Library—a Web site that provides the most current and accurate information on starting and running a business. The publications page lists more than 200 publications that you can download.

> A computerized telephone message system is available from SBA Answer Desk and can be accessed 24 hours a day, seven days a week.

The SBA home page contains detailed information on its services and other business services and provides a direct link to the SBA Online Library. For more information, log on at www.sba.gov. If you prefer to contact the SBA Answer Desk directly, use the phone number listed in Appendix B.

In addition to offering a myriad of services for the new or expanding business owner, the SBA provides business counseling and training through other service programs as described below.

SERVICE CORPS OF RETIRED EXECUTIVES (SCORE)

Sponsored by the SBA, the Service Corps of Retired Executives (SCORE) has more than 10,000 volunteers in nearly 400 offices throughout the nation. These retired businesspeople offer expert advice based on their many years of firsthand experience in virtually every phase of starting and operating a business. To set up a free appointment with a SCORE counselor nearest you, call your SBA field office or contact your nearest small business development center (SBDC). SBDCs are covered in more detail later in this chapter.

SMALL BUSINESS INCUBATORS

Although relatively new, small business incubators have become a breeding ground for a number of start-up businesses throughout the United States. Business incubation is a dynamic process of business enterprise development. Incubators nurture young firms, helping them to survive and grow during the start-up period when they are most vulnerable. These incubators sometimes offer a rent lower than market rate and shared housing with other new enterprises in one facility. These businesses can then share conference rooms, secretarial help, accounting expertise, research personnel, and on-site financial management counseling. Then, once a business is ready to stand on its own and the owner wants to relocate, the incubator program will help find a new location.

To qualify for participation in a small business incubator program, your business will have to go through a selection process. As part of this process, qualified individuals will review your business plan to determine if your business will fit into their program. To find out if there is an SBA-sponsored incubator program in Colorado, contact your local SBA office.

The National Business Incubation Association (NBIA) provides members with the resources needed to develop and manage successful business incubators. Whether you are exploring the concept of a business incubator for your community or already have an established incubation program, NBIA services are designed to keep you apprised of industry best practices and save you time and money.

> The National Business Incubation Association (NBIA) provides members with the resources needed to develop and manage successful business incubators.

With approximately 800 members worldwide, the NBIA is the largest membership organization of incubator developers and managers. Servicing technology, industrial, mixed-use, economic empowerment, and industry-specific incubators since 1985, the association provides members with critical tools and promotes awareness of the value of incubators for economic development. The NBIA's overall objectives include:

- Providing information, research, and networking resources to help members develop and manage successful incubation programs;
- Sponsoring annual conferences and training programs;
- Building awareness of business incubation as a valuable business development tool; and
- Informing and educating leaders, potential supporters, and stakeholders of the significant benefits of incubation.

To find out about private sector incubators, contact the NBIA. Refer to Appendix B for the contact information.

MINORITY ENTERPRISE DEVELOPMENT

The SBA offers two programs to foster business ownership for those who are socially and economically disadvantaged.

- *8(a) Small Disadvantaged Business Development—www.sba.gov/8abd.* Qualified minority small business owners can take advantage of the 8(a) program, which offers business development assistance through federal procurement opportunities.

- *7(j) Management and Technical Assistance—www.sba.gov/gcbd/7j.html.* The 7(j) program provides management and technical training in four main areas: accounting, marketing, proposal/bid preparation, and industry-specific technical assistance.

U.S. Department of Commerce

The U.S. Department of Commerce has developed a number of programs that assist small business owners. These programs are headed up by several bureaus and administrations:

- *Bureau of Economic Analysis,* which reports on the state of the U.S. economy and provides technical information that helps calculate the gross national product figures.
- *Census Bureau,* which produces statistical information in the forms of catalogs, guides, and directories that cover things such as U.S. population and housing, agriculture, state and local expenditures, transportation, and industries.
- *Economic Development Administration,* which helps generate new jobs, protect existing jobs, and stimulate commercial and industrial growth in economically distressed areas.
- *International Trade Administration,* which helps American exporters find assistance in locating, gaining access to, and developing foreign markets.
- *Minority Business Development Agency,* which helps minority business owners in their attempts to overcome the social and economic disadvantages that may have limited past participation in business.
- *Patent and Trademark Office*, which will help protect new products and trade names.

Although the department doesn't have the one-on-one relationship with small business owners that the SBA does, it does provide information that can help your business profit. To learn more about the U.S. Department of Commerce, contact it via phone or mail at the address listed in Appendix B.

> The U.S. Department of Commerce has developed a number of programs that assist small business owners.

U.S. Chamber of Commerce

The U.S. Chamber of Commerce was established in 1912 at the suggestion of President William Howard Taft to provide a strong link between business and government. Since then it has played a vital role in helping businesses, especially small businesses, succeed and prosper. In addition, the chamber represents businesses on critical legislative and regulatory issues.

One of the primary roles of the U.S. Chamber of Commerce is to help the public understand the danger that results from excessive government intervention in the economy. Costly and far-reaching federal programs and mandates on businesses raise the costs of doing business and weaken the competitive position of the U.S. in the global marketplace. To serve the needs of small businesses, the U.S. Chamber of Commerce has developed programs that are both affordable and effective. As a member, you can:

- Keep up to date on legislation that will affect your business and get tips and advice on running it more successfully, from the Chamber's monthly magazine, *uschamber.com*;
- Get news on legislative and regulatory developments, economic forecasts and analysis, and highlights from online small business toolkits, from the Chamber's weekly small business e-newsletter, *uschamber.com weekly*;
- Access information on small business legislative issues and SBA loans through the chamber's Small Business Center, with four sections— Toolkits (in-depth, specific information and advice on such topics as hiring, finance, and office management), Issues (policy areas that most affect small businesses), Business Documents and Forms (model business documents, templates, checklists, and official government forms, free to members), and Member Center (gateway to benefits, discounts, and services available only to members);
- Receive *Center News*, a monthly e-newsletter from The Center for Workforce Preparation (a non-profit affiliate of the U.S. Chamber of Commerce), with information about current workforce development initiatives, promising practices in training and education for employees, and the latest trends and research; and
- *Receive Corporate Citizenship*, a bimonthly e-newsletter devoted to covering responsible business practices and providing insight on the current trends, research, and policy developments that impact the active role of business in society.

To learn more about the U.S. Chamber of Commerce, you can go to its Web site or contact it via phone or mail. The information is in Appendix B.

LOCAL CHAMBERS OF COMMERCE

If you want to learn more about the region or community where you plan to locate your business, then turn to the local chamber of commerce for assistance. The staff will give you information about general business conditions, available space and rentals, and local business organizations and associations. Usually chambers of commerce are a good place for referrals. To locate the chamber nearest you, look in the white pages of your telephone directory.

Internal Revenue Service (IRS)

The Internal Revenue Service (IRS) has developed several programs to help you stay informed and one step ahead of the taxes for which you are responsible as a small business owner. Through its TeleTax program, the IRS offers quick and easy access to tax help on about 150 tax topics. In fact, you can order forms, instructions, and publications toll-free by phone. See Appendix B for contact information for the TeleTax program.

> The Internal Revenue Service (IRS) has developed several programs to help you stay informed and one step ahead of the taxes for which you are responsible.

If you prefer, go online to get the forms and information you need. The IRS's Web site contains not only forms, instructions, and publications, but also educational materials, IRS press releases and fact sheets, and answers to frequently asked questions. For more information on IRS assistance for your business, refer to Appendix B.

Equal Employment Opportunity Commission (EEOC)

As described in Chapter 11, a multitude of duties awaits employers in Colorado. If your business has employees, you will need to understand the laws that cover civil rights, age discrimination, and equal pay. These laws were created and are enforced by the Equal Employment Opportunity Commission (EEOC).

Created by Congress, the EEOC enforces Title VII of the Civil Rights Act of 1964. In addition, since 1979 the EEOC has also enforced the Age Discrimination in Employment Act of 1967, the Equal Pay Act of 1963, and Sections 501 and 505 of the Rehabilitation Act of 1973. In 1992, the EEOC began enforcing the Americans with Disabilities Act (ADA).

Every employer in the United States, including all employment agencies, labor organizations, and joint labor-management committees, must post and keep posted in a conspicuous place upon their premises a notice that describes the applicable provisions of Title VII and the ADA. Such notice must be posted in a prominent and accessible place where notices to employees, applicants, and members are customarily maintained. Failure to comply may result in fines to your business.

To obtain a poster or to learn how the laws mentioned above affect your business, consider obtaining a copy of *Laws Enforced by the U.S. Equal*

Employment Opportunity Commission. To order this free publication and poster, use the toll-free phone number listed in Appendix B.

State Resources

In order to attract new business and keep existing business, most states have adopted a "small business-friendly" philosophy. In line with this philosophy, you will find numerous state agency programs and services—most of them free-of-charge—simply for the asking. Take a moment to get to know what Colorado agencies are available to you and how you can best use their services. Addresses and phone numbers for the state agencies listed below are provided in Appendix C.

Colorado Secretary of State

The Colorado Secretary of State provides licensing and general information on the different types of business—sole proprietorship, partnership, corporation, limited liability company (LLC), and so on.

Colorado Office of Economic Development and International Trade

The Office of Economic Development and International Trade (OED) provides technical assistance on location, redevelopment, exporting, and other business needs. The OED also loans money to businesses in rural areas through revolving loan funds. The Colorado Business Center is operated under the auspices of this office and acts as a one-stop business assistance shop for state licensing and registration requirements.

Colorado Department of Revenue

The Colorado Department of Revenue answers all tax-related questions and offers many publications to businesses, in print and on the agency Web site. Of course, the Colorado Department of Revenue can also provide you with the necessary forms to cover all your business tax needs.

Colorado Department of Labor and Employment

The Colorado Department of Labor and Employment will answer questions regarding state labor laws affecting employers, including wage-hour regulations, child labor, minimum wage, and discrimination laws.

> In order to attract new business and keep existing business, most states have adopted a "small business-friendly" philosophy.

Colorado Department of Regulatory Agencies

The Civil Rights Division of the Colorado Department of Regulatory Agencies can help you understand and comply with the family and medical leave law requirements. It's also the place to start when checking into business and occupational licenses.

Small Business Development Centers

The small business development center (SBDC) network is a cooperative effort of the U.S. SBA, the state academic community, the private sector, and state and local governments. Over 900 SBDCs are located in colleges and universities throughout the nation. Similar to a SCORE counselor, your local SBDC can offer advice on a variety of start-up issues. Frequently, your local SBDC will sponsor business-oriented seminars. In 2005, SBDCs provided counseling at more than 1,100 service locations. To find the nearest SBDC, contact the lead center listed in Appendix B.

The Colorado SBDC network is dedicated to helping small businesses throughout Colorado achieve their goals of growth, expansion, innovation, increased productivity, management improvement, and success. Regulatory, management, financial, and marketing experts work in partnership with entrepreneurs to help them succeed.

> The Colorado SBDC network is dedicated to helping small businesses throughout Colorado achieve their goals of growth, expansion, innovation, increased productivity, management improvement, and success.

Private Sources of Help

In addition to the various state and federal resources, you will find a wealth of business information from private organizations and agencies. The private resources listed here represent some of the most popular and well-established organizations and by no means represent all the private resources available in Colorado. To learn about other private sources of help, do an Internet search or contact your local library for assistance.

State Business Publications

Colorado has many trade and business journals that will help you stay current on business activities and issues in the state. For a partial list of these helpful business publications, see Appendix C.

National Federation of Independent Businesses (NFIB)

The National Federation of Independent Businesses (NFIB) is the oldest and largest small business advocacy group in the nation. This nonprofit organization is the only business organization with the strength of a combined federal and state lobbying program. Representing approximately 600,000 small and independent business owners, NFIB has offices in every state capital and in Washington, DC.

You can become a member of NFIB. As a member you will receive:

- A bimonthly publication called *My Business*, which features articles geared toward the interests of small business owners;
- Copies of state and federal mandate ballots that show you how NFIB's legislative lobbying agenda is established; and
- An annual publication, *How Congress Voted*, which gives details of the Congressional voting record and how these votes affected and will affect you as a small business owner.
- Three e-mail newsletters: *MyBUSINESS Minute*, *VOICE*, and *InPolitics*.

To learn more about NFIB, see Appendix C.

National Association for the Self-Employed (NASE)

Another helpful membership organization is the National Association for the Self-Employed (NASE). Since 1981, NASE has established one of the largest business associations of its kind. Attributing its success to the "strength in numbers" theory, NASE has more than 250,000 members.

As a member of NASE, you will receive a variety of benefits, including free access to knowledgeable small business consultants via ShopTalk 800®—a toll-free hotline where you can get advice on issues that affect your business—and a bimonthly newsletter, *Self-Employed America*®, which gives you valuable information on how small businesses can survive and prosper in today's competitive environment.

NASE offers it members a chance to get involved with small business advocacy issues through its Micro-Business Crusader program.

NASE offers it members a chance to get involved with small business advocacy issues through its Micro-Business Crusader program. Further, members will have access to medical and dental plan savings, travel savings, and discounts on special business training, eye care, and legal services. To contact NASE, use the address and phone number in Appendix C.

National Association of Women Business Owners (NAWBO)

The National Association of Women Business Owners (NAWBO), headquartered in the Washington, DC metropolitan area, is the only dues-based national organization representing the interests of all women entrepreneurs in all types of businesses. The organization currently has over 75 chapters. Membership is open to sole proprietors, partners, and corporate owners with day-to-day management responsibility. Active members who live in a chapter area automatically join both chapter and national. Those who do not live in a chapter area join as at-large members. Contact information is provided in Appendix C.

National Minority Business Council, Inc. (NMBC)

This is a not-for-profit organization of small businesses that are owned by members of minorities and by women. Its primary goal is to promote the success and profitability of its members by providing services, programs, advocacy, and networking support. One of its programs is an International Trade Program that provides technical assistance, education, and training and acts as a clearinghouse for business leads and information on export and import. Contact information is provided in Appendix C.

Latin Business Association

The primary purpose of this organization is to promote the growth of Latino-owned businesses by connecting its members to business opportunities through automated business matching, networking events, informative e-newsletters, seminars and workshops, and its relationships within the business community. The LBA has a chapter in Mexico and partnerships with Chambers of Commerce in Central and South America. Appendix C provides contact information.

Hispanic Business Women's Alliance (HBWA)

This is an online community of Hispanic women who are entrepreneurs, professionals, consultants, executives, inventors, and investors throughout North America, Latin America, the Caribbean, and Spain who are interested in doing business and collaborating with each other. HBWA was established on the premise that few Hispanic women have all the resources they need to start or expand businesses and the belief that, no matter what they may need, there is most likely another Hispanic businesswoman who can help them succeed faster. Contact information is provided in Appendix C.

Asian Women in Business (AWIB)

This not-for-profit membership organization was founded in 1995 to help Asian women realize their entrepreneurial potential. AWIB fills a vital need for women who need information, education, and networking opportunities to start or expand businesses. It provides information, education, and networking opportunities for Asian women starting or expanding businesses. Appendix C provides contact information.

13 | *Welcome to Colorado*

While this quiet Western state is known to most of the world as home to some of the most spectacular mountains in creation (there are 53 peaks that tower more than 14,000 feet above sea level in Colorado's stretch of the Rocky Mountains), Colorado is still recognized by many Americans primarily for its glamorous, exclusive, star-studded ski resorts. Mention an impending trip to Colorado, and someone is certain to sigh dreamily about Vail or Aspen or Steamboat Springs, even if he or she doesn't know anyone who has ever been there. But Colorado is much more than a fabled playland for the rich and famous, as you will learn. So slip off your ski boots and snuggle up to the fire as we go over some of the reasons you are smart to be starting your business in this jeweled state.

Get to Know the Demographics of Colorado

Demographics, or the vital statistics of human populations, should be of great interest to any current or prospective small business owner. Things like size, growth, density, and distribution of the populations of the major counties and cities in Colorado will affect the way you do business—from your marketing strategy to how you will obtain financing.

The major source of demographic research for the United States is the U.S. Census Bureau. The major source of Colorado-specific data (including that from the U.S. Census Bureau) is the Colorado Department of Local Affairs. This department is responsible for keeping track of demographic data from numerous state and federal sources; it is a good source of population projections, economic shifts, and other data invaluable to your business planning decisions. Take a moment to understand the influence of the demographic makeup of Colorado on your proposed business. Start with a look at three main factors: population, major industries, and income and consumption rates.

Population Statistics

Colorado's population has increased more rapidly than the national average since the 1940s. In 1994–95, Colorado had the eighth-highest growth rate in the nation. Most of the growth experienced is from net in-migration—that is, more people entering the state than leaving it—and this migration rate can change dramatically from year to year, making Colorado demographics not easily predictable.

> Colorado's population has increased more rapidly than the national average since the 1940s. In 1994–95, Colorado had the eighth-highest growth rate in the nation.

TABLE 1: POPULATION STATISTICS

		Colorado	**United States**
Resident population	2000	4,301,261	281,421,906
	2005	4,665,177	296,410,404
Resident population change	2000–2005	8.4%	5.3%
Percent under 18 years old	2004	25.6%	25.0%
Percent 65 years or older	2004	9.8%	12.4%
Foreign-born persons	2004	9.7%	11.9%
High school graduates, age 25+	2004	88.8%	85.0%
Households	2000	1,658,238	105,480,101
Land area (square miles)	2006	103,718	3,537,438
Persons per square mile	2005	45	79.6
Population projections	2015	4,833,000	310,160,000
	2025	5,188,000	329,048,000

Source: U.S. Census Bureau

The state did not reach a population above 5 million by 2025, as expected. Colorado ranks 47th of the 50 states in the percentage of population age 65 or older. A healthy 65 percent of the population is of work age—good news if you will be hiring. The general population in Colorado is also better educated and more likely to be in the labor force than are the populations of most states.

Business and Employment

The state is a hub for communications and transportation. Colorado also has a strong manufacturing base, but the service sector is the largest employment base, led by business services and professional service sectors primarily composed of health, engineering, and computer-related services. The service industries outpace just about every other industry.

TABLE 2: BUSINESS AND EMPLOYMENT STATISTICS

		Colorado	United States
Private nonfarm establishments	2001	139,225	7,095,302
Private nonfarm employment	2001	1,986,570	115,061,184
Private nonfarm employment change	2000-2001	3.8%	0.9%
Manufacturers shipments ($1000)	1997	40,012,820	3,842,061,405
Retail sales ($1000)	1997	40,536,034	2,460,886,012
Retail sales per capita	1997	$10,417	$9,190
Civilian population employed	1990	67.4%	62.8%
	1997	70.4%	63.8%
Average annual pay	1997	$30,067	$30,336
	2004	$40,276	$39,354

Source: U.S. Census Bureau

Almost 90 percent of all Colorado establishments fall into the "very small" category, with fewer than 20 employees. The sectors with the largest establishments (more than 500 employees) are services and manufacturing. Colorado also has more (or more accessible) doctors and hospitals than many regions of the surrounding states, so its facilities serve out-of-state populations as well as its own. But the keys to this state are a forward-looking research sector (Colorado has a high concentration of science and high-tech research and development industries) and a highly diversified economy. The smaller business sectors have played a big part in holding Colorado together in the past, when the major industries weren't doing so well.

> Almost 90 percent of all Colorado establishments fall into the "very small" category, with fewer than 20 employees.

Although Colorado's labor boom of the 1990s—led by record employment in the construction and high-tech fields—was beginning to decline at the turn of the new millennium, the events of September 11, 2001 sent job growth and the overall state economy into a tailspin. Colorado was hit hard by the economic repercussions of the attack, particularly due to its dependence on tourism. In 2002, travel spending, which accounts for 8 percent of all Colorado's jobs, dropped as much as 20 percent. Employment in Colorado dropped by 4.4 percent from early 2001 to mid-2003, when employment in the U.S. dropped by 2.2 percent. Other factors, including the national recession, weak business spending, and the collapse of the telecom industry, resulted in the greatest loss of jobs in the state since the 1950s.

The good news is that the downturn has resulted in an abundant and eager labor pool from which to choose. In 2005 Colorado ranked 13th among the states in job growth, with job growth of 2.1 percent—its best year since 2000, before the recession.

Income and Consumption Rates

Colorado residents have considerably higher median household incomes than Americans in general, and this income, as indicated in Table 3, has been increasing steadily. The average personal income in Colorado is also higher than the national average. It is probably not surprising, given their relatively high income levels, that Colorado households spend more than the national average on retail goods and that Colorado ranks slightly above the national average in home ownership rates.

> Colorado residents have considerably higher median household incomes than Americans in general

TABLE 3: INCOME AND CONSUMPTION STATISTICS

		Colorado	**United States**
Personal income per capita	2000	$32,434	$29,469
	2004	$36,063	$32,937
Median household income	1999	$47,203	$41,994
	2003	$50,538	$43,564
Persons below poverty	2003	9.8%	12.7%
Energy consumption per capita (million BTUs)	1996	291	349
	2001	287	338
Homeownership rates	2000	68.3%	67.4%
	2004	71.1%	69.0%

Sources: U.S. Census Bureau

According to Table 3, energy consumption by Colorado residents is low, ranking it 39th in the nation in 2001, but this figure may be misleading as it probably reflects the widespread use of woodstoves for heat and cooking. Wood burned for heat or fuel is not as easily quantifiable by cost or by BTUs consumed per capita as are electricity, propane, or natural gas used for the same, especially in a state that is one-quarter covered in forests.

Colorado State Data Center

To break much of this census data down into manageable pieces, the Census Bureau created the State Data Center (SDC) program. Since 1978, state data centers have provided training and technical assistance in accessing and using census data for research, administration, planning, and decision making. Users of this information have ranged from state, county, and local governments to the business community and university researchers. Further, in 1988, the SDC expanded its services through the Business and Industry Data Center (BIDC) program of the U.S. Census Bureau. The BIDC program directly serves businesses through government, academic, and nonprofit organizations.

The Colorado Department of Local Affairs administers the State Data Center. The SDC is a federal-state cooperative program between the U.S. Census Bureau and the state of Colorado and is committed to providing current census data and related products for Colorado. The SDC strives to increase access to and awareness of census data.

You can learn more about the SDC/BIDC programs by contacting the Customer Liaison Office of the U.S. Census Bureau. Refer to Appendix B for the address and phone number of this agency. The contact information for the Colorado State Data Center can be found in Appendix C.

As you get to know the incentives for doing business in Colorado, you will notice how using this statistical information can give you the edge in understanding the potential market and customers for your product or service. The statistics here just begin to scratch the surface; for more detailed analyses and surveys of the makeup of Colorado, contact your state data center.

Incentives for Doing Business in Colorado

Colorado workers are highly trained and educated and are looking for employment that will keep them happy. Colorado provides many investment tax credits, enterprise zone tax credits, and sales tax exemptions. You will find that the state and local tax collections from personal income are less

> Since 1978, state data centers have provided training and technical assistance in accessing and using census data for research, administration, planning, and decision making.

than in the Western states of Washington, Oregon, Utah, Arizona, and California, as well as 31 other states. In 2004 Colorado ranked 41st of all states in per capita corporate income tax revenue, at $52, when the U.S. average was $118. And the state's transportation system—of vital importance to most businesses—is modern and sophisticated, yet simple enough to respond to customer demand.

All these factors ensure that Colorado business owners will stay in Colorado and new business owners will enjoy the many incentives that Colorado has to offer. The next few sections offer more details of the benefits to operating a business in this state.

Overall Business Climate

In its *2006 Development Report Card for the States*, the Corporation for Enterprise Development, an objective and well-respected policy organization in Washington, D.C., awarded Colorado A's in two of the three major indexes—Business Vitality and Development Capacity—and a B in Performance. The report assesses how well each state's economy is doing in more than 70 critical measures ranging from Employment and Resource Efficiency to Entrepreneurial Energy, Quality of Life, and Infrastructure Resources. It ranked Colorado third among the states. It has definitely been recovering well from its slump, which hit after the state had received straight A's for eight consecutive year when no other state had received a perfect report card for more than two consecutive years. This state is serious about attracting, developing, and retaining new businesses.

In 2005, a survey by the Small Business and Entrepreneurship Council (SBEC) in Washington, D.C., ranked Colorado the tenth "most entrepreneur-friendly" state for "policy environments."

Colorado offers numerous marketing, financial, research, and training programs and incentives to help the new businessperson obtain the advice and assistance he or she needs to succeeed. Add to this Colorado's high national standing in terms of wages, cost of living, quality of life, employment opportunities, and the growing importance of the Western states, and you will soon conclude that there is no better time than now to start your business in one of the developing cities of this state. And if you still have doubts, the next few sections should erase them.

> Colorado offers numerous marketing, financial, research, and training programs and incentives to help the new businessperson obtain the advice and assistance.

Access to Markets

Due to its strategic location on the edge of the New West, straddling the Continental Divide, Colorado is a major air travel hub: much of the east-west travel and commerce in America passes through this state. Access to markets will not be a problem; in fact, depending on your markets and needs, you may even find it to be superior to market access in larger states with less efficient systems and facilities.

Start with Denver International Airport (DIA), which opened in 1995 as the first major U.S. airport to be constructed in more than 20 years. DIA has one of the best on-time records of any of the nation's ten busiest airports and ranked second in the world in customer satisfaction among large airports in the most recent Global Airport Satisfaction Index Study[SM]. In addition to DIA, modern airport facilities exist statewide and there is a well-developed network of general aviation airports to serve both business and pleasure travelers.

> Colorado also has over 3,000 miles of Class-1 tracks and intermodal train/truck transfer facilities to efficiently move goods to their destinations without unloading and reloading.

Colorado also has over 3,000 miles of Class-1 tracks and intermodal train/truck transfer facilities to efficiently move goods to their destinations without unloading and reloading. Colorado's central location and interstate highway system helped make the heavily populated "Front Range" area (which includes Denver, Boulder, Colorado Springs, Fort Collins, and Pueblo) a growing distribution point for many wholesalers and retailers. I-25 is the major north-south interstate and I-70 the major east-west interstate. These two, well-maintained arteries ensure quick and efficient transport across the state. Colorado's interstates account for 955 miles of the 9,000-plus miles of the state's highway system.

Best of all, the situation, while good, is not static. Planned growth in the transportation system should encourage even more business growth and ensure continuing great service in the years to come.

Labor Force Outlook

One of the most important things to note about the Colorado labor force is that it is eager and growing. This is good for your business because it means you will have your choice of qualified candidates. Overall, employment showed an impressive 30 percent gain during the '90s and, despite the post-September 11 setbacks, state unemployment rates are at or lower than the national average 5.0 percent for 2005, when the national average was 5.1.

Also important is the fact that many of the new businesses are in high-tech and scientific research areas, which means that current workers are well educated and well trained. And, if your business requires truly specialized employees, the state offers numerous custom training programs to help ensure that workers are available to meet your needs. (See discussion at the end of this chapter.)

Colorado residents on the whole are a remarkably well-educated group. Nearly 90 percent of the adult population (25 years and older) have graduated from high school, and the state had the second-highest percentage of college graduates in the country in 2004: more than 35.5 percent of Colorado adults had at least a bachelor's degree, well above the national average of 27.7 percent.

Tax Structure and Incentives

Colorado's low business taxes are significant incentives for locating in the state. The corporate income tax rate, for example, is a flat 4.63 percent of federally adjusted income—one of the lowest rates in the country. And the definition of "net income" for state tax purposes is so lenient that Colorado ranks lowest in per capita corporate income tax revenue of all states that collect a corporate income tax. In addition, the state's tax policies on foreign corporations (both out-of-state and out-of-country holdings) are exceedingly liberal.

A 2.9 percent sales or use tax is collected on nonfood items; local municipalities may collect up to an additional 4.1 percent sales tax. However, manufacturing firms are offered a significant sales and use tax break on equipment and machine tools, which are not taxed after the first $500 in purchases each calendar year. And all businesses benefit from the fact that no sales or use taxes are collected on component parts, fuels, electricity, newsprint or ink, or packaging materials. Colorado does not assess inventory taxes.

There are many tax credit incentives for investment into the state. If you participate in the Colorado Enterprise Zone Tax Credit Program, you are eligible for numerous credits:

- A $500 credit is available to you for each new full-time employee working within the zone during your first year of operations—and an additional credit of $2,000 per new job for new business facilities located in a designated Enhanced Rural Enterprise Zone.
- An additional $500 credit is available for each new full-time employee working for a manufacturing or processing business that adds value to agricultural goods.
- During the first two years of business within a zone, a $200 credit is allowed for each new full-time employee covered by a company-pro-

> If you participate in the Colorado Enterprise Zone Tax Credit Program, you are eligible for numerous credits.

vided health insurance plan or program, providing more than 50 percent of the cost is borne by the employer.

- A 3 percent investment tax credit against Colorado income taxes may be claimed by businesses making investments in equipment used exclusively in an enterprise zone.
- Enterprise zone businesses are also exempt from the 2.9 percent sales tax for purchases on manufacturing machines and machine tools and tax credit of up to 3 percent is available on research and development activities in an enterprise zone.
- A credit is available for 25 percent of qualified expenditures (up to $50,000) to rehabilitate buildings 20 years or older that have been vacant for at least two years and contributors to qualifying projects within the zones may receive a 50 percent tax credit, up to $100,000.

Colorado has other tax incentive programs, ranging from investment tax credits to sales tax exemptions.

As you might imagine, given the wide variety of credit and incentive programs for enterprise zones alone, this state has other tax incentive programs, ranging from investment tax credits to sales tax exemptions. You can contact the Colorado Office of Economic Development and International Trade for details. Contact information is provided in Appendix C.

Research and Development, Financing, and Support Services

The Colorado Economic Development Commission (EDC) was created by the state legislature to promote economic development. Grants and loans from the economic development fund are approved by the EDC to public and private entities throughout the state to help existing businesses expand and new companies locate in Colorado. For more information on financing options, see Appendix D.

Research

The Colorado legislature created the Colorado Advanced Technology Institute (CATI) in 1983 as the state's science and technology development agency. The goal was to establish Colorado as an acknowledged world leader in selected high-tech industries so that more firms and institutions involved in education, research, product development, and manufacturing in these technologies would locate in the state. Although CATI ended in 1999, the state continues the commitment to technology that has made it a leader.

If your business is in a high-tech field, Colorado's prestigious colleges and universities—notably the University of Colorado, the Colorado School of Mines, and Colorado State University—are another resource you should tap for assistance with research and development issues.

Training

Colorado offers two significant industry-oriented training programs, both through the Office of Economic Development and International Trade, that might be useful to your new or expanding business. Colorado FIRST is a training assistance program developed to encourage businesses to locate in Colorado or businesses currently there to undertake major expansion by assuring them of a trained labor force. Existing Industry is a similar program aimed at encouraging Colorado companies that are implementing new technologies to remain competitive and keep jobs in Colorado. Both are designed particularly for high-paying, long-term positions requiring short-term, job-specific training. Companies are encouraged to coordinate their training through local community colleges and to contribute resources, machinery, and expertise.

Colorado also offers an array of educational and vocational training programs for both youths and adults through the Colorado Community College System (CCCS), *www.cccs.edu*. Training is provided for more than 400 specific occupations, for skills ranging from basic to highly technical.

Other Support

Other initiatives to promote high-tech business development include the following:

- The University of Colorado System has recently made technology transfer a high priority. Its Technology Transfer Office will help identify, protect, package, and license to business the intellectual property and know-how resulting from research.
- The University of Denver's University College offers nontraditional courses that are designed to stimulate new entrepreneurs.
- The University of Colorado-Colorado Springs established the Colorado Institute for Technology Transfer and Implementation (CITTI) in 1990. Its mission is to help creative individuals transform technological ideas into economic opportunities. CITTI enables unique public/private partnerships.

> Colorado offers two significant industry-oriented training programs, both through the Office of Economic Development and International Trade

Additional information on research and support available in Colorado is available through the small business development centers. See Appendix C for contact information. State financing options and incentives are described in Appendix D.

Lifestyle

Once the silver capital of the United States, Colorado has, throughout its history, attracted dreamers and schemers, the rich and powerful and those who merely hoped to be. But it has an even longer history as a land desired by people for the beauty and majesty of its natural features. First settled by the Anasazi, who flourished here from 300 to 1300 A.D., this land was once the home of the Arapaho, Cheyenne, Comanche, Kiowa, and Ute. It was claimed by both France and Spain, fought over by the United States and Mexico, and invaded in the second half of the 19th century by people in search of gold and silver and lead miners, cattle barons, and other settlers with an eye for the richness of the vast geography. History is as close as your back door in this breathtaking state, but a colorful past is by no means all that Colorado has to offer.

> Colorado has, throughout its history, attracted dreamers and schemers, the rich and powerful and those who merely hoped to be.

Colorado boasts a healthy economy and environment, impressive sports and recreational opportunities, respected schools and colleges, responsive government, diverse shopping opportunities, an effective transportation system, ethnic diversity, good neighborhoods, and excellent health care.

Home and Community

First and foremost is the quality of life you can expect here—low state income, sales, and property taxes; a cost of living (including urban housing rental and purchase costs) that is generally comparable to that of most other Western states and cities; and perhaps the lowest utility costs in the West. Colorado communities are very involved in volunteer activities to help area churches, schools, governments, hospitals, service groups, and nonprofit organizations.

Recreation

The state is probably best known for the Rocky Mountains, whose steep peaks form the Continental Divide. People travel from all over the world to see the mountains that are so high they split our country—shedding rivers to the Pacific on one side and to the Gulf of Mexico on the other—but there are many other exciting things to see and do. You can visit Mesa Verde National Park and see the Anasazi cliff dwellings, visit dozens of museums, explore breathtaking sandstone formations, take a ride on the historic railways, tour a gold mine, or enjoy one of the many festivals or events. For the outdoor enthusiast, Colorado offers hiking trails, rock climbing, snow skiing, water skiing, and various other exciting activities. If you don't like the outdoors, then take a look at some of the great indoor adventures that Colorado has to offer.

Culture

The Central City Opera Summer Festival draws tourists and residents alike with its continued artistic excellence. You can also visit the Boulder Ballet Ensemble and enjoy one of its many shows throughout the year, including the Nutcracker, Coppelia, and the children's favorite—Peter and the Wolf. You can obtain a Colorado Vacation Guide online at www.colorado.com or through your local chamber of commerce or business assistance center for a comprehensive list of where and when things are happening in Colorado.

Chapter Wrap-Up

Colorado is a technically and culturally advanced state with a fast-paced lifestyle. If you're looking for a state that will give you a chance in the business world, Colorado has it all, from a great tax system to educated and motivated workers. Colorado offers many incentives for business owners and many services to ease business start-up.

Map of Colorado

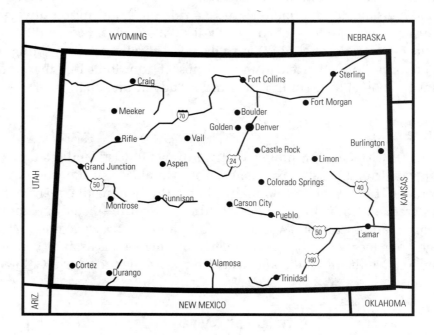

A | *Forms You'll Need to Get Started*

This appendix contains many of the referenced forms. The table identifies the chapter in which each form is mentioned and the page on which it is located in Appendix A. The government forms reproduced here must not be used for submission. Obtain full-sized forms from the appropriate government agency for that purpose.

Form 2553. Election by a Small Business Corporation

Form **2553** (Rev. March 2005) Department of the Treasury Internal Revenue Service	**Election by a Small Business Corporation** (Under section 1362 of the Internal Revenue Code) ▶ See Parts II and III on back and the separate instructions. ▶ The corporation may either send or fax this form to the IRS. See page 2 of the instructions.	OMB No. 1545-0146

Notes: 1. *Do not file Form 1120S*, U.S. Income Tax Return for an S Corporation, for any tax year before the year the election takes effect.
2. *This election to be an S corporation can be accepted only if all the tests are met under* **Who May Elect** *on page 1 of the instructions; all shareholders have signed the consent statement; an officer has signed this form; and the exact name and address of the corporation and other required form information are provided.*

Part I	**Election Information**		
Please Type or Print	Name (see instructions)	**A** Employer identification number	
	Number, street, and room or suite no. (If a P.O. box, see instructions.)	**B** Date incorporated	
	City or town, state, and ZIP code	**C** State of incorporation	

D Check the applicable box(es) if the corporation, after applying for the EIN shown in **A** above, changed its name ☐ or address ☐

E Election is to be effective for tax year beginning (month, day, year) . . . . ▶   /   /

F Name and title of officer or legal representative who the IRS may call for more information

G Telephone number of officer or legal representative
(   )

H If this election takes effect for the first tax year the corporation exists, enter month, day, and year of the **earliest** of the following: (1) date the corporation first had shareholders, (2) date the corporation first had assets, or (3) date the corporation began doing business . . . . ▶   /   /

I Selected tax year: Annual return will be filed for tax year ending (month and day) ▶ ....

If the tax year ends on any date other than December 31, except for a 52-53-week tax year ending with reference to the month of December, complete Part II on the back. If the date you enter is the ending date of a 52-53-week tax year, write "52-53-week year" to the right of the date.

J Name and address of each shareholder or former shareholder required to consent to the election. (See the instructions for column K)	**K** Shareholders' Consent Statement. Under penalties of perjury, we declare that we consent to the election of the above-named corporation to be an S corporation under section 1362(a) and that we have examined this consent statement, including accompanying schedules and statements, and to the best of our knowledge and belief, it is true, correct, and complete. We understand our consent is binding and may not be withdrawn after the corporation has made a valid election. (Sign and date below.)		**L** Stock owned or percentage of ownership (see instructions)		**M** Social security number or employer identification number (see instructions)	**N** Shareholder's tax year ends (month and day)
	Signature	Date	Number of shares or percentage of ownership	Date(s) acquired		

Under penalties of perjury, I declare that I have examined this election, including accompanying schedules and statements, and to the best of my knowledge and belief, it is true, correct, and complete.

Signature of officer ▶   Title ▶   Date ▶

For Paperwork Reduction Act Notice, see page 4 of the instructions.   Cat. No. 18629R   Form **2553** (Rev. 3-2005)

Form 2553. Election by a Small Business Corporation (continued)

Form 2553 (Rev. 3-2005)   Page **2**

Part II   **Selection of Fiscal Tax Year** (All corporations using this part must complete item O and item P, Q, or R.)

O   Check the applicable box to indicate whether the corporation is:

    1. ☐ A new corporation **adopting** the tax year entered in item I, Part I.

    2. ☐ An existing corporation **retaining** the tax year entered in item I, Part I.

    3. ☐ An existing corporation **changing** to the tax year entered in item I, Part I.

P   Complete item P if the corporation is using the automatic approval provisions of Rev. Proc. 2002-38, 2002-22 I.R.B. 1037, to request **(1)** a natural business year (as defined in section 5.05 of Rev. Proc. 2002-38) or **(2)** a year that satisfies the ownership tax year test (as defined in section 5.06 of Rev. Proc. 2002-38). Check the applicable box below to indicate the representation statement the corporation is making.

    1. Natural Business Year ▶ ☐ I represent that the corporation is adopting, retaining, or changing to a tax year that qualifies as its natural business year as defined in section 5.05 of Rev. Proc. 2002-38 and has attached a statement verifying that it satisfies the 25% gross receipts test (see instructions for content of statement). I also represent that the corporation is not precluded by section 4.02 of Rev. Proc. 2002-38 from obtaining automatic approval of such adoption, retention, or change in tax year.

    2. Ownership Tax Year ▶ ☐ I represent that shareholders (as described in section 5.06 of Rev. Proc. 2002-38) holding more than half of the shares of the stock (as of the first day of the tax year to which the request relates) of the corporation have the same tax year or are concurrently changing to the tax year that the corporation adopts, retains, or changes to per item I, Part I, and that such tax year satisfies the requirement of section 4.01(3) of Rev. Proc. 2002-38. I also represent that the corporation is not precluded by section 4.02 of Rev. Proc. 2002-38 from obtaining automatic approval of such adoption, retention, or change in tax year.

Note: *If you do not use item P and the corporation wants a fiscal tax year, complete either item Q or R below. Item Q is used to request a fiscal tax year based on a business purpose and to make a back-up section 444 election. Item R is used to make a regular section 444 election.*

Q   Business Purpose—To request a fiscal tax year based on a business purpose, check box Q1. See instructions for details including payment of a user fee. You may also check box Q2 and/or box Q3.

    1. Check here ▶ ☐ if the fiscal year entered in item I, Part I, is requested under the prior approval provisions of Rev. Proc. 2002-39, 2002-22 I.R.B. 1046. Attach to Form 2553 a statement describing the relevant facts and circumstances and, if applicable, the gross receipts from sales and services necessary to establish a business purpose. See the instructions for details regarding the gross receipts from sales and services. If the IRS proposes to disapprove the requested fiscal year, do you want a conference with the IRS National Office?
    ☐ Yes   ☐ No

    2. Check here ▶ ☐ to show that the corporation intends to make a back-up section 444 election in the event the corporation's business purpose request is not approved by the IRS. (See instructions for more information.)

    3. Check here ▶ ☐ to show that the corporation agrees to adopt or change to a tax year ending December 31 if necessary for the IRS to accept this election for S corporation status in the event (1) the corporation's business purpose request is not approved and the corporation makes a back-up section 444 election, but is ultimately not qualified to make a section 444 election, or (2) the corporation's business purpose request is not approved and the corporation did not make a back-up section 444 election.

R   Section 444 Election—To make a section 444 election, check box R1. You may also check box R2.

    1. Check here ▶ ☐ to show the corporation will make, if qualified, a section 444 election to have the fiscal tax year shown in item I, Part I. To make the election, you must complete **Form 8716,** Election To Have a Tax Year Other Than a Required Tax Year, and either attach it to Form 2553 or file it separately.

    2. Check here ▶ ☐ to show that the corporation agrees to adopt or change to a tax year ending December 31 if necessary for the IRS to accept this election for S corporation status in the event the corporation is ultimately not qualified to make a section 444 election.

Part III   **Qualified Subchapter S Trust (QSST) Election Under Section 1361(d)(2)***

Income beneficiary's name and address	Social security number
Trust's name and address	Employer identification number

Date on which stock of the corporation was transferred to the trust (month, day, year) . . . . ▶   /   /

In order for the trust named above to be a QSST and thus a qualifying shareholder of the S corporation for which this Form 2553 is filed, I hereby make the election under section 1361(d)(2). Under penalties of perjury, I certify that the trust meets the definitional requirements of section 1361(d)(3) and that all other information provided in Part III is true, correct, and complete.

Signature of income beneficiary or signature and title of legal representative or other qualified person making the election	Date

*Use Part III to make the QSST election only if stock of the corporation has been transferred to the trust on or before the date on which the corporation makes its election to be an S corporation. The QSST election must be made and filed separately if stock of the corporation is transferred to the trust **after** the date on which the corporation makes the S election.

Form **2553** (Rev. 3-2005)

Form SS-4. Application for Employer Identification Number

Form **SS-4** (Rev. February 2006) Department of the Treasury Internal Revenue Service	**Application for Employer Identification Number** (For use by employers, corporations, partnerships, trusts, estates, churches, government agencies, Indian tribal entities, certain individuals, and others.) ▶ See separate instructions for each line. ▶ Keep a copy for your records.	OMB No. 1545-0003 EIN

Type or print clearly.

1 Legal name of entity (or individual) for whom the EIN is being requested

2 Trade name of business (if different from name on line 1)	**3** Executor, administrator, trustee, "care of" name
4a Mailing address (room, apt., suite no. and street, or P.O. box)	**5a** Street address (if different) (Do not enter a P.O. box.)
4b City, state, and ZIP code	**5b** City, state, and ZIP code

6 County and state where principal business is located

7a Name of principal officer, general partner, grantor, owner, or trustor	**7b** SSN, ITIN, or EIN

8a Type of entity (check only one box)
- ☐ Sole proprietor (SSN) _____
- ☐ Partnership
- ☐ Corporation (enter form number to be filed) ▶ _____
- ☐ Personal service corporation
- ☐ Church or church-controlled organization
- ☐ Other nonprofit organization (specify) ▶ _____
- ☐ Other (specify) ▶

- ☐ Estate (SSN of decedent) _____
- ☐ Plan administrator (SSN) _____
- ☐ Trust (SSN of grantor) _____
- ☐ National Guard   ☐ State/local government
- ☐ Farmers' cooperative   ☐ Federal government/military
- ☐ REMIC   ☐ Indian tribal governments/enterprises
- Group Exemption Number (GEN) ▶ _____

8b If a corporation, name the state or foreign country (if applicable) where incorporated

State	Foreign country

9 Reason for applying (check only one box)
- ☐ Started new business (specify type) ▶ _____
- ☐ Hired employees (Check the box and see line 12.)
- ☐ Compliance with IRS withholding regulations
- ☐ Other (specify) ▶

- ☐ Banking purpose (specify purpose) ▶ _____
- ☐ Changed type of organization (specify new type) ▶ _____
- ☐ Purchased going business
- ☐ Created a trust (specify type) ▶ _____
- ☐ Created a pension plan (specify type) ▶ _____

10 Date business started or acquired (month, day, year). See instructions.	**11** Closing month of accounting year

12 First date wages or annuities were paid (month, day, year). **Note.** If applicant is a withholding agent, enter date income will first be paid to nonresident alien. (month, day, year) . . . . ▶

13 Highest number of employees expected in the next 12 months (enter -0- if none). Do you expect to have $1,000 or less in employment tax liability for the calendar year? ☐ Yes ☐ No. (If you expect to pay $4,000 or less in wages, you can mark yes.)	Agricultural	Household	Other

14 Check **one** box that best describes the principal activity of your business.
- ☐ Construction ☐ Rental & leasing ☐ Transportation & warehousing
- ☐ Real estate   ☐ Manufacturing   ☐ Finance & insurance
- ☐ Health care & social assistance ☐ Wholesale–agent/broker
- ☐ Accommodation & food service ☐ Wholesale–other ☐ Retail
- ☐ Other (specify)

15 Indicate principal line of merchandise sold, specific construction work done, products produced, or services provided.

16a Has the applicant ever applied for an employer identification number for this or any other business? . . . . . ☐ Yes ☐ No
Note. If "Yes," please complete lines 16b and 16c.

16b If you checked "Yes" on line 16a, give applicant's legal name and trade name shown on prior application if different from line 1 or 2 above.
Legal name ▶   Trade name ▶

16c Approximate date when, and city and state where, the application was filed. Enter previous employer identification number if known.

Approximate date when filed (mo., day, year)	City and state where filed	Previous EIN

Third Party Designee	Complete this section **only** if you want to authorize the named individual to receive the entity's EIN and answer questions about the completion of this form.	
	Designee's name	Designee's telephone number (include area code) ( )
	Address and ZIP code	Designee's fax number (include area code) ( )

Under penalties of perjury, I declare that I have examined this application, and to the best of my knowledge and belief, it is true, correct, and complete.

Name and title (type or print clearly) ▶

	Applicant's telephone number (include area code) ( )
Signature ▶ Date ▶	Applicant's fax number (include area code) ( )

For Privacy Act and Paperwork Reduction Act Notice, see separate instructions.   Cat. No. 16055N   Form **SS-4** (Rev. 2-2006)

Form SS-4. Application for Employer Identification Number
(continued)

Do I Need an EIN?

File Form SS-4 if the applicant entity does not already have an EIN but is required to show an EIN on any return, statement, or other document.[1] See also the separate instructions for each line on Form SS-4.

IF the applicant...	AND...	THEN...
Started a new business	Does not currently have (nor expect to have) employees	Complete lines 1, 2, 4a–8a, 8b (if applicable), and 9–16c.
Hired (or will hire) employees, including household employees	Does not already have an EIN	Complete lines 1, 2, 4a–6, 7a–b (if applicable), 8a, 8b (if applicable), and 9–16c.
Opened a bank account	Needs an EIN for banking purposes only	Complete lines 1–5b, 7a–b (if applicable), 8a, 9, and 16a–c.
Changed type of organization	Either the legal character of the organization or its ownership changed (for example, you incorporate a sole proprietorship or form a partnership)[2]	Complete lines 1–16c (as applicable).
Purchased a going business[3]	Does not already have an EIN	Complete lines 1–16c (as applicable).
Created a trust	The trust is other than a grantor trust or an IRA trust[4]	Complete lines 1–16c (as applicable).
Created a pension plan as a plan administrator[5]	Needs an EIN for reporting purposes	Complete lines 1, 3, 4a–b, 8a, 9, and 16a–c.
Is a foreign person needing an EIN to comply with IRS withholding regulations	Needs an EIN to complete a Form W-8 (other than Form W-8ECI), avoid withholding on portfolio assets, or claim tax treaty benefits[6]	Complete lines 1–5b, 7a–b (SSN or ITIN optional), 8a–9, and 16a–c.
Is administering an estate	Needs an EIN to report estate income on Form 1041	Complete lines 1, 2, 3, 4a–6, 8a, 9-11, 12-15 (if applicable), and 16a–c.
Is a withholding agent for taxes on non-wage income paid to an alien (i.e., individual, corporation, or partnership, etc.)	Is an agent, broker, fiduciary, manager, tenant, or spouse who is required to file Form 1042, Annual Withholding Tax Return for U.S. Source Income of Foreign Persons	Complete lines 1, 2, 3 (if applicable), 4a–5b, 7a–b (if applicable), 8a, 9, and 16a–c.
Is a state or local agency	Serves as a tax reporting agent for public assistance recipients under Rev. Proc. 80-4, 1980-1 C.B. 581[7]	Complete lines 1, 2, 4a–5b, 8a, 9, and 16a–c.
Is a single-member LLC	Needs an EIN to file Form 8832, Entity Classification Election, for filing employment tax returns, **or** for state reporting purposes[8]	Complete lines 1–16c (as applicable).
Is an S corporation	Needs an EIN to file Form 2553, Election by a Small Business Corporation[9]	Complete lines 1–16c (as applicable).

[1] For example, a sole proprietorship or self-employed farmer who establishes a qualified retirement plan, or is required to file excise, employment, alcohol, tobacco, or firearms returns, must have an EIN. A partnership, corporation, REMIC (real estate mortgage investment conduit), nonprofit organization (church, club, etc.), or farmers' cooperative must use an EIN for any tax-related purpose even if the entity does not have employees.

[2] However, do not apply for a new EIN if the existing entity only (a) changed its business name, (b) elected on Form 8832 to change the way it is taxed (or is covered by the default rules), or (c) terminated its partnership status because at least 50% of the total interests in partnership capital and profits were sold or exchanged within a 12-month period. The EIN of the terminated partnership should continue to be used. See Regulations section 301.6109-1(d)(2)(iii).

[3] Do not use the EIN of the prior business unless you became the "owner" of a corporation by acquiring its stock.

[4] However, grantor trusts that do not file using Optional Method 1 and IRA trusts that are required to file Form 990-T, Exempt Organization Business Income Tax Return, must have an EIN. For more information on grantor trusts, see the Instructions for Form 1041.

[5] A plan administrator is the person or group of persons specified as the administrator by the instrument under which the plan is operated.

[6] Entities applying to be a Qualified Intermediary (QI) need a QI-EIN even if they already have an EIN. See Rev. Proc. 2000-12.

[7] See also *Household employer* on page 3. **Note.** State or local agencies may need an EIN for other reasons, for example, hired employees.

[8] Most LLCs do not need to file Form 8832. See *Limited liability company (LLC)* on page 4 for details on completing Form SS-4 for an LLC.

[9] An existing corporation that is electing or revoking S corporation status should use its previously-assigned EIN.

Printed on recycled paper

Form SS-4. Application for Employer Identification Number
(continued)

Instructions for Form SS-4

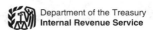

Department of the Treasury
Internal Revenue Service

(Rev. February 2006)

Application for Employer Identification Number

Section references are to the Internal Revenue Code unless otherwise noted.

General Instructions

Use these instructions to complete Form SS-4, Application for Employer Identification Number. Also see *Do I Need an EIN?* on page 2 of Form SS-4.

Purpose of Form

Use Form SS-4 to apply for an employer identification number (EIN). An EIN is a nine-digit number (for example, 12-3456789) assigned to sole proprietors, corporations, partnerships, estates, trusts, and other entities for tax filing and reporting purposes. The information you provide on this form will establish your business tax account.

 An EIN is for use in connection with your business activities only. Do not use your EIN in place of your social security number (SSN).

Reminders

Apply online. Generally, you can apply for and receive an EIN online using the Internet. See *How To Apply* below.

File only one Form SS-4. Generally, a sole proprietor should file only one Form SS-4 and needs only one EIN, regardless of the number of businesses operated as a sole proprietorship or trade names under which a business operates. However, if the proprietorship incorporates or enters into a partnership, a new EIN is required. Also, each corporation in an affiliated group must have its own EIN.

EIN applied for, but not received. If you do not have an EIN by the time a return is due, write "Applied For" and the date you applied in the space shown for the number. Do not show your SSN as an EIN on returns.

If you do not have an EIN by the time a tax deposit is due, send your payment to the Internal Revenue Service Center for your filing area as shown in the instructions for the form that you are filing. Make your check or money order payable to the "United States Treasury" and show your name (as shown on Form SS-4), address, type of tax, period covered, and date you applied for an EIN.

Federal tax deposits. New employers that have a federal tax obligation will be pre-enrolled in the Electronic Federal Tax Payment System (EFTPS). EFTPS allows you to make all of your federal tax payments online at *www.eftps.gov* or by telephone. Shortly after we have assigned you your EIN, you will receive instructions by mail for activating your EFTPS enrollment. You will also receive an EFTPS Personal Identification Number (PIN) that you will use to make your payments, as well as instructions for obtaining an Internet password you will need to make payments online.

If you are not required to make deposits by EFTPS, you can use Form 8109, Federal Tax Deposit (FTD) Coupon, to make deposits at an authorized depositary. If

you would like to receive Form 8109, call 1-800-829-4933. Allow 5 to 6 weeks for delivery. For more information on federal tax deposits, see Pub. 15 (Circular E).

How To Apply

You can apply for an EIN online, by telephone, by fax, or by mail depending on how soon you need to use the EIN. Use only one method for each entity so you do not receive more than one EIN for an entity.

Online. Generally, you can receive your EIN by Internet and use it immediately to file a return or make a payment. Go to the IRS website at *www.irs.gov/businesses* and click on Employer ID Numbers.

Applicants that may not apply online. The online application process is not yet available to:

Applicants with foreign addresses (including Puerto Rico),

Limited Liability Companies (LLCs) that have not yet determined their entity classification for federal tax purposes (see *Limited liability company (LLC)* on page 4),

Real Estate Investment Conduits (REMICs),

State and local governments,

Federal Government/Military, and

Indian Tribal Governments/Enterprises.

Telephone. You can receive your EIN by telephone and use it immediately to file a return or make a payment. Call the IRS at 1-800-829-4933. (International applicants must call 215-516-6999.) The hours of operation are 7:00 a.m. to 10:00 p.m. local time (Pacific time for Alaska and Hawaii). The person making the call must be authorized to sign the form or be an authorized designee. See *Signature* and *Third Party Designee* on page 6. Also see the *TIP* below.

If you are applying by telephone, it will be helpful to complete Form SS-4 before contacting the IRS. An IRS representative will use the information from the Form SS-4 to establish your account and assign you an EIN. Write the number you are given on the upper right corner of the form and sign and date it. Keep this copy for your records.

If requested by an IRS representative, mail or fax (facsimile) the signed Form SS-4 (including any Third Party Designee authorization) within 24 hours to the IRS address provided by the IRS representative.

TIP *Taxpayer representatives can apply for an EIN on behalf of their client and request that the EIN be faxed to their client on the same day.* **Note.** *By using this procedure, you are authorizing the IRS to fax the EIN without a cover sheet.*

Fax. Under the Fax-TIN program, you can receive your EIN by fax within 4 business days. Complete and fax Form SS-4 to the IRS using the Fax-TIN number listed on page 2 for your state. A long-distance charge to callers outside of the local calling area will apply. Fax-TIN

Cat. No. 62736F

Form SS-4. Application for Employer Identification Number
(continued)

numbers can only be used to apply for an EIN. The numbers may change without notice. Fax-TIN is available 24 hours a day, 7 days a week.

Be sure to provide your fax number so the IRS can fax the EIN back to you.

Note. By using this procedure, you are authorizing the IRS to fax the EIN without a cover sheet.

Mail. Complete Form SS-4 at least 4 to 5 weeks before you will need an EIN. Sign and date the application and mail it to the service center address for your state. You will receive your EIN in the mail in approximately 4 weeks. See also *Third Party Designee* on page 6.

Call 1-800-829-4933 to verify a number or to ask about the status of an application by mail.

Where to Fax or File

If your principal business, office or agency, or legal residence in the case of an individual, is located in:	Fax or file with the "Internal Revenue Service Center" at:
Connecticut, Delaware, District of Columbia, Florida, Georgia, Maine, Maryland, Massachusetts, New Hampshire, New Jersey, New York, North Carolina, Ohio, Pennsylvania, Rhode Island, South Carolina, Vermont, Virginia, West Virginia	Attn: EIN Operation Holtsville, NY 11742 Fax-TIN: 631-447-8960
Illinois, Indiana, Kentucky, Michigan	Attn: EIN Operation Cincinnati, OH 45999 Fax-TIN: 859-669-5760
Alabama, Alaska, Arizona, Arkansas, California, Colorado, Hawaii, Idaho, Iowa, Kansas, Louisiana, Minnesota, Mississippi, Missouri, Montana, Nebraska, Nevada, New Mexico, North Dakota, Oklahoma, Oregon, South Dakota, Tennessee, Texas, Utah, Washington, Wisconsin, Wyoming	Attn: EIN Operation Philadelphia, PA 19255 Fax-TIN: 859-669-5760
If you have no legal residence, principal place of business, or principal office or agency in any state:	Attn: EIN Operation Philadelphia, PA 19255 Fax-TIN: 215-516-1040

How To Get Forms and Publications

Phone. Call 1-800-TAX-FORM (1-800-829-3676) to order forms, instructions, and publications. You should receive your order or notification of its status within 10 workdays.

Internet. You can access the IRS website 24 hours a day, 7 days a week at *www.irs.gov* to download forms, instructions, and publications.

CD-ROM. For small businesses, return preparers, or others who may frequently need tax forms or publications, a CD-ROM containing over 2,000 tax products (including many prior year forms) can be purchased from the National Technical Information Service (NTIS).

To order Pub. 1796, IRS Tax Products CD, call 1-877-CDFORMS (1-877-233-6767) toll free or connect to *www.irs.gov/cdorders*.

Tax Help for Your Business

IRS-sponsored Small Business Workshops provide information about your federal and state tax obligations. For information about workshops in your area, call 1-800-829-4933.

Related Forms and Publications

The following forms and instructions may be useful to filers of Form SS-4.

Form 990-T, Exempt Organization Business Income Tax Return.

Instructions for Form 990-T.

Schedule C (Form 1040), Profit or Loss From Business.

Schedule F (Form 1040), Profit or Loss From Farming.

Instructions for Form 1041 and Schedules A, B, D, G, I, J, and K-1, U.S. Income Tax Return for Estates and Trusts.

Form 1042, Annual Withholding Tax Return for U.S. Source Income of Foreign Persons.

Instructions for Form 1065, U.S. Return of Partnership Income.

Instructions for Form 1066, U.S. Real Estate Mortgage Investment Conduit (REMIC) Income Tax Return.

Instructions for Forms 1120 and 1120-A.

Form 2553, Election by a Small Business Corporation.

Form 2848, Power of Attorney and Declaration of Representative.

Form 8821, Tax Information Authorization.

Form 8832, Entity Classification Election.

For more information about filing Form SS-4 and related issues, see:

Pub. 51 (Circular A), Agricultural Employer's Tax Guide;

Pub. 15 (Circular E), Employer's Tax Guide;

Pub. 538, Accounting Periods and Methods;

Pub. 542, Corporations;

Pub. 557, Tax-Exempt Status for Your Organization;

Pub. 583, Starting a Business and Keeping Records;

Pub. 966, The Secure Way to Pay Your Federal Taxes for Business and Individual Taxpayers;

Pub. 1635, Understanding Your EIN;

Package 1023, Application for Recognition of Exemption Under Section 501(c)(3) of the Internal Revenue Code; and

Package 1024, Application for Recognition of Exemption Under Section 501(a).

Specific Instructions

Print or type all entries on Form SS-4. Follow the instructions for each line to expedite processing and to avoid unnecessary IRS requests for additional information. Enter "N/A" (nonapplicable) on the lines that do not apply.

Line 1—Legal name of entity (or individual) for whom the EIN is being requested. Enter the legal name of the entity (or individual) applying for the EIN exactly as it appears on the social security card, charter, or other applicable legal document. An entry is required.

Form SS-4. Application for Employer Identification Number

(continued)

Individuals. Enter your first name, middle initial, and last name. If you are a sole proprietor, enter your individual name, not your business name. Enter your business name on line 2. Do not use abbreviations or nicknames on line 1.

Trusts. Enter the name of the trust.

Estate of a decedent. Enter the name of the estate. For an estate that has no legal name, enter the name of the decedent followed by "Estate."

Partnerships. Enter the legal name of the partnership as it appears in the partnership agreement.

Corporations. Enter the corporate name as it appears in the corporate charter or other legal document creating it.

Plan administrators. Enter the name of the plan administrator. A plan administrator who already has an EIN should use that number.

Line 2—Trade name of business. Enter the trade name of the business if different from the legal name. The trade name is the "doing business as " (DBA) name.

 Use the full legal name shown on line 1 on all tax returns filed for the entity. (However, if you enter a trade name on line 2 and choose to use the trade name instead of the legal name, enter the trade name on all returns you file.) To prevent processing delays and errors, always use the legal name only (or the trade name only) on all tax returns.

Line 3—Executor, administrator, trustee, "care of" name. Trusts enter the name of the trustee. Estates enter the name of the executor, administrator, or other fiduciary. If the entity applying has a designated person to receive tax information, enter that person's name as the "care of" person. Enter the individual's first name, middle initial, and last name.

Lines 4a-b—Mailing address. Enter the mailing address for the entity's correspondence. If line 3 is completed, enter the address for the executor, trustee or "care of" person. Generally, this address will be used on all tax returns.

TIP *File Form 8822, Change of Address, to report any subsequent changes to the entity's mailing address.*

Lines 5a-b—Street address. Provide the entity's physical address only if different from its mailing address shown in lines 4a-b. Do not enter a P.O. box number here.

Line 6—County and state where principal business is located. Enter the entity's primary physical location.

Lines 7a-b—Name of principal officer, general partner, grantor, owner, or trustor. Enter the first name, middle initial, last name, and SSN of (a) the principal officer if the business is a corporation, (b) a general partner if a partnership, (c) the owner of an entity that is disregarded as separate from its owner (disregarded entities owned by a corporation enter the corporation's name and EIN), or (d) a grantor, owner, or trustor if a trust.

If the person in question is an alien individual with a previously assigned individual taxpayer identification number (ITIN), enter the ITIN in the space provided and submit a copy of an official identifying document. If necessary, complete Form W-7, Application for IRS Individual Taxpayer Identification Number, to obtain an ITIN.

You must enter an SSN, ITIN, or EIN unless the only reason you are applying for an EIN is to make an entity classification election (see Regulations sections 301.7701-1 through 301.7701-3) and you are a nonresident alien or other foreign entity with no effectively connected income from sources within the United States.

Line 8a—Type of entity. Check the box that best describes the type of entity applying for the EIN. If you are an alien individual with an ITIN previously assigned to you, enter the ITIN in place of a requested SSN.

 This is not an election for a tax classification of an entity. See Limited liability company (LLC) *on page 4.*

Other. If not specifically listed, check the "Other" box, enter the type of entity and the type of return, if any, that will be filed (for example, "Common Trust Fund, Form 1065" or "Created a Pension Plan"). Do not enter "N/A." If you are an alien individual applying for an EIN, see the *Lines 7a-b* instructions above.

Household employer. If you are an individual, check the "Other" box and enter "Household Employer" and your SSN. If you are a state or local agency serving as a tax reporting agent for public assistance recipients who become household employers, check the "Other" box and enter "Household Employer Agent." If you are a trust that qualifies as a household employer, you do not need a separate EIN for reporting tax information relating to household employees; use the EIN of the trust.

QSub. For a qualified subchapter S subsidiary (QSub) check the "Other" box and specify "QSub."

Withholding agent. If you are a withholding agent required to file Form 1042, check the "Other" box and enter "Withholding Agent."

Sole proprietor. Check this box if you file Schedule C, C-EZ, or F (Form 1040) and have a qualified plan, or are required to file excise, employment, alcohol, tobacco, or firearms returns, or are a payer of gambling winnings. Enter your SSN (or ITIN) in the space provided. If you are a nonresident alien with no effectively connected income from sources within the United States, you do not need to enter an SSN or ITIN.

Corporation. This box is for any corporation other than a personal service corporation. If you check this box, enter the income tax form number to be filed by the entity in the space provided.

 If you entered "1120S" after the "Corporation" checkbox, the corporation must file Form 2553 no later than the 15th day of the 3rd month of the tax year the election is to take effect. Until Form 2553 has been received and approved, you will be considered a Form 1120 filer. See the Instructions for Form 2553.

Personal service corporation. Check this box if the entity is a personal service corporation. An entity is a personal service corporation for a tax year only if:

The principal activity of the entity during the testing period (prior tax year) for the tax year is the performance of personal services substantially by employee-owners, and

The employee-owners own at least 10% of the fair market value of the outstanding stock in the entity on the last day of the testing period.

Personal services include performance of services in such fields as health, law, accounting, or consulting. For more information about personal service corporations,

Form SS-4. Application for Employer Identification Number
(continued)

see the Instructions for Forms 1120 and 1120-A and Pub. 542.

Other nonprofit organization. Check this box if the nonprofit organization is other than a church or church-controlled organization and specify the type of nonprofit organization (for example, an educational organization).

 If the organization also seeks tax-exempt status, you must file either Package 1023 or Package 1024. See Pub. 557 for more information.

If the organization is covered by a group exemption letter, enter the four-digit group exemption number (GEN). (Do not confuse the GEN with the nine-digit EIN.) If you do not know the GEN, contact the parent organization. Get Pub. 557 for more information about group exemption numbers.

If the organization is a section 527 political organization, check the box for *Other nonprofit organization* and specify "section 527 organization" in the space to the right. To be recognized as exempt from tax, a section 527 political organization must electronically file Form 8871, Political Organization Notice of Section 527 Status, within 24 hours of the date on which the organization was established. The organization may also have to file Form 8872, Political Organization Report of Contributions and Expenditures. See *www.irs.gov/polorgs* for more information.

Plan administrator. If the plan administrator is an individual, enter the plan administrator's SSN in the space provided.

REMIC. Check this box if the entity has elected to be treated as a real estate mortgage investment conduit (REMIC). See the Instructions for Form 1066 for more information.

State/local government. If you are a government employer and you are not sure of your social security and Medicare coverage options, go to *www.ncsssa.org/ssaframes.html* to obtain the contact information for your state's Social Security Administrator.

Limited liability company (LLC). An LLC is an entity organized under the laws of a state or foreign country as a limited liability company. For federal tax purposes, an LLC may be treated as a partnership or corporation or be disregarded as an entity separate from its owner.

By default, a domestic LLC with only one member is disregarded as an entity separate from its owner and must include all of its income and expenses on the owner's tax return (for example, Schedule C (Form 1040)). Also by default, a domestic LLC with two or more members is treated as a partnership. A domestic LLC may file Form 8832 to avoid either default classification and elect to be classified as an association taxable as a corporation. For more information on entity classifications (including the rules for foreign entities), see the instructions for Form 8832.

 Do not file Form 8832 if the LLC accepts the default classifications above. If the LLC is eligible to be treated as a corporation that meets certain tests and it will be electing S corporation status, it must timely file Form 2553. The LLC will be treated as a corporation as of the effective date of the S corporation election and does not need to file Form 8832. See the Instructions for Form 2553.

Complete Form SS-4 for LLCs as follows.

A single-member domestic LLC that accepts the default classification (above) does not need an EIN and generally should not file Form SS-4. Generally, the LLC should use the name and EIN of its owner for all federal tax purposes. However, the reporting and payment of employment taxes for employees of the LLC may be made using the name and EIN of either the owner or the LLC as explained in Notice 99-6. You can find Notice 99-6 on page 12 of Internal Revenue Bulletin 1999-3 at *www.irs.gov/pub/irs-irbs/irb99-03.pdf.* (**Note.** If the LLC applicant indicates in box 13 that it has employees or expects to have employees, the owner (whether an individual or other entity) of a single-member domestic LLC will also be assigned its own EIN (if it does not already have one) even if the LLC will be filing the employment tax returns.)

A single-member, domestic LLC that accepts the default classification (above) and wants an EIN for filing employment tax returns (see above) or non-federal purposes, such as a state requirement, must check the "Other" box and write "Disregarded Entity" or, when applicable, "Disregarded Entity—Sole Proprietorship" in the space provided.

A multi-member, domestic LLC that accepts the default classification (above) must check the "Partnership" box.

A domestic LLC that will be filing Form 8832 to elect corporate status must check the "Corporation" box and write in "Single-Member" or "Multi-Member" immediately below the "form number" entry line.

Line 9—Reason for applying. Check only one box. Do not enter "N/A."

Started new business. Check this box if you are starting a new business that requires an EIN. If you check this box, enter the type of business being started. Do not apply if you already have an EIN and are only adding another place of business.

Hired employees. Check this box if the existing business is requesting an EIN because it has hired or is hiring employees and is therefore required to file employment tax returns. Do not apply if you already have an EIN and are only hiring employees. For information on employment taxes (for example, for family members), see Pub. 15 (Circular E).

 You may have to make electronic deposits of all depository taxes (such as employment tax, excise tax, and corporate income tax) using the Electronic Federal Tax Payment System (EFTPS). See Federal tax deposits on page 1; section 11, Depositing Taxes, of Pub. 15 (Circular E); and Pub. 966.

Created a pension plan. Check this box if you have created a pension plan and need an EIN for reporting purposes. Also, enter the type of plan in the space provided.

TIP *Check this box if you are applying for a trust EIN when a new pension plan is established. In addition, check the "Other" box in line 8a and write "Created a Pension Plan" in the space provided.*

Banking purpose. Check this box if you are requesting an EIN for banking purposes only, and enter the banking purpose (for example, a bowling league for depositing dues or an investment club for dividend and interest reporting).

Changed type of organization. Check this box if the business is changing its type of organization. For example, the business was a sole proprietorship and has

Form SS-4. Application for Employer Identification Number
(continued)

been incorporated or has become a partnership. If you check this box, specify in the space provided (including available space immediately below) the type of change made. For example, "From Sole Proprietorship to Partnership."

Purchased going business. Check this box if you purchased an existing business. Do not use the former owner's EIN unless you became the "owner" of a corporation by acquiring its stock.

Created a trust. Check this box if you created a trust, and enter the type of trust created. For example, indicate if the trust is a nonexempt charitable trust or a split-interest trust.

Exception. Do not file this form for certain grantor-type trusts. The trustee does not need an EIN for the trust if the trustee furnishes the name and TIN of the grantor/owner and the address of the trust to all payors. However, grantor trusts that do not file using Optional Method 1 and IRA trusts that are required to file Form 990-T, Exempt Organization Business Income Tax Return, must have an EIN. For more information on grantor trusts, see the Instructions for Form 1041.

 TIP *Do not check this box if you are applying for a trust EIN when a new pension plan is established. Check "Created a pension plan."*

Other. Check this box if you are requesting an EIN for any other reason; and enter the reason. For example, a newly-formed state government entity should enter "Newly-Formed State Government Entity" in the space provided.

Line 10—Date business started or acquired. If you are starting a new business, enter the starting date of the business. If the business you acquired is already operating, enter the date you acquired the business. If you are changing the form of ownership of your business, enter the date the new ownership entity began. Trusts should enter the date the trust was funded. Estates should enter the date of death of the decedent whose name appears on line 1 or the date when the estate was legally funded.

Line 11—Closing month of accounting year. Enter the last month of your accounting year or tax year. An accounting or tax year is usually 12 consecutive months, either a calendar year or a fiscal year (including a period of 52 or 53 weeks). A calendar year is 12 consecutive months ending on December 31. A fiscal year is either 12 consecutive months ending on the last day of any month other than December or a 52-53 week year. For more information on accounting periods, see Pub. 538.

Individuals. Your tax year generally will be a calendar year.

Partnerships. Partnerships must adopt one of the following tax years.
   The tax year of the majority of its partners.
   The tax year common to all of its principal partners.
   The tax year that results in the least aggregate deferral of income.
   In certain cases, some other tax year.

   See the Instructions for Form 1065 for more information.

REMICs. REMICs must have a calendar year as their tax year.

Personal service corporations. A personal service corporation generally must adopt a calendar year unless it meets one of the following requirements.
   It can establish a business purpose for having a different tax year.
   It elects under section 444 to have a tax year other than a calendar year.

Trusts. Generally, a trust must adopt a calendar year except for the following trusts.
   Tax-exempt trusts.
   Charitable trusts.
   Grantor-owned trusts.

Line 12—First date wages or annuities were paid. If the business has employees, enter the date on which the business began to pay wages. If the business does not plan to have employees, enter "N/A."

Withholding agent. Enter the date you began or will begin to pay income (including annuities) to a nonresident alien. This also applies to individuals who are required to file Form 1042 to report alimony paid to a nonresident alien.

Line 13—Highest number of employees expected in the next 12 months. Complete each box by entering the number (including zero ("-0-")) of "Agricultural," "Household," or "Other" employees expected by the applicant in the next 12 months. Check the appropriate box to indicate if you expect your annual employment tax liability to be $1,000 or less. Generally, if you pay $4,000 or less in wages subject to social security and Medicare taxes and federal income tax withholding, you are likely to pay $1,000 or less in employment taxes.

   For more information on employment taxes, see Pub. 15 (Circular E); or Pub. 51 (Circular A) if you have agricultural employees (farmworkers).

Lines 14 and 15. Check the one box in line 14 that best describes the principal activity of the applicant's business. Check the "Other" box (and specify the applicant's principal activity) if none of the listed boxes applies. You must check a box.

   Use line 15 to describe the applicant's principal line of business in more detail. For example, if you checked the "Construction" box in line 14, enter additional detail such as "General contractor for residential buildings" in line 15. An entry is required.

Construction. Check this box if the applicant is engaged in erecting buildings or engineering projects, (for example, streets, highways, bridges, tunnels). The term "Construction" also includes special trade contractors, (for example, plumbing, HVAC, electrical, carpentry, concrete, excavation, etc. contractors).

Real estate. Check this box if the applicant is engaged in renting or leasing real estate to others; managing, selling, buying or renting real estate for others; or providing related real estate services (for example, appraisal services).

Rental and leasing. Check this box if the applicant is engaged in providing tangible goods such as autos, computers, consumer goods, or industrial machinery and equipment to customers in return for a periodic rental or lease payment.

Manufacturing. Check this box if the applicant is engaged in the mechanical, physical, or chemical transformation of materials, substances, or components into new products. The assembling of component parts of

Form SS-4. Application for Employer Identification Number
(continued)

manufactured products is also considered to be manufacturing.

Transportation & warehousing. Check this box if the applicant provides transportation of passengers or cargo; warehousing or storage of goods; scenic or sight-seeing transportation; or support activities related to transportation.

Finance & insurance. Check this box if the applicant is engaged in transactions involving the creation, liquidation, or change of ownership of financial assets and/or facilitating such financial transactions; underwriting annuities/insurance policies; facilitating such underwriting by selling insurance policies; or by providing other insurance or employee-benefit related services.

Health care and social assistance. Check this box if the applicant is engaged in providing physical, medical, or psychiatric care or providing social assistance activities such as youth centers, adoption agencies, individual/family services, temporary shelters, daycare, etc.

Accommodation & food services. Check this box if the applicant is engaged in providing customers with lodging, meal preparation, snacks, or beverages for immediate consumption.

Wholesale–agent/broker. Check this box if the applicant is engaged in arranging for the purchase or sale of goods owned by others or purchasing goods on a commission basis for goods traded in the wholesale market, usually between businesses.

Wholesale–other. Check this box if the applicant is engaged in selling goods in the wholesale market generally to other businesses for resale on their own account, goods used in production, or capital or durable nonconsumer goods.

Retail. Check this box if the applicant is engaged in selling merchandise to the general public from a fixed store; by direct, mail-order, or electronic sales; or by using vending machines.

Other. Check this box if the applicant is engaged in an activity not described above. Describe the applicant's principal business activity in the space provided.

Lines 16a-c. Check the applicable box in line 16a to indicate whether or not the entity (or individual) applying for an EIN was issued one previously. Complete lines 16b and 16c only if the "Yes" box in line 16a is checked. If the applicant previously applied for more than one EIN, write "See Attached" in the empty space in line 16a and attach a separate sheet providing the line 16b and 16c information for each EIN previously requested.

Third Party Designee. Complete this section only if you want to authorize the named individual to receive the entity's EIN and answer questions about the completion of Form SS-4. The designee's authority terminates at the time the EIN is assigned and released to the designee. You must complete the signature area for the authorization to be valid.

Signature. When required, the application must be signed by (a) the individual, if the applicant is an individual, (b) the president, vice president, or other principal officer, if the applicant is a corporation, (c) a responsible and duly authorized member or officer having knowledge of its affairs, if the applicant is a partnership, government entity, or other unincorporated organization, or (d) the fiduciary, if the applicant is a trust or an estate. Foreign applicants may have any duly-authorized person, (for example, division manager), sign Form SS-4.

Privacy Act and Paperwork Reduction Act Notice. We ask for the information on this form to carry out the Internal Revenue laws of the United States. We need it to comply with section 6109 and the regulations thereunder, which generally require the inclusion of an employer identification number (EIN) on certain returns, statements, or other documents filed with the Internal Revenue Service. If your entity is required to obtain an EIN, you are required to provide all of the information requested on this form. Information on this form may be used to determine which federal tax returns you are required to file and to provide you with related forms and publications.

We disclose this form to the Social Security Administration (SSA) for their use in determining compliance with applicable laws. We may give this information to the Department of Justice for use in civil and criminal litigation, and to the cities, states, and the District of Columbia for use in administering their tax laws. We may also disclose this information to other countries under a tax treaty, to federal and state agencies to enforce federal nontax criminal laws, and to federal law enforcement and intelligence agencies to combat terrorism.

We will be unable to issue an EIN to you unless you provide all of the requested information that applies to your entity. Providing false information could subject you to penalties.

You are not required to provide the information requested on a form that is subject to the Paperwork Reduction Act unless the form displays a valid OMB control number. Books or records relating to a form or its instructions must be retained as long as their contents may become material in the administration of any Internal Revenue law. Generally, tax returns and return information are confidential, as required by section 6103.

The time needed to complete and file this form will vary depending on individual circumstances. The estimated average time is:

Recordkeeping	8 hrs., 22 min.
Learning about the law or the form	42 min.
Preparing the form	52 min.
Copying, assembling, and sending the form to the IRS	- - - - -

If you have comments concerning the accuracy of these time estimates or suggestions for making this form simpler, we would be happy to hear from you. You can write to Internal Revenue Service, Tax Products Coordinating Committee, SE:W:CAR:MP:T:T:SP, IR-6406, 1111 Constitution Avenue, NW, Washington, DC 20224. Do not send the form to this address. Instead, see *Where to Fax or File* on page 2.

Form I-9. Employment Eligibility Verification

Department of Homeland Security
U.S. Citizenship and Immigration Services

OMB No. 1615-0047; Expires 03/31/07
Employment Eligibility Verification

INSTRUCTIONS
PLEASE READ ALL INSTRUCTIONS CAREFULLY BEFORE COMPLETING THIS FORM.

Anti-Discrimination Notice. It is illegal to discriminate against any individual (other than an alien not authorized to work in the U.S.) in hiring, discharging, or recruiting or referring for a fee because of that individual's national origin or citizenship status. It is illegal to discriminate against work eligible individuals. Employers **CANNOT** specify which document(s) they will accept from an employee. The refusal to hire an individual because of a future expiration date may also constitute illegal discrimination.

Section 1- Employee. All employees, citizens and noncitizens, hired after November 6, 1986, must complete Section 1 of this form at the time of hire, which is the actual beginning of employment. **The employer is responsible for ensuring that Section 1 is timely and properly completed.**

Preparer/Translator Certification. The Preparer/Translator Certification must be completed if Section 1 is prepared by a person other than the employee. A preparer/translator may be used only when the employee is unable to complete Section 1 on his/her own. However, the employee must still sign Section 1 personally.

Section 2 - Employer. For the purpose of completing this form, the term "employer" includes those recruiters and referrers for a fee who are agricultural associations, agricultural employers or farm labor contractors.

Employers must complete Section 2 by examining evidence of identity and employment eligibility within three (3) business days of the date employment begins. If employees are authorized to work, but are unable to present the required document(s) within three business days, they must present a receipt for the application of the document(s) within three business days and the actual document(s) within ninety (90) days. However, if employers hire individuals for a duration of less than three business days, Section 2 must be completed at the time employment begins. **Employers must record: 1)** document title; **2)** issuing authority; **3)** document number, **4)** expiration date, if any; and **5)** the date employment begins. Employers must sign and date the certification. Employees must present original documents. Employers may, but are not required to, photocopy the document(s) presented. These photocopies may only be used for the verification process and must be retained with the I-9. **However, employers are still responsible for completing the I-9.**

Section 3 - Updating and Reverification. Employers must complete Section 3 when updating and/or reverifying the I-9. Employers must reverify employment eligibility of their employees on or before the expiration date recorded in Section 1. Employers **CANNOT** specify which document(s) they will accept from an employee.

- If an employee's name has changed at the time this form is being updated/reverified, complete Block A.

- If an employee is rehired within three (3) years of the date this form was originally completed and the employee is still eligible to be employed on the same basis as previously indicated on this form (updating), complete Block B and the signature block.

- If an employee is rehired within three (3) years of the date this form was originally completed and the employee's work authorization has expired **or** if a current employee's work authorization is about to expire (reverification), complete Block B and:

- examine any document that reflects that the employee is authorized to work in the U.S. (see List A **or** C),

- record the document title, document number and expiration date (if any) in Block C, and

- complete the signature block.

Photocopying and Retaining Form I-9. A blank I-9 may be reproduced, provided both sides are copied. The Instructions must be available to all employees completing this form. Employers must retain completed I-9s for three (3) years after the date of hire or one (1) year after the date employment ends, whichever is later.

For more detailed information, you may refer to the Department of Homeland Security (DHS) Handbook for Employers, (Form M-274). You may obtain the handbook at your local U.S. Citizenship and Immigration Services (USCIS) office.

NOTE: This is the 1991 edition of the Form I-9 that has been rebranded with a current printing date to reflect the recent transition from the INS to DHS and its components.

EMPLOYERS MUST RETAIN COMPLETED FORM I-9
PLEASE DO NOT MAIL COMPLETED FORM I-9 TO ICE OR USCIS

Form I-9 (Rev. 05/31/05)Y

Form I-9. Employment Eligibility Verification (continued)

Department of Homeland Security
U.S. Citizenship and Immigration Services

OMB No. 1615-0047; Expires 03/31/07
Employment Eligibility Verification

Please read instructions carefully before completing this form. The instructions must be available during completion of this form. ANTI-DISCRIMINATION NOTICE: It is illegal to discriminate against work eligible individuals. Employers CANNOT specify which document(s) they will accept from an employee. The refusal to hire an individual because of a future expiration date may also constitute illegal discrimination.

Section 1. Employee Information and Verification. To be completed and signed by employee at the time employment begins.

Print Name: Last	First	Middle Initial	Maiden Name

Address (Street Name and Number)		Apt. #	Date of Birth (month/day/year)

City	State	Zip Code	Social Security #

I am aware that federal law provides for imprisonment and/or fines for false statements or use of false documents in connection with the completion of this form.

I attest, under penalty of perjury, that I am (check one of the following):
☐ A citizen or national of the United States
☐ A Lawful Permanent Resident (Alien #) A _____
☐ An alien authorized to work until _____
(Alien # or Admission #)

Employee's Signature	Date (month/day/year)

Preparer and/or Translator Certification. (To be completed and signed if Section 1 is prepared by a person other than the employee.) I attest, under penalty of perjury, that I have assisted in the completion of this form and that to the best of my knowledge the information is true and correct.

Preparer's/Translator's Signature	Print Name

Address (Street Name and Number, City, State, Zip Code)	Date (month/day/year)

Section 2. Employer Review and Verification. To be completed and signed by employer. Examine one document from List A OR examine one document from List B and one from List C, as listed on the reverse of this form, and record the title, number and expiration date, if any, of the document(s).

List A	OR	List B	AND	List C
Document title:				
Issuing authority:				
Document #:				
Expiration Date (if any):				
Document #:				
Expiration Date (if any):				

CERTIFICATION - Iattest, under penalty of perjury, that I have examined the document(s) presented by the above-named employee, that the above-listed document(s) appear to be genuine and to relate to the employee named, that the employee began employment on (month/day/year) _____ and that to the best of my knowledge the employee is eligible to work in the United States. (State employment agencies may omit the date the employee began employment.)

Signature of Employer or Authorized Representative	Print Name	Title

Business or Organization Name	Address (Street Name and Number, City, State, Zip Code)	Date (month/day/year)

Section 3. Updating and Reverification. To be completed and signed by employer.

A. New Name (if applicable)	B. Date of Rehire (month/day/year) (if applicable)

C. If employee's previous grant of work authorization has expired, provide the information below for the document that establishes current employment eligibility.

Document Title:	Document #:	Expiration Date (if any):

I attest, under penalty of perjury, that to the best of my knowledge, this employee is eligible to work in the United States, and if the employee presented document(s), the document(s) I have examined appear to be genuine and to relate to the individual.

Signature of Employer or Authorized Representative	Date (month/day/year)

NOTE: This is the 1991 edition of the Form I-9 that has been rebranded with a current printing date to reflect the recent transition from the INS to DHS and its components.

Form I-9 (Rev. 05/31/05)Y Page 2

Sample Income Statement (Profit & Loss Statement)

For Year: _____	January	February	March	April	May
INCOME					
Gross Sales					
Less returns and allowances					
Net Sales					
Cost of Goods					
Gross Profit					
GENERAL & ADMINISTRATIVE (G&A) EXPENSES					
Salaries and wages					
Employee benefits					
Payroll taxes					
Sales commissions					
Professional services					
Rent					
Maintenance					
Equipment rental					
Furniture and equipment purchase					
Depreciation and amortization					
Insurance					
Interest expenses					
Utilities					
Telephone					
Office supplies					
Postage and shipping					
Marketing and advertising					
Travel					
Entertainment					
Other					
Other					
TOTAL G&A EXPENSES					
Net income before taxes					
Provision for taxes on income					
NET INCOME AFTER TAXES (Net Profit)					

Sample Income Statement (continued)

June	July	August	September	October	November	December	TOTAL

Sample Cash Flow Statement

For the period of: _____	January	February	March	April	May
SALES Cash sales					
CREDIT SALES COLLECTIBLE For this month					
From last month					
From prior months					
OTHER CASH INFLOWS Sale of equipment					
Loan proceeds					
TOTAL INFLOWS					
PURCHASES Accounts payable that will be paid this month					
Salaries, wages, and benefits					
Other operating costs					
Tax payments					
Loan fees, principal, interest					
Equipment purchases					
Dividends					
Other _____					
Total Outflows					
INFLOWS MINUS OUTFLOWS EQUALS NET CASH					
COMPANY CASH BUDGET					
Opening cash balance					
Cash inflows					
Cash available					
Cash outflows					
Net end of month cash					

Sample Cash Flow Statement (continued)

June	July	August	September	October	November	December	TOTAL

Sample Balance Sheet

Company Name: _____

Balance Sheet as of: _____

ASSETS:		LIABILITIES:	
Cash	_____	Accounts payable	_____
Marketable securities	_____	Sales tax payable	_____
Accounts receivable	_____	Payroll payable	_____
Inventory	_____	Payroll taxes payable	_____
Prepaid expenses	_____	Income taxes payable	_____
_____	_____	Accruals	_____
TOTAL CURRENT ASSETS	_____	TOTAL CURRENT LIABILITIES	_____
Land	_____	Notes Payable	
Buildings	_____	_____	_____
Equipment	_____	_____	_____
Accumulated depreciation	_____	_____	_____
Leasehold improvements	_____	_____	_____
Amortization of leasehold improvements	_____	_____	_____
TOTAL FIXED ASSETS	_____	TOTAL LONG-TERM LIABILITIES	_____
Deposits	_____	Draws	_____
Long-term investments	_____	Paid-in capital	_____
Deferred Assets	_____	Retained earnings prior	_____
_____	_____	Retained earnings current	_____
LONG-TERM ASSETS	_____	TOTAL EQUITY	_____
TOTAL ASSETS	$ _____	TOTAL EQUITY & LIABILITIES	$ _____

Note: Total Assets must equal Total Equity and Liabilities.

Sample Purchase Order

Purchase Order Number _____

From _____ Phone _____

Address _____

_____

Vendor   Ship to

_____   _____

_____   _____

_____   _____

_____   _____

____

Job Reference # _____   Ship Via _____

Delivery Date _____   Terms _____

Quantity	Item Number	Description	Unit Cost	Extended Price
_____	_____	_____	_____	_____
_____	_____	_____	_____	_____
_____	_____	_____	_____	_____
_____	_____	_____	_____	_____
_____	_____	_____	_____	_____
_____	_____	_____	_____	_____
_____	_____	_____	_____	_____

Conditions:

Our purchase order number must appear on
all invoices, bills of lading, shipping memos,
and packing lists. Goods are subject to our   Subtotals $_____
inspection and approval. If shipment will be
delayed for any reason, advise us   Freight $_____
immediately and state all necessary facts. To
avoid errors, note specifications carefully   Tax $_____
and let us know if unable to complete orders
as written.   Total $_____

Approved by _____   Date_____

Sample Invoice

Invoice Number _____

From _____ Phone _____

Address _____

_____ Order Taken by _____

To _____ Phone _____

Address _____ Date of Order _____

_____ Purchase Order # _____

Job Location _____ Ordered by

_____ Starting Time

Quantity	Material	Price	Amount	Description of Work
_____	_____	_____	_____	_____
_____	_____	_____	_____	_____
_____	_____	_____	_____	_____
_____	_____	_____	_____	_____
_____	_____	_____	_____	_____
_____	_____	_____	_____	_____
_____	_____	_____	_____	_____

Date Hours Rate Amount

__ __ __ ____

__ __ __ ____

__ __ __ ____

__ __ __ ____

Total Labor $_____

Other Charges

__ __ __ ____

__ __ __ ____

__ __ __ ____

__ __ __ ____

Recap of Job Invoice

Terms _____

Date Completed _____

I hereby acknowledge the satisfactory completion of the above work.

Authorized Signature _____

Total Materials $_____

Total Labor $_____

Total Other Charges $_____

Tax $_____

Total Due _____

Sample Job Description

POSITION MINIMUM REQUIREMENTS:

Education _____
_____
_____

Experience _____
_____
_____

Responsibility _____
_____
_____

Initiative _____
_____
_____

Skills _____
_____
_____

Physical Requirements _____
_____
_____

Mental Requirements _____
_____
_____

Supervision _____
_____
_____

Equipment Used _____
_____
_____

Other Supervision _____
_____
_____

Prepared by_____   Date _____
Approved by _____   Date _____

Sample Job Application

Our policy is to provide equal employment opportunity to all qualified persons without regard to race, creed, color, religious belief, sex, age, national origin, physical or mental disability, or veteran status.

PERSONAL INFORMATION

Name _____

Home Address _____

Day Phone _____ Evening Phone _____

Social Security Number _____

Are you a citizen or authorized by INS to work? (Documentation may be required.) ☐ Yes ☐ No

Have you ever been convicted of a felony? (This will not necessarily affect your application.)

                                                  ☐ Yes ☐ No

EMPLOYMENT DESIRED

Have you ever applied for employment here? ☐ Yes ☐ No

When? _____

Have you ever been employed by this company? ☐ Yes ☐ No

When? _____ Where? _____

Are you presently employed? ☐ Yes ☐ No

May we contact your employer? ☐ Yes ☐ No

Are you available for full-time work? ☐ Yes ☐ No

Are you available for part-time work? ☐ Yes ☐ No

Will you relocate? ☐ Yes ☐ No

Are you willing to travel? ☐ Yes ☐ No If yes, what percent? _____

Date you can start: _____

Desired position: _____

Desired starting salary: _____

Please list applicable skills: _____

EDUCATION

School	Location	Major	Degree	Grade Average
_____	_____	_____	_____	_____
_____	_____	_____	_____	_____
_____	_____	_____	_____	_____
_____	_____	_____	_____	_____

Please list any scholastic honors received and offices held in school: _____

_____

Are you planning to continue your studies? ☐ Yes ☐ No

If yes, where and what courses of study? _____

_____

Sample Job Application (continued)

WORK EXPERIENCE

Please list employment from the last ten years, starting with the most recent employer.

Company Name _____

Address _____

Job Title _____

Responsibilities _____

_____

Dates of Employment — From _____ To _____

Reason for Leaving _____

Company Name _____

Address _____

Job Title _____

Responsibilities _____

_____

Dates of Employment — From _____ To _____

Reason for Leaving _____

Company Name _____

Address _____

Job Title _____

Responsibilities _____

_____

Dates of Employment — From _____ To _____

Reason for Leaving _____

Company Name _____

Address _____

Job Title _____

Responsibilities _____

_____

Dates of Employment — From _____ To _____

Reason for Leaving _____

Attach additional sheet if necessary.

Sample Job Application (continued)

REFERENCES

List three personal references, not related to you, whom have known you more than one year:

Name _____ Phone _____ Years Known _____

Address _____

Name _____ Phone _____ Years Known _____

Address _____

Name _____ Phone _____ Years Known _____

Address _____

EMERGENCY CONTACT

In case of emergency, please notify: _____

Name _____ Phone _____

Address _____

Name _____ Phone _____

Address _____

PLEASE READ BEFORE SIGNING

I certify that all information provided by me on this application is true and complete to the best of my knowledge and that I have withheld nothing which, if disclosed, would alter the integrity of this application.

I authorize my previous employers, schools or persons listed as references to give any information regarding my employment or educational record. I agree that this company and my previous employers will not be held liable in any respect if a job is not extended, or is withdrawn, or employment is terminated because of false statements, omissions or answers made by myself on this application. In the event of any employment with this company I will comply with all rules and regulations as set by the company in any communication distributed to the employees.

In compliance with the Immigration Reform and Control Act of 1986, I understand that I am required to provide approved documentation to the company, which verifies my right to work in the United States on the first day of employment. I have received from the company a list of approved documents which are required.

I understand that employment at this company is "at will" which means that either I or this company can terminate the employment relationship at any time, with or without prior notice, and for any reason not prohibited by statute. All employment is continued on that basis. I hereby acknowledge that I have read and understand the above statements.

Signature _____ Date _____

Sample Job Application (continued)

LISTS OF ACCEPTABLE DOCUMENTS

LIST A		LIST B		LIST C
Documents that Establish Both Identity and Employment Eligibility	**OR**	**Documents that Establish Identity**	**AND**	**Documents that Establish Employment Eligibility**

LIST A — Documents that Establish Both Identity and Employment Eligibility

1. U.S. Passport (unexpired or expired)

2. Certificate of U.S. Citizenship (Form N-560 or N-561)

3. Certificate of Naturalization (Form N-550 or N-570)

4. Unexpired foreign passport, with I-551 stamp or attached Form I-94 indicating unexpired employment authorization

5. Permanent Resident Card or Alien Registration Receipt Card with photograph (Form I-151 or I-551)

6. Unexpired Temporary Resident Card (Form I-688)

7. Unexpired Employment Authorization Card (Form I-688A)

8. Unexpired Reentry Permit (Form I-327)

9. Unexpired Refugee Travel Document (Form 1-571)

10. Unexpired Employment Authorization Document issued by DHS that contains a photograph (Form I-688B)

OR

LIST B — Documents that Establish Identity

1. Driver's license or ID card issued by a state or outlying possession of the United States provided it contains a photograph or information such as name, date of birth, gender, height, eye color and address

2. ID card issued by federal, state or local government agencies or entities, provided it contains a photograph or information such as name, date of birth, gender, height, eye color and address

3. School ID card with a photograph

4. Voter's registration card

5. U.S. Military card or draft record

6. Military dependent's ID card

7. U.S. Coast Guard Merchant Mariner Card

8. Native American tribal document

9. Driver's license issued by a Canadian government authority

For persons under age 18 who are unable to present a document listed above:

10. School record or report card

11. Clinic, doctor or hospital record

12. Day-care or nursery school record

AND

LIST C — Documents that Establish Employment Eligibility

1. U.S. social security card issued by the Social Security Administration (other than a card stating it is not valid for employment)

2. Certification of Birth Abroad issued by the Department of State (Form FS-545 or Form DS-1350)

3. Original or certified copy of a birth certificate issued by a state, county, municipal authority or outlying possession of the United States bearing an official seal

4. Native American tribal document

5. U.S. Citizen ID Card (Form I-197)

6. ID Card for use of Resident Citizen in the United States (Form I-179)

7. Unexpired employment authorization document issued by DHS (other than those listed under List A)

Illustrations of many of these documents appear in Part 8 of the Handbook for Employers (M-274)

Form I-9 (Rev. 05/31/05)Y Page 3

Sample Form W-4. Employee Withholding Allowance Certification

Form W-4 (2006)

Purpose. Complete Form W-4 so that your employer can withhold the correct federal income tax from your pay. Because your tax situation may change, you may want to refigure your withholding each year.

Exemption from withholding. If you are exempt, complete only lines 1, 2, 3, 4, and 7 and sign the form to validate it. Your exemption for 2006 expires February 16, 2007. See Pub. 505, Tax Withholding and Estimated Tax.

Note. You cannot claim exemption from withholding if (a) your income exceeds $850 and includes more than $300 of unearned income (for example, interest and dividends) and (b) another person can claim you as a dependent on their tax return.

Basic instructions. If you are not exempt, complete the **Personal Allowances Worksheet** below. The worksheets on page 2 adjust your withholding allowances based on itemized deductions, certain credits, adjustments to income, or two-

earner/two-job situations. Complete all worksheets that apply. However, you may claim fewer (or zero) allowances.

Head of household. Generally, you may claim head of household filing status on your tax return only if you are unmarried and pay more than 50% of the costs of keeping up a home for yourself and your dependent(s) or other qualifying individuals. See line **E** below.

Tax credits. You can take projected tax credits into account in figuring your allowable number of withholding allowances. Credits for child or dependent care expenses and the child tax credit may be claimed using the **Personal Allowances Worksheet** below. See Pub. 919, How Do I Adjust My Tax Withholding, for information on converting your other credits into withholding allowances.

Nonwage income. If you have a large amount of nonwage income, such as interest or dividends, consider making estimated tax payments using Form 1040-ES, Estimated Tax for Individuals. Otherwise, you may owe additional tax.

Two earners/two jobs. If you have a working spouse or more than one job, figure the total number of allowances you are entitled to claim on all jobs using worksheets from only one Form W-4. Your withholding usually will be most accurate when all allowances are claimed on the Form W-4 for the highest paying job and zero allowances are claimed on the others.

Nonresident alien. If you are a nonresident alien, see the Instructions for Form 8233 before completing this Form W-4.

Check your withholding. After your Form W-4 takes effect, use Pub. 919 to see how the dollar amount you are having withheld compares to your projected total tax for 2006. See Pub. 919, especially if your earnings exceed $130,000 (Single) or $180,000 (Married).

Recent name change? If your name on line 1 differs from that shown on your social security card, call 1-800-772-1213 to initiate a name change and obtain a social security card showing your correct name.

Personal Allowances Worksheet (Keep for your records.)

A   Enter "1" for **yourself** if no one else can claim you as a dependent . . . . **A** _____

B   Enter "1" if: {
- You are single and have only one job; or
- You are married, have only one job, and your spouse does not work; or
- Your wages from a second job or your spouse's wages (or the total of both) are $1,000 or less. } **B** _____

C   Enter "1" for your **spouse.** But, you may choose to enter "-0-" if you are married and have either a working spouse or more than one job. (Entering "-0-" may help you avoid having too little tax withheld.) . . . . **C** _____

D   Enter number of **dependents** (other than your spouse or yourself) you will claim on your tax return . . . **D** _____

E   Enter "1" if you will file as **head of household** on your tax return (see conditions under **Head of household** above) . **E** _____

F   Enter "1" if you have at least $1,500 of **child or dependent care expenses** for which you plan to claim a credit . . **F** _____
     (**Note.** Do **not** include child support payments. See Pub. **503**, Child and Dependent Care Expenses, for details.)

G   **Child Tax Credit** (including additional child tax credit):
- If your total income will be less than $55,000 ($82,000 if married), enter "2" for each eligible child.
- If your total income will be between $55,000 and $84,000 ($82,000 and $119,000 if married), enter "1" for each eligible child plus "1" **additional** if you have four or more eligible children. **G** _____

H   Add lines A through G and enter total here. (**Note.** This may be different from the number of exemptions you claim on your tax return.) ▶ **H** _____

For accuracy, complete all worksheets that apply.
- If you plan to **itemize or claim adjustments to income** and want to reduce your withholding, see the **Deductions and Adjustments Worksheet** on page 2.
- If you have **more than one job** or are **married and you and your spouse both work** and the combined earnings from all jobs exceed $35,000 ($25,000 if married) see the **Two-Earner/Two-Job Worksheet** on page 2 to avoid having too little tax withheld.
- If **neither** of the above situations applies, **stop here** and enter the number from line H on line 5 of Form W-4 below.

- - - - - - - - - - - - - - -   **Cut here and give Form W-4 to your employer. Keep the top part for your records.**   - - - - - - - - - - - - - - -

Form **W-4**
Department of the Treasury
Internal Revenue Service

Employee's Withholding Allowance Certificate

▶ Whether you are entitled to claim a certain number of allowances or exemption from withholding is subject to review by the IRS. Your employer may be required to send a copy of this form to the IRS.

OMB No. 1545-0074

20**06**

1 Type or print your first name and middle initial.	Last name		2 Your social security number
Home address (number and street or rural route)		3 ☐ Single ☐ Married ☐ Married, but withhold at higher Single rate. **Note.** If married, but legally separated, or spouse is a nonresident alien, check the "Single" box.	
City or town, state, and ZIP code		4 **If your last name differs from that shown on your social security card, check here. You must call 1-800-772-1213 for a new card.** ▶ ☐	

5   Total number of allowances you are claiming (from line **H** above **or** from the applicable worksheet on page 2)   **5** _____

6   Additional amount, if any, you want withheld from each paycheck . . . . **6** $ _____

7   I claim exemption from withholding for 2006, and I certify that I meet **both** of the following conditions for exemption.
- Last year I had a right to a refund of **all** federal income tax withheld because I had **no** tax liability **and**
- This year I expect a refund of **all** federal income tax withheld because I expect to have **no** tax liability.

   If you meet both conditions, write "Exempt" here . . . . ▶   **7** _____

Under penalties of perjury, I declare that I have examined this certificate and to the best of my knowledge and belief, it is true, correct, and complete.

Employee's signature
(Form is not valid unless you sign it.) ▶ _____   Date ▶ _____

8 Employer's name and address (Employer: Complete lines 8 and 10 only if sending to the IRS.)	9 Office code (optional)	10 Employer identification number (EIN)

For Privacy Act and Paperwork Reduction Act Notice, see page 2.   Cat. No. 10220Q   Form **W-4** (2006)

Sample Form W-4. Employee Withholding Allowance Certification (continued)

Form W-4 (2006)   Page **2**

Deductions and Adjustments Worksheet

Note. Use this worksheet *only* if you plan to itemize deductions, claim certain credits, or claim adjustments to income on your 2006 tax return.

1	Enter an estimate of your 2006 itemized deductions. These include qualifying home mortgage interest, charitable contributions, state and local taxes, medical expenses in excess of 7.5% of your income, and miscellaneous deductions. (For 2006, you may have to reduce your itemized deductions if your income is over $150,500 ($75,250 if married filing separately). See *Worksheet 3* in Pub. 919 for details.) . . .	**1** $ _____
2	Enter: { $10,300 if married filing jointly or qualifying widow(er) $ 7,550 if head of household $ 5,150 if single or married filing separately }	**2** $ _____
3	**Subtract** line 2 from line 1. If line 2 is greater than line 1, enter "-0-"	**3** $ _____
4	Enter an estimate of your 2006 adjustments to income, including alimony, deductible IRA contributions, and student loan interest	**4** $ _____
5	**Add** lines 3 and 4 and enter the total. (Include any amount for credits from *Worksheet 7* in Pub. 919) .	**5** $ _____
6	Enter an estimate of your 2006 nonwage income (such as dividends or interest)	**6** $ _____
7	**Subtract** line 6 from line 5. Enter the result, but not less than "-0-"	**7** $ _____
8	**Divide** the amount on line 7 by $3,300 and enter the result here. Drop any fraction	**8** _____
9	Enter the number from the **Personal Allowances Worksheet**, line H, page 1	**9** _____
10	**Add** lines 8 and 9 and enter the total here. If you plan to use the **Two-Earner/Two-Job Worksheet**, also enter this total on line 1 below. Otherwise, **stop here** and enter this total on Form W-4, line 5, page 1 .	**10** _____

Two-Earner/Two-Job Worksheet (See *Two earners/two jobs* on page 1.)

Note. Use this worksheet *only* if the instructions under line H on page 1 direct you here.

1	Enter the number from line H, page 1 (or from line 10 above if you used the **Deductions and Adjustments Worksheet**)	**1** _____
2	Find the number in **Table 1** below that applies to the **LOWEST** paying job and enter it here	**2** _____
3	If line 1 is **more than or equal to** line 2, subtract line 2 from line 1. Enter the result here (if zero, enter "-0-") and on Form W-4, line 5, page 1. **Do not** use the rest of this worksheet	**3** _____

Note. If line 1 is *less than* line 2, enter "-0-" on Form W-4, line 5, page 1. Complete lines 4–9 below to calculate the additional withholding amount necessary to avoid a year-end tax bill.

4	Enter the number from line 2 of this worksheet . . . . **4** _____	
5	Enter the number from line 1 of this worksheet . . . . **5** _____	
6	**Subtract** line 5 from line 4	**6** _____
7	Find the amount in **Table 2** below that applies to the **HIGHEST** paying job and enter it here	**7** $ _____
8	**Multiply** line 7 by line 6 and enter the result here. This is the additional annual withholding needed . .	**8** $ _____
9	Divide line 8 by the number of pay periods remaining in 2006. For example, divide by 26 if you are paid every two weeks and you complete this form in December 2005. Enter the result here and on Form W-4, line 6, page 1. This is the additional amount to be withheld from each paycheck	**9** $ _____

Table 1: Two-Earner/Two-Job Worksheet

Married Filing Jointly						All Others		
If wages from **HIGHEST** paying job are—	AND, wages from **LOWEST** paying job are—	Enter on line 2 above	If wages from **HIGHEST** paying job are—	AND, wages from **LOWEST** paying job are—	Enter on line 2 above	If wages from **LOWEST** paying job are—	Enter on line 2 above	
$0 - $42,000	$0 - $4,500	0	$42,001 and over	32,001 - 38,000	6	$0 - $6,000	0	
	4,501 - 9,000	1		38,001 - 46,000	7	6,001 - 12,000	1	
	9,001 - 18,000	2		46,001 - 55,000	8	12,001 - 19,000	2	
	18,001 and over	3		55,001 - 60,000	9	19,001 - 26,000	3	
$42,001 and over	$0 - $4,500	0		60,001 - 65,000	10	26,001 - 35,000	4	
	4,501 - 9,000	1		65,001 - 75,000	11	35,001 - 50,000	5	
	9,001 - 18,000	2		75,001 - 95,000	12	50,001 - 65,000	6	
	18,001 - 22,000	3		95,001 - 105,000	13	65,001 - 80,000	7	
	22,001 - 26,000	4		105,001 - 120,000	14	80,001 - 90,000	8	
	26,001 - 32,000	5		120,001 and over	15	90,001 - 120,000	9	
						120,001 and over	10	

Table 2: Two-Earner/Two-Job Worksheet

Married Filing Jointly		All Others	
If wages from **HIGHEST** paying job are—	Enter on line 7 above	If wages from **HIGHEST** paying job are—	Enter on line 7 above
$0 - $60,000	$500	$0 - $30,000	$500
60,001 - 115,000	830	30,001 - 75,000	830
115,001 - 165,000	920	75,001 - 145,000	920
165,001 - 290,000	1,090	145,001 - 330,000	1,090
290,001 and over	1,160	330,001 and over	1,160

Printed on recycled paper

Sample Performance Review

Name _____

Job Title _____

Department _____

Supervisor _____

Date Hired _____Last Review Date _____ Today's Date _____

The following definitions apply to each factor rated below.

Level 6 — Far exceeds job requirements
Level 5 — Consistently exceeds job requirements
Level 4 — Meets and usually exceeds job requirements
Level 3 — Consistently meets job requirements
Level 2 — Inconsistent in meeting job requirements
Level 1 — Does not meet job requirements
   (Circle appropriate number.)

Quantity of Work _____ Level   1   2   3   4   5   6

Volume of work regularly produced. Speed and consistency of output.

Comments: _____

_____

_____

_____

Quality of Work _____ Level   1   2   3   4   5   6

Extent to which employee can be counted upon to carry out assignments to completion.

Comments: _____

_____

_____

_____

Job Cooperation _____ Level   1   2   3   4   5   6

Amount of interest and enthusiasm shown in work.

Comments: _____

_____

_____

_____

Sample Performance Review (continued)

Ability to work with others   Level   1   2   3   4   5   6

Extent to which employee effectively interacts with others in the performance of his/her job.

Comments: _____

_____

_____

_____

Adaptability   Level   1   2   3   4   5   6

Extent to which employee is able to perform a variety of tasks within the scope of his/her job.

Comments: _____

_____

_____

_____

Job Knowledge   Level   1   2   3   4   5   6

Extent of job information and understanding possessed by employee.

Comments: _____

_____

_____

_____

Initiative   Level   1   2   3   4   5   6

Extent to which employee is a self starter in attaining objectives of the job.

Comments: _____

_____

_____

_____

Overall Performance Evaluation   Level   1   2   3   4   5   6

Comments: _____

_____

_____

_____

_____

_____

_____

Sample Performance Review (continued)

Attendance   ☐ Problem ☐ No Problem

Volume of work regularly produced. Speed and consistency of output

Comments: _____

_____

_____

_____

EMPLOYEE'S CAREER DEVELOPMENT

Strengths: _____

_____

_____

_____

_____

Development Needs: _____

_____

_____

_____

_____

Development Plan (include Long Range): _____

_____

_____

_____

EMPLOYEE'S COMMENTS (optional)

General comments about your performance: _____

_____

_____

_____

_____

Read and Acknowledged by:

Employee _____ Date _____

Approvals

Supervisor _____ Date _____

Department Manager _____ Date _____

Personnel _____ Date _____

Owner or CEO _____ Date _____

B | *Federal Agency Contacts*

Federal Information Center
(800) 688-9889
Purpose: To provide other federal numbers.

U.S. Small Business Administration (SBA) Field Offices
Purpose: Free financial assistance and counseling on creating a marketing plan and developing a business plan.

Headquarters
409 Third Street, SW
Washington, DC 20416
(800) U-ASK-SBA (827-5722)
www.sba.gov

Denver Regional Office
721 19th Street, Suite 400
Denver, CO 80202
(303) 844-0500
(303) 844-0506 (fax)
(303) 844-0507 (TTY/TDD)

Colorado District Office
721 19th Street, Suite 426
Denver, CO 80202
(303) 844-2607
(303) 844-6468 (fax)
(303) 844-5638 (TTY/TDD)
SBA Online Library
www.sba.gov/library

Publications:
www.sba.gov/library/pubs.html

SBA Answer Desk
Purpose: For 24-hour information
relating to small business.
(800) UASK-SBA
www.sba.gov.answerdesk.html

U.S. Business Advisor

Purpose: Electronic one-stop center for
making electronic links to all government business sites.

Office of Technology
Mail Code 6470
409 3rd Street, SW
Washington, DC 20416
(202) 205-6450
(202) 205-7754
www.business.gov

Small Business Development Centers (SBDC)

Purpose: This lead center will direct you
to the nearest SBDC counselor for free
training and start-up assistance.

Colorado SBDC
Colorado Office of Economic
Development
1625 Broadway, Suite 1700

Denver, CO 80202
(303) 892-3840
(303) 892-3848 (fax)
www.state.co.us/oed/sbdc/sbdc-
list.cfm

National Business Incubation Association (NBIA)

Purpose: Will help you locate the nearest
business incubator.

Headquarters
20 East Circle Drive, , #37198
Athens, OH 45701-3751
(740) 593-4331
(740) 593-1996 (fax)
www.nbia.org

U.S. Department of Commerce

Purpose: Serves as the umbrella agency
for a variety of programs geared toward
business.

Headquarters
1401 Constitution Avenue, NW
Washington, DC 20230
(202) 482-2000
(202) 482-5270 (fax)
www.doc.gov

Bureau of Economic Analysis (BEA)
Public Information Office
1441 L Street
Washington, DC 20230
(202) 606-9900
(202) 606-5355 (TDD)
For information on services:
STAT-USA
(202) 482-1986
www.bea.gov

U.S. Census Bureau
www.census.gov
U.S. Census Bureau
6900 West Jefferson Avenue, Suite 100
Denver, CO 80235-2032
(303) 264-0202 or (800) 852-6159
(303) 969-6777 (fax)
(303) 969-6767 (TDD)
denver.regional.office@census.gov
www.census.gov

Economic Development
Administration (EDA)
14th and Constitution Avenue
Washington, DC 20230
(202) 482-5081
www.eda.gov
EDA Regional Office
1244 Speer Boulevard, Suite 670
Denver, CO 80204-3591
(303) 844-4715
(303) 844-3968 (fax)

International Trade Administration
(ITA)
www.ita.doc.gov
Trade Information Center
(800) USA-TRADE (872-8723)
(800) TDD-TRADE (833-8723)
(202) 482-4473 (fax)
tic@ita.doc.gov
www.trade.gov/td/tic

MinorityBusiness Development
Agency (MBDA)
U.S. Department of Commerce
14th and Constitution Avenue, NW,
Room 5053
Washington, DC 20230

(202) 482-0404
(202) 482-2678 (fax)
help@mbda.gov
www.mbda.gov

Dallas Regional MBDA Office (serving
Colorado)
1100 Commerce Street, Room 726
Dallas, TX 75242
(214) 767-8001
(214) 767-0613 (fax)
dro-info@mbda.gov

U.S. Chamber of Commerce
Purpose: Provides a link between small
business and government, and is the
main center for a nationwide network of
local chambers of commerce.

Chamber Headquarters
1615 H Street, NW
Washington, DC 20062-2000
(202) 659-6000
www.uschamber.org

Internal Revenue Service (IRS)
www.irs.gov
Purpose: Where to register to pay withholding tax (FUTA, unemployment, SSI,
FICA), income, and corporate taxes.

Taxpayer Assistance Centers
Colorado Springs
2864 S. Circle Drive
Colorado Springs, CO 80906
(719) 579-5227

Denver
600 17th Street
Denver, CO 80202
(303) 446-1675

Ft. Collins
301 S. Howes Street
Ft. Collins, CO 80521
(970) 221-0688

Grand Junction
400 Rood Avenue
Grand Junction, CO 81502
(970) 241-6265

IRS Live telephone assistance
(800) 829-1040

Employer Identification Number (EIN)
Apply by phone, Business and
Specialty Tax Line:
(800) 829-4933 (7:00 a.m.-10:00 p.m.
local time, Monday through Friday)
Apply by fax, send Form SS-4:
(215) 516-3990 (fax)
Apply by mail:
Internal Revenue Service Center
Attn: EIN Operations
Philadelphia, PA 19255

TeleTax
(800) 829-4477 (nationwide)
Purpose: Provides recorded information, 24 hours a day, on tax-related
subjects.

Tax Forms
(800) TAX-FORM (829-3676)
(800) 829-4059 (TTY/TDD)
www.irs.gov/formspubs

U.S. Department of Labor

Frances Perkins Building
200 Constitution Avenue, NW
Washington, DC 20210

(866) 4-USA-DOL (487-2365)
(877) 889-5627 (TTY)
www.dol.gov

Information about the Family and
Medical Leave Act:
www.dol.gov/esa/whd/fmla/index.htm

Fair Labor Standards Act Minimum
Wage Poster:
www.dol.gov/esa/regs/compliance/
posters/flsa.htm

Workplace Poster Requirements for
Small Businesses:
www.dol.gov/osbp/sbrefa/poster/
matrix.htm

Department of Labor, Employment and
Training Administration
www.doleta.gov

DOLETA Regional Administrator
U.S. Department of Labor/ETA
525 Griffin Street Room 317
Dallas, TX 75202
(214) 767-8263
(214) 767-5113 (fax)

Occupational Safety and Health
Administration
200 Constitution Avenue, NW
Washington, DC 20210
(800) 321-OSHA (6742)
www.osha.gov

Publications:
www.osha.gov/pls/publications/pubin
dex.list
Recordkeeping Handbook:
www.osha.gov/recordkeeping/
index.html

Equal Employment Opportunity Commission (EEOC)
Purpose: To provide posters and information about employer responsibilities under the Americans with Disabilities Act.

Headquarters
1801 L Street, NW
Washington, DC 20507
(202) 663-4900
(202) 663-4494 (TDD)
(800) 669-4000 (connection to nearest EEOC field office)
(800) 669-6820 (TDD) (connection to nearest EEOC field office)
www.eeoc.gov

Publications Information Center
P.O. Box 12549
Cincinnati, OH 45212-0549
(800) 669-3362
(800) 800-3302 (TDD/TTY)

Posters:
www.eeoc.gov/posterform.html

Publications:
www.eeoc.gov/publications.html

EEOC District Office
3300 North Central Avenue, Suite 690
Phoenix, AZ 85012-2504
(602) 640-5000
(602) 640-5072 (TTY)
(602) 640-5071 (fax)

Environmental Protection Agency
Purpose: To provide assistance for compliance with federal EPA requirements.

Ariel Rios Building
1200 Pennsylvania Avenue, N.
Washington, DC 20460
(202) 272-0167
www.epa.gov

EPA Region 8
999 18th Street, Suite 500
Denver, CO 80202-2466
(303) 312-6312, (800) 227-8917
(303) 312-6339 (fax)
r8eisc@epa.gov
www.epa.gov/region8

Federal Trade Commission (FTC)
Purpose: Provides federal disclosure information on franchise opportunities.

Headquarters
600 Pennsylvania Avenue, NW
Washington, DC 20580
(877) FTC-HELP (382-4357)
(866) 653-4261 (TTY)
(consumer response centers)
www.ftc.gov/bcp/franchise/netfran.htm

FTC Western Regional Office
901 Market Street, Suite 570
San Francisco, CA 94103
(877) 382-4351

Bureau of Consumer Protection
Division of Marketing Practices
601 Pennsylvania Avenue, NW
Washington, DC 20580
(202) 326-3222 (general questions)
www.ftc.gov/bcp/bcp.htm

U.S. Citizenship and Immigration Services

Purpose: Where to find the employer relations office nearest you for assistance with Form I-9, Employment Eligibility Verification.

> 20 Massachusetts Avenue, NW
> Washington, DC 20529
> (800) 375-5283
> (800) 767-1833 (TTY)
> uscis.gov

National Committee for Employer Support of the Guard and Reserve

Purpose: To provide information and mediation for understanding and applying the law related to military leave.

> National Committee
> 1555 Wilson Boulevard, Suite 200
> Arlington, VA 22209-2405
> (800) 336-4590
> (703) 696-1411 (fax)
> www.esgr.org

U.S. Patent and Trademark Office

www.uspto.gov

Purpose: To provide federal protection of trademarks, service marks, and trade names.

> Patent and Trademark Office
> (800) 786-9199 (U.S. and Canada),
> (571) 272-1000
> (571) 273-8300 (fax)
> usptoinfo@uspto.gov
> www.uspto.gov

> Trademark Electronic Application
> System (TEAS)
> www.uspto.gov/teas/index.html
> (800) 786-9199
> (703) 308-HELP (4357)
> (703) 305-7785 (TDD)
> (703) 305-7786 (fax)

> Trademark Assistance Office
> (703) 308-9000
> (703) 308-7016 (fax)
> TrademarkAssistanceOffice@uspto.gov

C | *State and Private Agency Contacts*

Colorado Secretary of State

Purpose: To file as any type of business entity.

Business Center
Colorado Secretary of State
1560 Broadway, Suite 200
Denver, CO 80290
(303) 894-2200
(303) 869-4864 (fax)
business@sos.state.co.us
www.sos.state.co.us

Colorado Office of Economic Development and International Trade

Purpose: Works with companies starting, expanding, or relocating in Colorado.

1625 Broadway, Suite 1700
Denver, CO 80202
(303) 892-3840
(303) 892-3848 (fax)
www.state.co.us/oed

Colorado Department of Revenue

Purpose: Answers all tax-related questions and provides publications to taxpayers.

Taxpayer Service Division
Denver Service Center
1375 Sherman Street
Denver, CO 80261
(303) 238-SERV (7378)
(303) 592-8107 (fax)
www.revenue.state.co.us/TPS_Dir/home.asp

Division of Property Taxation
Colorado Department of Local Affairs
1313 Sherman Street, Suite 419
Denver, CO 80203
(303) 866-2371
(303) 866-4000 (fax)
dola.helpdesk@state.co.us
www.dola.state.co.us/propertytax/index.htm

Colorado Department of Labor and Employment

Purpose: For questions affecting employers, including wage-hour regulations, child labor, minimum wage, and discrimination laws.

633 17th Street
Denver, CO 80202-3660
(303) 318-8000 (general information)
www.coworkforce.com

Division of Labor (Labor Standards Unit)
(303) 318-8441, (888) 390-7936
(303) 318-8400 (fax)
www.coworkforce.com/LAB/Posting%20Requirements.pdf

Division of Employment and Training
P.O. Box 8789
Denver, CO 80201-8789
(303) 318-9100 (Denver metro area), (800) 480-8299
(303) 318-9016 (TTD Denver metro area), (303) 894-7730 (TTD outside Denver metro area)
unemp.tax@state.co.us
www.coworkforce.com/UIT/EmployersHandbook

Division of Workers' Compensation
(303) 318-8640 (Employer Services)

Pinnacol Assurance

Purpose: To obtain workers' compensation.

7502 E. Lowry Boulevard
Denver, CO 80230-7006
(303) 361-4000, (800) 873-7242
www.pinnacol.com

Colorado Department of Regulatory Agencies

Purpose: To obtain information about business licensing, securities, insurance, and other business-related regulations.

1560 Broadway, Suite 1550
Denver, CO 80202
(303) 894-7855
(303) 894-7885 (fax)
edo@dora.state.co.us
www.dora.state.co.us

Division of Civil Rights
1560 Broadway, Suite 1050
Denver, CO 80202
(303) 894-2997
(303) 894-7830 (fax)
ccrd@dora.state.co.us
www.dora.state.co.us/civil-rights

Colorado State Directory of New Hires

Purpose: To report new hires.

P.O. Box 2920
Denver, CO 80201-2920
(303) 297-2849, (800) 696-1468
(303) 297-2595 (fax)
cse.employer.outreach@state.co.us
newhire.state.co.us/newhire/do

Occupational Health and Safety Consultation

Purpose: Offers free OSHA consultation services.

Colorado State University
Occupational Health and Safety
Section
Environmental and Radiological

Health Sciences
Environmental Health Building 155
Fort Collins, CO 80523-1681
(970) 491-6151
(970) 491-7778 (fax)
ohss@lamar.colostate.edu
www.bernardino.colostate.edu/public

Colorado Department of Public Health and Environment

Purpose: To help small businesses comply with state regulations.

Environmental Customer Assistance
4300 Cherry Creek Drive South
Denver, CO 80246-1530
(303) 692-2000, (800) 886-7689 (in Colorado)
(303) 691-7700 (TTD)
cdphe.information@state.co.us
www.cdphe.state.co.us

Air Pollution Control Division
(303) 692-3100
(303) 782-0278 (fax)
www.cdphe.state.co.us/ap

Hazardous Materials and Waste
Management Division
(303) 692-3300, (888) 569-1831
(303) 759-5355 (fax)
www.cdphe.state.co.us/hm

Water Quality Control Division
(303) 692-3500
(303) 782-0390 (fax)
www.cdphe.state.co.us/wq

Small Business Ombudsman
(303) 692-2135

Colorado State Data Center

Purpose: To provide the most up-to-date census data for the state.

Colorado Department of Local Affairs
Demography Section
1313 Sherman Street, Room 521
Denver, CO 80203
(303) 866-3190
(303) 866-4819 (fax)
www.dola.state.co.us/is/cedishom.htm

State Business Publications

The Boulder County Business Report
3180 Sterling Circle
Boulder, CO 80301-2338
(303) 440-4950
(303) 440-8954 (fax)
www.bcbr.com

Business Times of Western Colorado
2591 B 3/4 Road
Grand Junction, CO 81503
(970) 241-0177
(970) 241-9730 (fax)
www.thebusinesstimes.com

Colorado Biz
7009 South Potomac Street, Suite 200
Englewood, CO 80112
(303) 397-7600
(303) 397-7619 (fax)
www.cobizmag.com

Colorado Construction
1114 W. 7th Avenue, Suite 100
Denver, CO 80204
(303) 756-9995
(303) 756-4465 (fax)
www.coloradoconstructionmag.com

Colorado Municipalities
Colorado Municipal League
1144 Sherman Street
Denver, CO 80203-2207
(303) 831-6411
www.cml.org/publications/colorado_
municipalities.html

Colorado Springs Business Journal
31 E. Platte Avenue, Suite 300
Colorado Springs, CO 80903-1246
(719) 634-5905
csbj.clickdata.com

Denver Business Journal
1700 Broadway, Suite 515
Denver, CO 80290-9908
(303) 837-3500
(303) 837-3535 (fax)
denver@bizjournals.com
www.bizjournals.com/denver

Northern Colorado Business Report
Northern Colorado Business Report, Inc.
141 S. College Avenue
Fort Collins, CO 80524
(970) 221-5400
(970) 221-5432 (fax)
cwood@ncbr.com
www.ncbr.com

National Federation of Independent Businesses (nfib)

Purpose: A nonprofit small business advocacy group that lobbies at the state and federal levels.

Membership Services Office
53 Century Boulevard, Suite 250

Nashville, TN 37214
(800) NFIB-NOW (232-6273),
(615) 872-5800
www.nfib.com

National Association for the Self-Employed® (NASE)

Purpose: A membership organization that gives small business owners advice and competitive information.

P.O. Box 612067
DFW Airport
Dallas, TX 75261-2067
(800) 232-NASE (232-6273)
(800) 551-4446 (fax)
www.nase.org

Society of Risk Management Consultants (SRMC)

Purpose: To assist in finding a professional and ethical insurance consultant.

330 S. Executive Drive, Suite 301
Brookfield, WI 53005-4275
(800) 765-SRMC (765-7762)
www.srmcsociety.org

National Venture Capital Association (NVCA)

Purpose: To find sources of venture capital.

1655 North Fort Myer Drive, Suite 850
Arlington, VA 22209
(703) 524-2549
(703) 524-3940 (fax)
www.nvca.org

National Association of Small Business Investment Companies (NASBIC)

Purpose: Central contact agency to find SBICs throughout the nation.

666 11th Street, NW, Suite 750
Washington, DC 20001
(202) 628-5055
(202) 628-5080 (fax)
nasbic@nasbic.org
www.nasbic.org

National Association of Women Business Owners (NAWBO)

Purpose: Provides networking and business assistance to businesses owned by women.

8405 Greensboro Drive, Suite 800
McLean, VA 22102
(703) 506-3268, (800) 55-NAWBO (556-2926)
(703) 506-3266 (fax)
www.nawbo.org

National Minority Business Council, Inc. (NMBC)

Purpose: Helps small minority- and women-owned businesses.

25 West 45th Street, Suite 301
New York, NY 10036
(212) 997-4753
(212) 997-5102 (fax)
www.nmbc.org

Latin Business Association

Purpose: Promotes the growth of Latino-owned businesses.

> 120 South San Pedro Street, Suite 530
> Los Angeles CA 90012
> (213) 628-8510
> www.lbausa.com

Hispanic Business Women's Alliance

Purpose: Fosters collaboration among Hispanic women who are entrepreneurs, professionals, consultants, executives, inventors, and investors in North America, Latin America, the Caribbean, and Spain.

> The Atrium Center
> 530 Avenida de la Constitución
> San Juan, PR 00901-2304
> (787) 289-7843, (787) 289-8779
> www.hbwa.net

Asian Women in Business

Purpose: Provides information, education, and networking opportunities for Asian women starting or expanding businesses.

> 358 Fifth Avenue, Suite 504
> New York, NY 10001
> (212) 868-1368
> (212) 868-1373 (fax)
> www.awib.org

D| *State Loan Programs*

Colorado has a small but efficient system for financing business start-up and expansion. The state doesn't offer a large number of loans, but there are no catches. Most of Colorado's loans are simple and easy to obtain.

Financial incentive programs are available throughout Colorado for new or expanding businesses. A few of the larger state-administered programs are presented here.

Colorado Housing and Finance Authority

Several financial programs are administered through the Colorado Housing and Finance Authority (CHFA). Several of the programs offered through the CHFA are listed below:

- The SBA 504 Loan Program provides real estate financing in conjunction with the SBA's 504 program. This program allows the borrower to obtain a fixed interest rate on the first mortgage for the entire term of the loan, with a minimal equity contribution of ten percent.

- CHFA Direct provides owner-occupied real estate financing for loan amounts ranging from $50,000 to $20,000,000 with down payments as low as 15 percent. It features a fully amortizing, fixed rate with loan terms up to 20 years.
- CHFA rural business loan are available for existing businesses located in rural areas of the state, communities with populations of less than 50,000, with some exclusions.
- Colorado businesses involved in waste diversion are eligible for the RENEW Loan Program, to finance real estate and equipment used in waste diversion and recycling.
- The New Markets Tax Credit Program (NMTC) encourages small businesses in low-income urban and rural communities.

If you cannot get bank financing, you may be eligible for export financing (if you qualify for export insurance). For more information, contact:

Colorado Housing and Finance Authority
Business Finance Division
1981 Blake Street, Suite 200
Denver, CO 80202-1272
(303) 297-7329, (800) 877-CHFA (2432) (in Colorado)
(303) 297-7305 TDD
www.colohfa.org/business

Community Development Block Grants (CDBG)

The U.S. Department of Housing and Urban Development provides funding for Community Development Block Grants (CDBG), which help communities develop. There are three types—housing, public facilities projects, and economic development; they are administered by three state agencies. The Colorado Office of Business Development and International Trade administers the CDBGs for economic development, to encourage the creation or retention of low- and moderate-income jobs.

The CDBG Infrastructure Program allocates funds for infrastructure projects in support of specific businesses. Local government-sponsored projects may receive grants of up to $500,000 and may require a local equivalent.

The Office of Business Development also funds 15 regional revolving loan fund programs through the CDBG. Funds available vary up to a ceiling of $100,000. Applicants for these loans may be either new or existing businesses. For businesses that require larger loans, these are available through the CDBG business loans program.

There are also business incentive funds available for businesses that commit to meeting job-creation requirements. Incentives vary based on a number of factors; however, requests generally range between $1,000 and $3,000 for each full-time job created. The local community must also provide matching funds/incentives to the business. The Economic Development Commission reviews and approves all requests for funding.

Finally, the Colorado FIRST Program (targeting new jobs that require training) and the Existing Industry Program (targeted to existing jobs that require retraining for the business to remain competitive), the state makes funds available to help business train their employees. Generally, the programs provide up to $800 per employee trained. Businesses must pay for at least 40 percent of the total training costs. The Office of Economic Development and International Trade reviews and approves requests for funding, in conjunction with the Colorado Community College System.

For more information on any of these programs, contact:

Office of Economic Development and International Trade
1625 Broadway, Suite 1710
Denver, CO 80202
(303) 892-3840
(303) 892-3848 (fax)
www.state.co.us/oed

Infrastructure Assistance Program
www.state.co.us/oed/business-finance/infrastructure.cfm

Regional Revolving Loans Funds
www.state.co.us/oed/finance/fundsmap.shtml

Economic Development Commission
Business Finance Division
www.advancecolorado.com/business-finance

Enterprise Zones

Colorado has an Enterprise Zone program, established by the Urban and Rural Enterprise Zone Act of 1986, that provides tax incentives to encourage businesses to locate and expand in designated economically distressed areas of the state. There are currently 18 enterprise zones and subzones. Businesses located in a zone may qualify for ten types of Enterprise Zone Tax Credits and Incentives to encourage job creation and investment in these zones. The Colorado Office of Business Development and International Trade administers the Enterprise Zone program with the Colorado Department of Revenue.

Office of Economic Development and International Trade
1625 Broadway, Room 1700
Denver, CO 80202
(303) 892-3840
(303) 892-3848 (fax)
www.state.co.us/oed/enterprise-zone

Colorado Department of Revenue
Taxpayer Service Division
1375 Sherman Street
Denver, CO 80261-0005
(303) 238-SERV (7378) (assistance)
(303) 238-FAST (3278) (forms and other services)
www.taxcolorado.com

Index